Concepts and Practices
of
DevSecOps

Crack the DevSecOps interviews

Ashwini Kumar Rath

www.bpbonline.com

First Edition 2024

Copyright © BPB Publications, India

ISBN: 978-93-55519-320

To View Complete
BPB Publications Catalogue
Scan the QR Code:

Dedicated to

My mother, the first architect of my words

About the Author

Ashwini Kumar Rath is an accomplished entrepreneur, prolific writer, and seasoned DevSecOps consultant with extensive computer programming experience. As the Director and CEO of Batoi, he has shaped its strategic vision and product development while extending his leadership to several tech companies he co-founded in India and internationally. Rath's educational background in theoretical physics and software management has fueled his successful transition into technology, culminating in the establishing of multiple tech startups. His academic interests encompass cloud computing, AI, and mathematical sciences, driving his contributions to numerous scholarly articles and business features in leading publications. As a frequent speaker at international forums, his expertise and insights are highly sought after. Committed to leveraging knowledge for socio-economic development, Rath also serves on various educational and business leadership boards.

About the Reviewers

❖ **Rakesh** is a seasoned technologist who has worked in the fast-paced technology field for 23 years. He gained expertise at Hewlett Packard, where he exhibited his passion for technology in positions like Technical Architect and Senior Software Engineer. Rakesh has been the Chief Technology Officer at In Time Tec for the past fifteen years, fulfilling his dream of helping clients worldwide overcome technology challenges. With a focus on IoT/Embedded Systems and Highly Scalable Cloud Solutions, his leadership experience ranges from creating low-level embedded software to creating high-performance cloud-based applications.

Rakesh strongly believes in the power of effective communication, analytical thinking, and team-building. Outside the boardroom, he remains current on the most recent technological advancements and supports open-source initiatives, showcasing his commitment to creativity and lifelong learning. Rakesh is always eager to collaborate on worthwhile initiatives with like-minded enthusiasts, highlighting the positive impact of technology on our daily lives. His diverse technological background reflects a commitment to expanding the possibilities of technology.

❖ **Ankit** is a senior cloud data architect with Google and has over a decade of progressive work experience in Cloud, Data, AI, and ethical machine learning practices. He works with customers to develop scalable, reliable, and performant data and machine learning platforms and has worked across companies like Amazon, CVS, Deloitte, and Infosys. He is a technical reviewer for various books focused on data governance, ethical AI, AI governance, Data and AI platforms, Python for AI, and other material related to the promotion of AI ethically and responsibly in society. He earned his master's from the esteemed Kelley School of Business and serves as the advisory board member for the Institute of Business Analytics, Indiana University Bloomington.

Acknowledgement

My most profound appreciation goes out to my beloved family and steadfast friends, whose constant support and motivation served as my guiding star throughout the creation of this book. In particular, my wife, Mita, deserves a special mention for her unwavering encouragement and patience during my perpetual travels and work, gently nudging me to complete each chapter.

I owe a significant debt of gratitude to BPB Publications. Their expertise and professional guidance were pivotal in transforming the raw manuscript into this finished work. It has been an enriching journey, enriched further by the diligent reviewers, technical experts, and editors whose input significantly enhanced the content and structure of this book.

My time in the tech industry, filled with the teachings and insights from my esteemed colleagues and peers from industry and academics, has been instrumental in my growth and understanding. Their generous contributions have immeasurably shaped the narratives and perspectives within these pages.

Last but not least, my sincere thanks to you, the readers, whose interest and support fuel the purpose of this work. Your enthusiasm is the heart of this endeavor, and your encouragement has been priceless. Thank you for making this book a reality.

Preface

Welcome to **Concepts and Practices of DevSecOps**!

As we find ourselves in the midst of a digital revolution, one thing has become evident – the importance of integrating security into our development and operational practices. This has given rise to the practice of DevSecOps, a discipline that builds upon the principles of DevOps with a sharpened focus on security.

This book aims to demystify the DevSecOps field, from its foundational concepts to the advanced practices and technologies that define it today. This comprehensive guide has been designed to equip you with the knowledge you need to excel in DevSecOps roles and to confidently face interviews that test your understanding and application of these principles.

The chapters in this book walk you through different aspects of DevSecOps, including Application Security, Infrastructure as Code, Containers and Security, Automation and Integration, and the Frameworks and Best Practices underpinning the discipline. As we journey into the world of DevSecOps together, we will explore how it plays a pivotal role in the current era of Digital Transformation.

Whether you are a DevOps engineer, project manager, product manager, software developer, or any professional seeking to fortify your understanding of DevSecOps, this book is a crucial resource. With a working knowledge of DevOps, you will find the content accessible and enlightening, helping you to contribute to or lead a DevSecOps team effectively.

Each chapter is structured to answer the pressing questions surrounding each topic, supplemented with practical use cases that bring the theoretical concepts to life. I have also included resources for further reading at the end of each section, allowing you to delve deeper into the subjects that interest you the most.

The world of DevSecOps is as fascinating as it is intricate. This book prepares you for your career progress in this field and ignites a passion for security's vital role in our ever-evolving digital landscape.

May this book serve as your compass, guiding you through the complex terrain of DevSecOps and helping you become an influential team member as you work together to build secure, efficient, and innovative solutions.

Chapter 1: Security in DevOps – It delves into the interweaving of security within DevOps culture, providing insights into the transformation of security measures within software systems management. It establishes a comprehensive framework for understanding DevSecOps, laying a foundation for the forthcoming chapters.

Chapter 2: Application Security – It offers an in-depth exploration of application security, discussing the intricate details of various application architectures and their inherent security aspects. Readers will gain a firm grasp of the tools and technologies that fortify applications, accompanied by a practical case study on constructing and sustaining an enterprise application.

Chapter 3: Infrastructure as Code – It acquaints the reader with different cloud platforms and essential infrastructure management tools instrumental in executing successful DevSecOps projects. Covering several leading vendors, it offers insights into tool selection for specific scenarios while focusing on scalability and change management for contemporary IT systems.

Chapter 4: Containers and Security – It offers a thorough understanding of security measures surrounding popular container technologies, emphasizing an understanding of various vulnerabilities. It examines solutions and processes for vulnerability management and discusses the optimal tools and techniques available.

Chapter 5: Automation and Integration – It introduces platforms and tools for comprehensive security management, particularly crucial in managing enterprise systems and large-scale software with substantial attack surfaces. It discusses a range of cloud security solutions, including CWPP, CSPM, CASB, and CNAPP, supplemented with a practical use case to demonstrate the substantial benefits of integration.

Chapter 6: Frameworks and Best Practices – It provides a detailed view of leading security frameworks and their management in the DevSecOps process, including audit, compliance, reporting, visualization, and threat modeling.

Chapter 7: Digital Transformation and DevSecOps – It discusses a lean approach to digital transformation projects with a spotlight on DevSecOps management. It touches upon cultural aspects, skills, roles, and responsibilities, managing technical liabilities, and establishing secure development practices.

Code Bundle and Coloured Images

Please follow the link to download the
Code Bundle and the *Coloured Images* of the book:

https://rebrand.ly/4c8758

The code bundle for the book is also hosted on GitHub at
https://github.com/bpbpublications/Concepts-and-Practices-of-DevSecOps.
In case there's an update to the code, it will be updated on the existing GitHub repository.

We have code bundles from our rich catalogue of books and videos available at
https://github.com/bpbpublications. Check them out!

Errata

We take immense pride in our work at BPB Publications and follow best practices to ensure the accuracy of our content to provide with an indulging reading experience to our subscribers. Our readers are our mirrors, and we use their inputs to reflect and improve upon human errors, if any, that may have occurred during the publishing processes involved. To let us maintain the quality and help us reach out to any readers who might be having difficulties due to any unforeseen errors, please write to us at :

errata@bpbonline.com

Your support, suggestions and feedbacks are highly appreciated by the BPB Publications' Family.

> Did you know that BPB offers eBook versions of every book published, with PDF and ePub files available? You can upgrade to the eBook version at www.bpbonline. com and as a print book customer, you are entitled to a discount on the eBook copy. Get in touch with us at :
>
> **business@bpbonline.com** for more details.
>
> At **www.bpbonline.com**, you can also read a collection of free technical articles, sign up for a range of free newsletters, and receive exclusive discounts and offers on BPB books and eBooks.

Piracy

If you come across any illegal copies of our works in any form on the internet, we would be grateful if you would provide us with the location address or website name. Please contact us at **business@bpbonline.com** with a link to the material.

If you are interested in becoming an author

If there is a topic that you have expertise in, and you are interested in either writing or contributing to a book, please visit **www.bpbonline.com**. We have worked with thousands of developers and tech professionals, just like you, to help them share their insights with the global tech community. You can make a general application, apply for a specific hot topic that we are recruiting an author for, or submit your own idea.

Reviews

Please leave a review. Once you have read and used this book, why not leave a review on the site that you purchased it from? Potential readers can then see and use your unbiased opinion to make purchase decisions. We at BPB can understand what you think about our products, and our authors can see your feedback on their book. Thank you!

For more information about BPB, please visit **www.bpbonline.com**.

Join our book's Discord space

Join the book's Discord Workspace for Latest updates, Offers, Tech happenings around the world, New Release and Sessions with the Authors:

https://discord.bpbonline.com

Table of Contents

CHAPTER 1
Security in DevOps

Introduction

While DevOps promises a great deal to different stakeholders, security has long been an exclusive focus for any software development team. Traditionally, companies outsource the security audit to an external agency or keep the stuff separate for a group of security experts. Moreover, all security management functions start after a software version is deployed into production. Such a scenario experiences a few to and fro exchanges that include tool-based scanning and manual testing by the security team on the one hand and the resulting effort of troubleshooting by the software or IT team on the other. Consequently, it significantly increases the time of a DevOps cycle and nullifies the fundamental purpose of DevOps, which commits to faster software delivery.

Let us dive into the first chapter.

Structure

In this chapter, we will discuss the following topics:

- Relooking at security operations
- Shifting security left
- Adopting DevSecOps: Key changes

- Security controls
- Documentation and security
- Threat modelling and security policies
- Infrastructure provisioning and security
- Code commit, release and security
- A use case: IoT application

Objectives

This chapter offers an insight into the security aspects of software systems and their management from the perspective of DevOps culture. We discuss the significant technological advancements, tools, and practices that have changed how we treat and incorporate security into the scheme of things. While the chapter serves as a solid introduction to DevSecOps, it also builds a broader framework for the later chapters.

Relooking at security operations

With the rapid adoption of cloud computing and remote working, the IT infrastructure is moving out of the cozy confines of office networks. Security has been more important than ever before. In this section, we shall relook at the **security operations** (**SecOps**) and how it fits into DevOps. Before we proceed further, let us review what a DevOps cycle looks like.

A DevOps cycle

It is famously illustrated with an infinity loop (*Figure 1.1*) broadly running over six stages:

- **Design:** You design new software, an improvement to existing software, or even a modification to the software to align with requirements.

- **Code:** The phase includes programming activities of coding, compiling (when needed) and testing the software units.

- **Integrate:** While different software developers work on different units, integration does the process of merging the changes into a codebase that will function as the designated software system.

- **Deploy:** After integration, the software system needs to be deployed at one or multiple server locations as per the deployment architecture.

- **Operate:** Users start using the system, they can be a selected user group (for doing a pilot) or the actual end users for whom the software is designed.

- **Monitor:** While the software is in use, its accuracy, usability, and performance must be monitored, and adequate feedback is gathered for the next cycle in the loop.

The 'monitor' stage of a cycle feeds the 'design' stage of the next loop cycle, thus creating an infinitely evolving software system's lifecycle. Every business owner or manager loves it, but they would expect the software to have minimal defects yet great security controls. They would also expect that each cycle should be as fast as possible to match the business goals and should lower the effective cost of software development and IT operation management.

It should be noted that different authors or practitioners describe the loop in slightly different ways. However, they fall broadly into the ones that we have described above.

The function of the DevOps infinite Loop is illustrated in *Figure 1.1*:

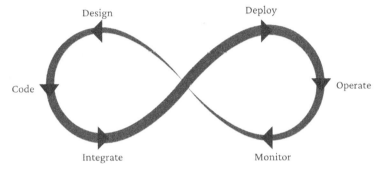

Figure 1.1: *DevOps infinite loop*

Conventional SecOps with DevOps

Let us cite an example to understand the traditional method of SecOps or security operations. Once, a software agency, which had recently adopted DevOps, was tasked with developing an application for its customer. The customer had their own chief security officer and chief risk officer. During one of the project review meetings, these two officers wanted to understand the software development cycle to eliminate process-related risks and have a transparent process for software development and management. The agency had automated the infrastructure provisioning on the Cloud and CI/CD pipeline. They could complete one DevOps cycle in less than a day. However, after each software release (software moving to production), they will refer to the security vendor, who will do a round of penetration testing and provide the list of findings (security issues observed) for the software development team to review and respond. The software team would do the following:

- If a finding is a false positive, they will ignore it.
- If a finding is of a high-risk category, they will fix it.
- If a finding refers to a low-risk category, they may fix or ignore it.

After the above tasks, the software team will respond to the security team. The security team will do another round of penetration testing. Here, the security team may add them to the configuration to ignore for this round if they accept the items marked as false-positive. Then they issue the findings for the development and system admin teams to review and address.

Issues with conventional SecOps

This process would continue until the security team is happy to give a thumbs up. The disadvantages of this process are:

- Penetration testing and addressing the issues may take up to a week at least; and

- Development and System Admin Teams only become aware of the security issues after the software goes to production.

We may argue why we cannot do similar penetration testing rounds when the software goes to beta rather than waiting for production release. Well, it depends on how much the business can wait, as such an effort will further push the release date by more than a week.

An illustration of the relative time lapse due to the conventional SecOps in comparison to a DevOps cycle is given in *Figure 1.2*:

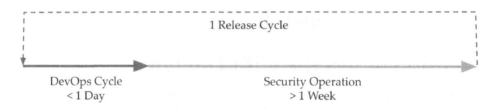

Figure 1.2: *Symbolic depiction of time spent for DevOps and traditional security operations*

Essentially, the above two reasons trigger a transformation in acquiring a new security perspective while practicing DevOps. The resulting process, tools and techniques come in a framework called **DevSecOps**.

Shifting security left

Security is immersed in the DevOps cycle in this new paradigm. To understand this, let us understand the kind of security interventions we can make (given a chance) in different stages of a DevOps cycle, now onwards, we shall call **DevSecOps Cycle**. Thus yes, the infinity loop of DevOps is still valid in DevSecOps.

The above discussion points to the requirement that security is treated in an integrated way with DevOps; it should not be managed separately. We still need to answer how security integrates.

First, it is pretty clear that security comes in the middle of the word DevOps, saying that the security aspect is to be considered at each stage of the infinity loop. This is what we call **shift left**, we no longer think about security after we finish a cycle; instead, we think about it all the time. Such a perspective transforms the culture, process, and tooling we need in DevSecOps.

Let us first look at the difference between the traditional and the new ways. *Table 1.1* explains this lucidly:

Traditional security management	New way
Security outsourced.	Security team is part of the team.
Security operation happens after each software release.	Security operation is integrated into each stage.
Manual and tool-based security scanning.	Least manual intervention. Scanning and data segregation are automated.
The development team only knows about the security issues after the release, and the security team provides feedback.	Each member of the software development and IT operation must be aware of the security aspect.

Table 1.1: Security operations, traditional versus DevSecOps

Basically, we see a clear difference in our approach and process in adopting DevSecOps for an organization. The culture will change, and the process will incorporate the security controls at each stage with engagement from each member of the team. We shall discuss this in the following sections.

Adopting DevSecOps: Key changes

DevSecOps blends software development and IT operations with tightly integrated security operations. We look at the whole process from a new perspective now. The team is now closely integrated; the team culture reflects the close collaboration of variously skilled people for the common goal - secured agile digital infrastructure.

As we have outlined before, the processes, tools and techniques are now different. However, these can be understood through the key changes:

- Lean
- Automation
- Measurement
- Ecosystem interoperability

Figure 1.3 reemphasizes this point:

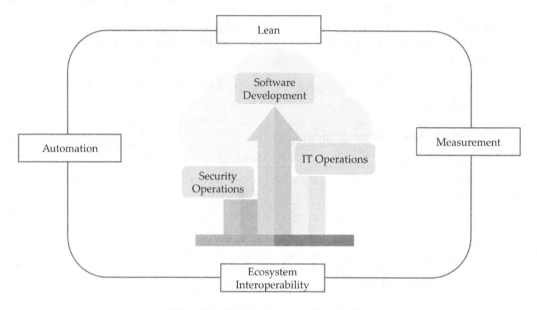

Figure 1.3: *Four key drivers in DevSecOps*

We shall discuss these four key changes in detail for a better understanding of DevSecOps and to prepare us to adopt the new paradigm.

Lean process

It is widely popular to adopt lean processes in project management. This approach in the software industry is embodied by the Agile Methodology. It asks to split the project into many small phases, each spanning over a week or two. Each phase runs in quick succession with a cycle of planning, execution, and feedback. This approach restricts the team from straying from the project scope, timeline, or cost (discussion on challenges to be discussed in *Chapter 7, Digital Transformation and DevSecOps*). It also encourages minimal yet meaningful documentation to maintain and track.

Figure 1.4 illustrates a typical lean agile cycle:

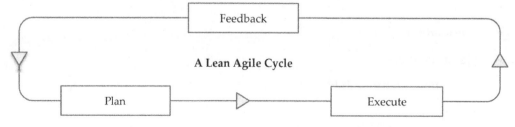

Figure 1.4: *Illustrating a lean agile cycle that is expected to be a bedrock of DevSecOps*

Agile versus DevSecOps: No contradiction

Agile methodology is extended and enhanced in DevSecOps. Each stage of the DevSecOps cycle follows the agile process within itself. We shall see how this is implemented as we make our journey through the book.

We shall discuss planning and security in detail later in this chapter. The execute pertains to the activity pointed by the name of the stage of the DevSecOps cycle. The feedback is rapid after each stage. The speed itself leads to the next driver, automation.

Automation

Like any other industry, software making, and management strives to reduce costs and defects. Of course, there is another aspect, increasing the speed of delivery. The exponential growth in the requirements of software applications happened due to the unhindered intervention of digital technologies in the business landscape.

Moreover, the rapid evolution in digital technologies makes the changes to current software architecture, technologies, and distribution faster. The essential point here is that the ever-increasing delivery speed of software or IT is the order of the day. It is important for a successful customer journey (to be covered in detail in *Chapter 7, Digital Transformation and DevSecOps*), better adoption of a software product and greater satisfaction of customers.

The only way we can move fast is by automating the process. However, automation would need a significant change in our perspective and approach through adopting the right tools and techniques, to be covered in *Chapter 5, Automation and Integration*.

Measurement

We strive to do our best while managing software development, IT operations or even security operations, it would undoubtedly be an advantage to understand the progress, enhancement, and success quantitatively. It is further important as we must choose from many available programming languages, platforms, architectures, frameworks, and databases based on performance, long-term costs, technical liabilities, and debts.

> **Note: A technical liability is a poorly designed software or a component of the software. On the other hand, technical debt is the liability that results from poor design, coding or choice of technologies or codebases.**

> **We shall discuss technical liability and debt in *Chapter 7, Digital Transformation and DevSecOps*. But we shall learn the tools and techniques for measuring the performance of a process and a product in the next chapter.**

The whole process is the **Value Stream Management** (**VSM**) that promotes tracking and controlling software delivery to the organization. For DevSecOps, we use two sets of metrics to measure:

- **DORA Metrics:** DORA stands for The DevOps Research and Assessment team. Its four metrics are **Deployment Frequency (DF)**, **Lead Time for changes (LT)**, **Man Time To Recovery (MTTR)**, and **Change Failure Rate (CFR)**.

- **Flow Metrics:** It measures how value moves through the value stream of a software product with its five metrics: velocity, efficiency, time, load, and distribution.

While the latter is more comprehensive, the first one is popular due to its simplicity. We shall discuss these in great detail in *Chapter 7, Digital Transformation and DevSecOps.*

Ecosystem interoperability

Even though the trinity of the cloud, AWS, GCP and Azure is currently ruling, you may have to opt for tools available in other cloud ecosystems (entirely or partly). Even if you work with the mainstream (read popular) cloud ecosystems, you may have to work across more than one. Also, this will be our approach throughout the book; we shall discuss the advantages and disadvantages of adopting cloud services of a particular ecosystem when we cover a usage scenario.

Figure 1.5 presents four major influencers that demand interoperability across the clouds and hybrid systems:

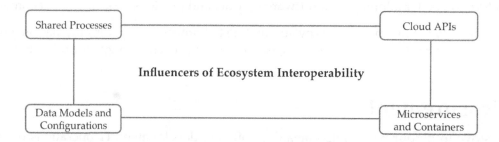

Figure 1.5: Influencers of ecosystem interoperability

The major challenge of multi-cloud management is identifying and aligning the shared processes. DevSecOps culture must permeate across ecosystems. Development tools across the aisles must be integrated. Security process and visibility must be uniform. Configuration management across clouds must be aligned.

One good thing about all the available ecosystems is that they support Microservices (to be discussed in *Chapter 2, Application Security* in great detail) and ReST APIs to integrate different parts of your software system. They may also provide code samples in your preferred programming languages. However, sometimes you may want to migrate from one service in one ecosystem to its counterpart in another, the reason can be the cost, performance, regulatory compliance, or even customer demand. Such a situation, though usual, challenges the resiliency of our solution. While we will discuss this with several examples in the book, this is a typical case of migration. It can be simple, like moving transactional emailing from Mailgun to Twillio. It can be complex, like a SaaS application deployed in multiple geographical regions on one Cloud ecosystem to be moved to another.

Another way to move across ecosystems is using containers like docker and Kubernetes (to be discussed in *Chapter 4, Containers and Security* in detail). Unlike microservices, these enable us to move the software units to different clouds.

While traditional infrastructure provisioning requires an elaborate process, provisioning of infrastructure on the cloud is fast and simple to scale and manage. We will discuss further on this later in this chapter.

Here it is imperative to understand the difference between design and documentation processes in old and new ways, which are responsible for successful software and digital infrastructure lifecycle management.

Documentation of new and old ways

The need for documentation has become more relevant with the speed of changes due to faster software development and infrastructure configuration management. The documentation is now treated as an actionable item during the design phase – you can generate code and configuration based on the design. On the other hand, documentation must self-validate with the actual system for audit and availability.

Table 1.2 lists the differences between the old and new design methods:

Old way	New way
Architectural details are maintained through extensive documentation in the form of e-books, including UML diagrams and data flow diagrams.	Architectural diagrams with notes specific to the public cloud ecosystem, low-code platforms or programming frameworks are recorded.
Infrastructure details are recorded in the form of network diagrams with each asset listed, their configurations, and the way they are linked with one another.	While the top-level infrastructure diagram is maintained for the business team's consumption, the configuration details are kept in special configuration files that are generated or managed through cloud-specific tools (or even simply editing JSON or YML files), these special files, for example, named profiles in AWS, store settings and credentials.
UI designs are usually in graphics with notes associated with these.	UI is more functional, with the possibility of generating front-end code.
Test cases are maintained through spreadsheets or sometimes with software like Smartbear's Zephyr.	Test cases are managed with cloud-based software while intimately connected to the CI/CD pipeline.

Old way	New way
Coding is done through code editors. Versioning is managed through different version control programs like SVN or Git. Deployment is managed manually.	Coding is done through a code editor (either locally or on the Cloud); tools available on low-code platforms may also be used. The versioning control system integrates with CI/CD pipelines and static and dynamic testing tools.

Table 1.2: *Difference in the way we document, in the old way and the DevSecOps Regime*

These are the equivalents when we make the transition from the traditional way of planning to DevSecOps. Security interventions are planned at each step.

Security controls

While working on DevSecOps, we need to understand the security interventions during each cycle. These are **Security Controls** and help us deliver secure software. *Table 1.3* provides the lists of security controls at each stage of DevSecOps.

S. No	DevOps Stage	Security Intervention
I	Design	Threat Modelling, Secure Coding Standard, Security Policies
II	Code	Static Application Security Testing, Security Unit and Functional Testing
III	Integrate	Software Dependency Management, Dynamic Application Security Testing
IV	Deploy	Live Site Penetration Testing, Web Application Firewall Configuration Testing, Digital Inventory Management and Configuration Testing
V	Operate	OperateContinuous Monitoring, Infrastructure Scanning, Access, and Activity Logging
VI	Monitor	Security Audit and Monitoring Feedback, Security Training and Assessment

Table 1.3: *Security intervention at different stages of DevSecOps cycle*

However, it is important that we understand the goal of having security controls. In the following sub-section, we shall discuss the broad goals of security.

Goals of security

There are three goals which act like pillars and guide us to implement security controls in the DevSecOps process:

- **Confidentiality:** The confidentiality of data is very critical when the data is in storage, when it is in process, or when it is in transit. It is about making the data accessible to only those who have permission. The confidentiality of data in storage is ensured by different encryption mechanisms (more in *Chapter 2, Application Security*). The mechanism of protecting data during its process is known as confidential computing (more in *Chapter 3, Infrastructure as a Code*). Data in transit gets its protection from HTTPS encryption (more in *Chapter 5, Automation and Integration*).

- **Integrity:** Integrity of data means that data cannot be changed in an undesired manner. Only valid users can access and modify the data in the expected way for which the application has been designed. We shall discuss this in *Chapter 2, Application Security,* the encryption and decryption of data, maintaining immutable data records during the workflows.

- **Availability:** The software system must be accessible any time the valid end-users need it; the system must be available. We shall discuss this in the context of infrastructure provisioning (high availability architecture) later in this chapter. We shall also discuss the availability of the application (fall to secure default) even when one or more parts are unavailable (we will discuss in *Chapter 2, Application Security*).

We will decipher and elaborate in the remaining sections of this chapter (in fact, we will expand in a big way with practical examples throughout the book).

Documentation and security

The most critical component of all activities in DevSecOps is documentation, actionable and trackable documentation. The documentation must be prepared concerning architecture, infrastructure provisioning, UI, database, functional system, and test cases. Usually, such a thing is initiated at the start of the project; but then evolves (as the project progresses).

There are multiple frameworks for document management. While agile practices, **Information Technology Infrastructure Library (ITIL)**, **IT Service Management (ITSM)**, for example, ISO/IEC 20000, and **Information Security Management (ISM)**, for example, ISO/IEC 27001, are quite popular in documenting different aspects, DevSecOps pushes actionable character in such efforts. We will discuss these more in *Chapter 6, Frameworks and Best Practices*.

While it would have been a happy situation in the pre-DevSecOps regime to manage the documentation in word processor programs (of course, illustrations and diagrams are done through respective programs), we aim now for automated document creation and validation after we input the high-level details.

With a major focus on automation and speed, auto-validation of configurations, databases and codes against the best practices and standards is the way to go.

Moreover, the feedback at each stage and auto-mitigation is a cardinal feature of the DevSecOps process. Feedback can be in the form of an alert to the responsible party (The individual with a specific role with a clear set of access privileges to the DevSecOps tools and systems and a list of tasks to perform).

Threat modelling and security policies

Threat modelling is the process of identifying the threats to the software product and its delivery and mitigating them proactively and cost-effectively. A threat may be a failure due to wrong or inadequate configurations in the system or unwanted external intervention (like a DoS attack).

Different frameworks exist to guide threat modelling; the list is in *Table 1.4*:

Framework	Description
STRIDE	Created by Microsoft, it draws its name from the acronym - Spoofing (impersonate attack), Tampering, Repudiation, Information disclosure, **Denial of service (DoS)**, and Elevation of Privilege.
CVSS	Acronym for Visual, Agile, and Simple Threat, uses an automated threat modelling method by ThreatModeler.
PASTA	Acronym for Process for Attack Simulation and Threat Analysis, uses seven step process
hTMM	Hybrid Threat Modelling Method developed by **Security Equipment Inc. (SEI)**.
Trike	Uses a method to define the system's assets and actors; a five-point probability scale for each CRUD action and actor.
Attack Trees	Uses charts to display the possible paths of security attacks into the system
Security Cards	Uses creative thinking and brainstorming rather than structured threat modelling approaches.

Table 1.4: Popular threat modelling frameworks

Some tools support the DevSecOps cycle and one or more of these frameworks; examples include OWASP Threat Dragon (**https://owasp.org/www-project-threat-dragon**) and ThreatModeler platform (**https://threatmodeler.com**), etc. We will discuss threat modelling frameworks and tools in detail in *Chapter 6, Frameworks and Best Practices*.

While Threat Modeling helps ascertain security threats, we need well-laid policies and procedures for planning, secure coding standard, change management, and progress auditing. ISO **Information Security Management System (ISMS)** leads in laying such a framework.

The way we write such policies has undergone significant changes in the past decade. The considerable increase in security threats and speed of software deliveries have put the onus on continuous tracking of process parameters and actions based on feedback received. And it can be possible by gearing up our infrastructure and code management toward this.

Infrastructure provisioning and security

With the level of automation that we expect, the traditional way of managing infrastructure provisioning and security has become a thing of the past. We need rapid provisioning and scaling while ensuring that the application remains available to its end users. This is possible through the configuration of infrastructure with high availability architecture.

A high availability configuration

A real-life high availability configuration has many complexities: hardware, virtualization, network, and operating system among others. The process also considers the cloud ecosystem(s) and any other private infrastructure that you will engage. Such an in-depth discussion may require a book to itself, and we shall avoid it in this book. Rather, we will discuss a typical architecture; though simple, it can be implemented at an enterprise level.

Figure 1.6 illustrates a typical high availability architecture where a scalable software application is hosted:

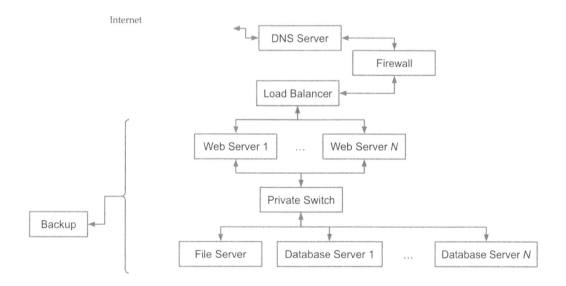

Figure 1.6: *A typical architecture of a scalable and high availability infrastructure*

The request from the user is received at the DNS server (please note that DNS management infrastructure may take a similar high availability architecture itself). The request is then filtered by the firewall before getting routed by Load Balancer, which routes (distributes) the traffic to redundant web servers (having the same application). Here, the request and response between the web servers and file/database servers are routed through a private switch making the data access exclusive to the web servers. Backups (preferably in a different location) are configured for further redundancy to meet **disaster recovery (DR)** safeguards. The failover is ensured by the redundancy of infrastructure, a standard character of the high availability architecture.

Managing infrastructure in the Cloud

With a cloud ecosystem, each component in the configuration, as mentioned above, finds a counterpart (a service on the cloud), be it a server, network, DNS, database, file storage, or backups. Please note that this situation is simplistic, and we will enhance it in the upcoming chapters.

Figure 1.7 is the flow of how one sets up a simple infrastructure deployment on the AWS Cloud:

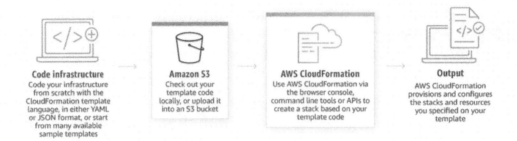

Code infrastructure
Code your infrastructure from scratch with the CloudFormation template language, in either YAML or JSON format, or start from many available sample templates

Amazon S3
Check out your template code locally, or upload it into an S3 bucket

AWS CloudFormation
Use AWS CloudFormation via the browser console, command line tools or APIs to create a stack based on your template code

Output
AWS CloudFormation provisions and configures the stacks and resources you specified on your template

Figure 1.7: *AWS CloudFormation, a simple process for infrastructure deployment*
(***Source****: https://aws.amazon.com/cloudformation/)*

When we provision infrastructure on the cloud, we use predefined templates or custom-designed templates (usually a file written in JSON, YML, etc.). We call this model **Infrastructure a Code (IaC)**, which we shall discuss in detail in *Chapter 3, Infrastructure as a Code*. However, for now, we have discussed the concept in the context of the utility regarding the speed of infrastructure deployment and the ease of validating security requirements.

Security intervention for infrastructure provisioning

Security validation (read testing) can now be done by checking the integrity of the content of this file. The entire process of configuration (provided we have the specifications), deployment (provided we decide to go for cloud-based infrastructure) and security validation (provided we use automated tools for the purpose) now take minutes instead of days. This is the level of automation and the speed level we are looking for.

Code commit, release and security

The coding activities and tools have seen many improvements in recent years regarding rapid code scaffolding, code suggestions and validation. While many languages are used based on their adaptability to the situation, programming frameworks have also received considerable attention from software development teams.

A programming framework

Here is a clarification for the uninitiated: A programming framework employs design patterns, code scaffolding, tools, and best practices to create a way to use the programming languages for building and managing software applications quicker and with the least defects. A few popular frameworks are listed in *Table 1.5*:

Language	Framework	Website
Python	Django	www.djangoproject.com
CSS	Bootstrap	getbootstrap.com
JavaScript	Node JS	nodejs.org
PHP	Laravel	laravel.com

Table 1.5: Popular programming languages and their popular frameworks

We will not dive any further into programming frameworks; We have only mentioned the ones that we will refer to later in the book for use cases and examples.

While discussing frameworks or languages themselves, you need to choose a code editor. Some of the frameworks have their own editors or a full-fledged **Integrated Development Environment (IDE)**. IDEs are also being made available on the cloud to increase access flexibility.

A few examples of popular Cloud code editors and IDEs are given in *Table 1.6*. We will use some of these while discussing use cases and examples in the book:

Cloud IDE	Website link
Google Cloud Shell	cloud.google.com/shell
AWS Cloud9	aws.amazon.com/cloud9/
Azure Notebook	visualstudio.microsoft.com/vs/features/notebooks-at-microsoft/
CodeAnywhere	codeanywhere.com
Red Hat OpenShift Dev Spaces	developers.redhat.com/products/openshift-dev-spaces/overview
Replit	replit.com

Table 1.6: Popular Cloud editors and IDEs

The next thing we need to draw our attention to is version control management systems. Whether pre-DevSecOps or DevSecOps, the version control programs like SVN and Git have been used as shown in *Figure 1.8*:

Figure 1.8: *Different version control systems*

From the standpoint of DevSecOps, we look at these version control systems and IDEs and how they are integrated with security validation and testing programs, test management systems, bug tracking systems, project or task management systems and code deployment systems.

The software code starts its journey from the coder to the live location where end users access it. A bug-free and secure software is managed through different environments during this process:

- **PR environment:** This Pull Request environment is where coders pull the code from the repository to their own dedicated environment for revisions. As we have discussed, such an environment can be in their local machine or on the cloud.

- **QA or Alpha Environment:** This environment is maintained (usually on the Cloud), which the manual testing team can access. QA stands for Quality and Assurance.

- **Staging or beta environment:** This environment on the Cloud is maintained for a pilot group of users (mostly chosen from end users) before the code moves to production.

- **Production or Live Environment:** This is the actual location for software for business use as illustrated in *Figure 1.9*:

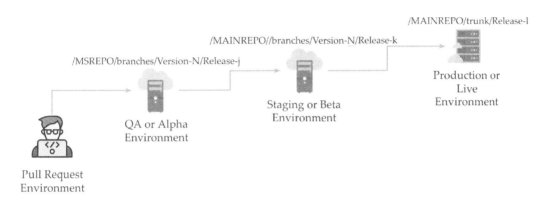

Figure 1.9: *Code deployment into different stages (PR, alpha, beta, and live), particularly from branches and trunk, their relationships*

It is important to learn how different instances of the codebase are integrated from different coders into the repository; also, how different branches in the repository merge into the trunk. You may find the illustration (*Figure 1.9*) useful. We will, of course, refer to and elaborate further in *Chapter 2, Application Security*.

All environments should have the same programming languages, databases, web servers, etc. The Staging Environment should be an exact replica of the Production Environment (maybe on a smaller scale).

Automated security tools in software environments

The automated scanning of the codebase is known as **Static Application Security Testing (SAST)**, and tools are connected to the repository. On the other hand, the code in action (when in staging and production environments, as shown in *Figure 1.10*) must be tested for security; it is known as **Dynamic Application Security Testing (DAST)**.

Version Control Systems provide **Hooks** (like SVN Hooks and Git Hooks) to run tests with the code in the PR environment, eliminating many issues before the code base even goes to the QA team or undergoes SAST. A Hook script runs when an event is triggered in the repository like a new revision.

Figure 1.10 illustrates how these tools are linked with repository and software environments:

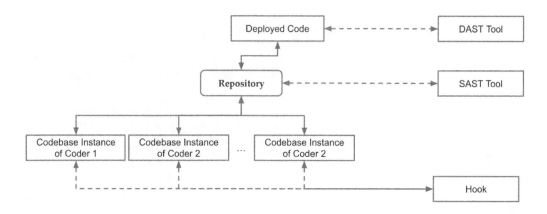

Figure 1.10: *Automated security interventions of DevSecOps during coding, release and deployment*

A use case: IoT application

While we build a robust conceptual foundation about DevSecOps through this book, we will also acquire practical skills for using tools and techniques. To achieve this systematically, let us have a use case in hand. Though the use case has actually been taken from a real-life case study, we will change the company's name and certain workflows to maintain anonymity.

The Use Case is about creating a real-time dashboard for the safety of workers on the factory floor while integrating the company's ERP data for a seamless experience. The company name is FitPractice Inc., and it is engaged in manufacturing and assembling a set of fitness equipment. The Company is a large enterprise and is well-known in the market. The IT in the company is managed in-house through several things sourced from different vendors.

The project is part of their digital transformation initiative (to be discussed in **Chapter 7, Digital Transformation and DevSecOps**), and the **Key Performance Indicator (KPI)** for our requirements are:

- Identify the workers on the factory floor

- Alert if a worker strays into the unsafe perimeter

- Record if a worker stays away from their work area

We shall limit ourselves to discussing only those specific aspects of digital infrastructure and processes that directly connect with our requirements. It must be understood that I have simplified the requirements of data management and application, as the focus of this book is not on coding the software. You may refer to a particular language or tool, but the objective will not be to bind you in any way; we shall also refer to different alternatives.

Upon reviewing the requirements vis-à-vis the available digital infrastructure at the company, the following tasks have been done:

- Creating a sensor network on the factory floor and transmitting the data in real-time to the Cloud.

- Provisioning the Cloud infrastructure and creating a data pipeline that will stream data into Cloud.

- Build dashboards.

- Making data of entry and exit of workers to and from the factory floor available by connecting the ERP attendance management module (that in turn receives data from the RFID tag attached to the workers' identity cards).

The desired system has been illustrated in *Figure 1.11*:

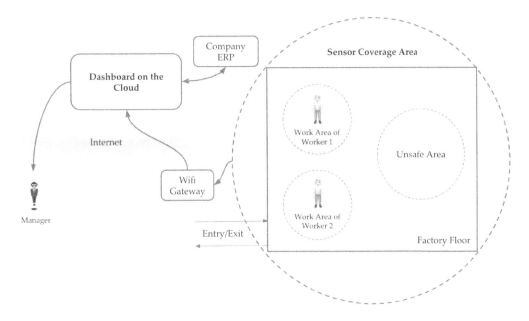

Figure 1.11: Top-level illustration of the data flow in the use case

The Factory Floor is fitted with sensors that take data from the RFID tags to identify the position of the workers who carry those. Each worker's allowed (work) area is estimated with a predefined mapping, similarly to unsafe areas (for the workers to go). The data pipeline is built with the help of a Wi-Fi gateway installed on the premises with continual data streaming to a public cloud platform like **Google Cloud Platform** (**GCP**). Please remember that you may choose another public cloud platform like AWS or Azure; we will discuss those comparisons and guidelines for making choices in *Chapter 3, Infrastructure as a Code*.

For this project, a group of people have been selected that includes software developers, a project manager, a system administrator, a solution architect, and a security expert:

- **Project Manager:** The person should be well-versed in software development process management.

- **Solution Architect:** The person understands how the solution can be implemented - cloud provisioning, database design, microservice design, sensor network deployment, data pipeline establishment, dashboard design and API integration.

- **System Administrator:** The person must have strong skills in provisioning cloud for the project, configuration management and automating the CI/CD pipeline.

- **Full-stack Developers:** Software developers with knowledge of comprehensive hands-on skills with UI, front-end and back-end programming, and database designing expertise. For this project, the individuals must have an understanding of IoT and knowledge of the Company's ERP and its APIs.

- **Security Expert:** The person must understand application security and penetration testing well.

Each of these individuals (read 'roles') intend to be skilled with DevSecOps methodology as we progress. Requisite information will be provided through the chapters of this book that will implement a robust DevSecOps framework, it will result in a secure application that evolves fast and continually matches the business expectation. If you are in any of the above five roles, you, after reading the book, will understand what will make a successful DevSecOps in your project.

In the following three sections, we shall demonstrate how the DevSecOps cycle is introduced into the project. Though we shall take through the Use Case for this, the purpose is generic. You can apply the principle to any of your projects.

It is premature to start the project without a list of KPIs and a robust architecture to support it. Right tools and technologies must also be chosen considering the long-term costs and liabilities (to be discussed in *Chapters 6, Frameworks and Best Practices*, and *Chapter 7, Digital Transformation and DevSecOps*).

Conclusion

We have learnt why security is important in DevOps and what a DevSecOps journey looks like. We received an understanding of the DevSecOps process and various concepts involved therein. We also saw how the intervention of security at each stage of the DevSecOps cycle and the available technological developments offer a new perspective on how we manage software delivery in an organization.

We shall dive deeper into the concepts learnt and employ those in the Use Case (described in the last section) in the next chapters.

Questions

1. What does a DevOps cycle look like?

2. How would we manage security operations along with DevOps if we stick to the conventional way?

3. What are the issues if we treat security operations separately?

4. Why do we include Security as an integrated part of DevOps that makes what we call, DevSecOps?

5. Is the famed Infinite Loop of DevOps still valid in DevSecOps?

6. How does security integrate with development and operation? What is the concept of 'shift left' in DevSecOps?

7. What are the key changes when adopting DevSecOps?

8. Is the Agile Methodology in direct contradiction with DevSecOps?

9. Why is automation critical in DevSecOps?

10. Why, what, and how to measure success in DevSecOps?

11. How do the old and new design methods compare when we transition to DevSecOps?

12. Where can we have security intervention in DevSecOps?

13. How is documentation important in the planning stage of DevSecOps, and how shall we approach the same?

14. What is Threat Modelling, and why is it needed?

15. What is a typical high availability architecture?

16. How do we manage infrastructure provisioning in a cloud environment?

17. How does security intervention happen for infrastructure provisioning?

18. What does a code commit process look like?

19. How are the automated tools linked with the code repository and software environments?

Join our book's Discord space

Join the book's Discord Workspace for Latest updates, Offers, Tech happenings around the world, New Release and Sessions with the Authors:

https://discord.bpbonline.com

## CHAPTER 2

Application Security

Introduction

With a broad understanding of the contours of DevSecOps, we shall focus on each aspect in substantial detail from now on. The core objective of any software development management exercise is to make the application robust, secure, scalable, and distributed; hence, we will first concentrate on application security from such contexts within the framework of DevSecOps.

Cloud computing makes it possible to achieve a software-centric approach to end-to-end IT management. In this perspective, we view application, hardware, and network infrastructure as pieces of code. Thus, it has been imperative to relook at the software architecture.

Different methods and tools have transformed how we design and implement modern applications. Understanding how various components work together in an application will pave the way for analyzing its scalability and security. Over the past several years, we have acquired advanced tools and techniques in this direction and will present these in the current chapter.

Structure

In this chapter, we will discuss the following topics:

- An app on the Cloud

- CI/CD pipeline and security

- Low-code and no-code platforms

- Application security

- Use case: Making a secure application

Objectives

This chapter dives deep into application security. First, we shall learn what makes a modern software application the tools and technologies involved. Our focus will majorly be on cloud-based distributed apps; in fact, the whole industry of software making strives for it. A comprehensive discussion about the architecture will bring awareness and understanding of the security requirements in designing, developing, deploying, and managing a software application. Later, we shall cover different frameworks, tools, and techniques to achieve this. Lastly, we shall apply these in the use case described in the previous chapter.

An app on the Cloud

With a wide acceptance of Cloud computing, justifiably so, the architecture of a software application has undergone transformative changes. We speak about microservices, serverless architectures, etc. However, before discussing these, let us understand how apps deliver data and functions on the Cloud that we call **cloud services**.

Delivery of Cloud services

A Cloud computing platform is essentially built through **virtualization**, a process that masks actual hardware and network infrastructure. In a typical situation, the deployment can be massive and may also be distributed geographically.

On the other hand, a software application may use a limited computing infrastructure at a single location for hosting a small private cloud for a niche application. In either scenario, we can still abstract how cloud services are delivered, as shown in *Figure 2.1*.

We can think of a piece of application software as an app. We can consider software that manages a server (creating the server, editing the server's configuration, or even deleting the server) as an app. Some overlook this subtle difference and instead refer to the server as an app. A cloud platform hosts multiple apps (usually tens or hundreds). These apps can be accessed by one another and by apps outside the platform through an **Application Programming Interface (API)**. The external apps can be in:

- The same platform but with different tenants

- Different public cloud

- A vanilla server placed on-premises

- A simple laptop hosting a piece of software with HTTPS access to the outside world

Refer to *Figure 2.1*:

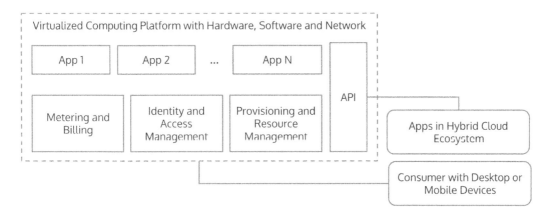

Figure 2.1: *Delivery of Cloud services, the multi-layered architecture of software in the cloud*

End-users can also access apps on the Cloud Platform. However, the following three special tools (software apps only) are mandatory before accessing apps:

- **Identity and Access Management (IAM)**

- **Metering and Billing (MB)**

- **Provisioning and Resource Management (PRM)**

We shall discuss these in the following three subsections. We shall see how they comply with our **Confidentiality, Integrity, and Availability (CIA)** security goals addressed in *Chapter 1, Security in DevOps*.

Identity and access management

The access control mechanism in an app is most important for the security of data and the functions that change the data states within it. A simple login goes a long way to ensure the app's security. Still, it is essential to manage the security aspects well. Two critical things that we track are:

- Management of cookies and sessions

- Matching the password in the database

When a user intends to access a resource (a URL or a program file), it is verified if the user has valid access. The access token is usually stored as a cookie value on the user device or a session value at the server location. This token is validated each time the user accesses the resource. Users who do not have such tokens are redirected to the login (or sign-in) screen. The user provides a username and a password on the login screen for checking against the existing user record. If the information (provided by the user) matches, a cookie or a session token is created for future use (validation). Otherwise, the user sees the error message. This process is called **user authentication**.

Today, with computing resources moving outside the cozy boundary of the corporate office, the authentication mechanism is in focus for modern software applications. With the growing sophistication of attack techniques, the authentication mechanism has evolved into a rather complex one. Only the username-password pair is no longer adequate, and we have more stages of verifying the authenticity of the user. The technique in practice is **Multi-Factor Authentication (MFA)**.

An email is sent to the email address matching the record corresponding to the username-password pair in the user database. The process may be designed to send an SMS instead of an email or both email and SMS. The rightful user verifies through a **One-Time Passcode (OTP)** received. People ascribe the process to two-factor authentication if only one (email or SMS) is used apart from the username-password pair for authentication.

Another modern technique is **Single Sign-On (SSO)**. It eliminates the need for a separate username-password pair for each application. Rather, it enables the user to have a single pair for authenticating multiple applications that support such a feature. There are many providers for SSO, like Google, Yahoo, Microsoft, Twitter, etc. You need to check which one is supported by your application. While modern SaaS applications support popular SSO tools like Google or Twitter, you may seek custom integrations with your preferred SSO provider for enterprise applications. The hybrid working and increased mobility of business users have led to an increased focus on these **Identity Governance and Administration (IGA)** technologies.

When the application authenticates a user, the next important thing is checking if the user is authorized to access the desired resource. It is known as **authorization**, checking if the user has access to the exact resource or permission to perform a particular action.

> **Note: User authentication establishes whether it is a valid user on the system. On the other hand, authorization confirms if the user has access to particular resources. For example, an authenticated user may not have permission to edit a specific data record.**

Figure 2.2 illustrates a typical authentication and authorization process for a user request to access protected cloud resources:

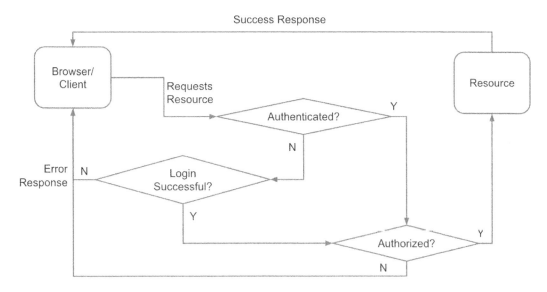

Figure 2.2: *A typical authentication and authorization of resources (data and functions)*

After authentications and authorizations are done, the user gets access to the resource. The cloud services offer a pay-per-use basis, and the meter is switched on. Of course, cloud vendors also provide a price for a fixed period that renews. Let us discuss the process in detail in the next section.

Metering and billing

The cloud service providers create the pricing along different parameters. It is based on whether the provisioning is at the level of **Infrastructure-as-a-Service (IaaS)**, **Platform-as-a-Service (PaaS)**, and **Software-as-a-Service (SaaS)**. The broad parameters are:

- Hardware and network infrastructure

- Operating systems and programming platform

- Value-added software development and maintenance

- Software to manage resource provisioning and billing

- Software for security and regulatory compliance requirements

The tools that operate the metering and billing process are critical for delivering a cloud service. The process can be complex if a service depends on other cloud services on a different platform, a typical case of hybrid architecture. API integration and microservices form the basis of such an outlook. Automation, as usual, increases the speed of activities;

on the other hand, it inflates the risk of disaster if full-proof contracts are not in place between two different cloud services (we shall learn more about it from the perspective of microservices in a later section).

Provisioning and resource management

One of the characteristics of cloud computing is resource pooling while delivering the infrastructure, platform or software services to the users. Provisioning and resource management adhere to this principle.

> **Note: Cloud Computing model has five characteristics, and cooperative resource management among the tenants of the computing infrastructure is one of them. If you want to read more on the model of cloud computing, please refer to https://www.nist.gov/news-events/news/2011/10/final-version-nist-cloud-computing-definition-published.**

In the context of the above tools for the successful delivery of cloud services, let us look at the constituents of an App (in the modern context).

Constituents of an app

As discussed earlier in this chapter, it is pertinent to see an app as a piece of software that orchestrates hardware infrastructure or platform or even a software application for end-users. Such varying usage has given rise to the requirement of relooking at the definition of an app.

The following are the four major constituents of an app:

- **Business Ops:** An App is meant to serve a purpose. A system administration app allows you to manage your operating system and networking. A storefront app provides the necessary tools to display your products online and to accept payment. Even when a business suite like ERP or CRM is used, the apps inside it do specific tasks; apps have well-defined data management functions. Business **Operations (Ops)** define those specific functions.

- **Disconnected Ops:** In real situations, there can be disruptions in the internet, thus throwing the cloud-based software out of action. Disconnected Ops is about managing situations where the accessing client of the user (mostly a browser with which the app is accessed) loses connection with the app on the cloud.

- **API:** API consists of two basic elements: the protocol and format of data for communication between two apps. Adherence to a standard protocol and a data format opens unlimited opportunities for scaling the business systems in a distributed manner. The popular protocols are SOAP, **Representational State Transfer (ReST)** and XML-RPC, even though ReST is the most adopted. Popular formats are XML and JSON; the latter has recently gained immense popularity.

- **IAM:** We have already discussed in detail about this earlier in this chapter. The basic premise of IAM is to create a mechanism where only valid users get access to the system and access the resources they have been assigned for. While the authentication may be done through the SSO tools using OAuth, OpenID or SAML, the authorization process depends on a **Role Based Access Control (RBAC)** scheme.

Refer to *Figure 2.3* for an illustration of the constituents of an app:

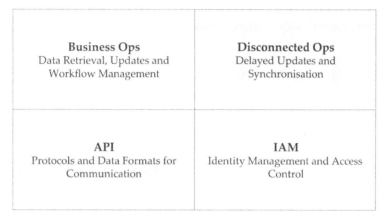

Figure 2.3: *The constituents of an app*

App and workflow

Within an app, a user's request may trigger an action to add a new record or change a record. Programmers write a method for each action. However, a data record goes through several states in a multi-user environment. A select group of users can access these states and their transitions to other states. We call any of these states a workflow state. The transition of one state to another may trigger an action that can change the same record or do something else.

Figure 2.4 illustrates the possibility of multiple states of data records in a multi-user environment:

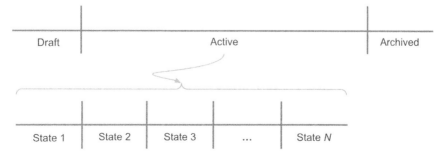

Figure 2.4: *The workflow in app*

An active data record undergoes transition through different states to fulfil the workflow requirements of the business rules. Here, a data record can be in the draft phase when created and made active (depending on the business rule). Also, an allowed user may mark the record as archived. While a data record is in the active phase, it can move through N (N > 0) number of states (workflow states). If N = 1, there is no workflow. If N > 1, workflow is initiated.

To cite an example of an article submission and review workflow for an online magazine, we would consider each article as a data record. A record can be in the draft phase when created by an author. It does not have a real value to the publishing workflow until it is made active. When active, a record can be marked as submitted. Then the article may be reviewed by another user to be labelled as reviewed and approved, such a record is published online. If the article is rejected or withdrawn, the state of the record is marked as rejected or withdrawn. N = 3 here. This scenario is one of the simplest workflows in online publishing.

We must remember that the data records in an app must be traceable and transparent concerning any operation. Some call this feature of data record immutability, the values of a data record must be obtained by going to its past versions. We adopt to implement this versioning procedure within the app architecture. Such a record is known as an **electronic record**; it helps to maintain the traceability of a data record in an app. On the other hand, any change in a data record is maintained by the audit log, a must-have for any app. Traceability and transparency in data record management help regulate app usage in a business environment.

Today, it is a mandatory requirement to monitor access to the app and data operations within the app. The quantitative measurement along different performance parameters and appropriate actions based on various conditions have become a must too.

Now, let us understand the microservices and their role in building a scalable and easily-maintainable app.

Session management: Cookie and JSON web token

The HTTP protocol is a stateless one. When you send a request to the server, it does not get any clue about the previous request or does not leave any indication for the subsequent request. It means transactions over HTTP (also HTTPS, transactions over the secured port) do not facilitate any memory regarding the user they are accessing the application. The session offers a token which is the key to such a memory. Session token, if not secured, leads to a disastrous situation where unwanted people can access the user data.

Figure 2.5 illustrates the working of the session management:

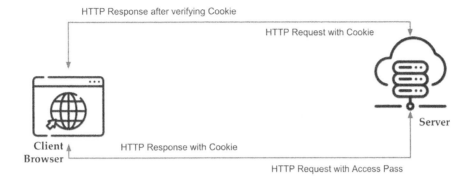

Figure 2.5: Creating session for an application

A user requests authentication with a username and password pair (we term this an access pass). A cookie is generated and stored at the client browser end if authenticated. It is a piece of string and is usually encrypted for vulnerability due to its client-side location. Post the first authentication, the HTTP request from the client browser carries the cookie to the server for validation and obtaining the application resource that it seeks.

The above authentication process is the simplest. In actual life, we use MFA for more stringent authentication (as discussed earlier in this chapter). On the other hand, modern enterprise computing requires applications on various servers to be approached by the same user with a single credential (or access pass). Such a credential is called a **federated identity**. As a standard that has been quite popular, **JSON Web Token (JWT)** is a widely adopted standard for transacting information with federated identity.

Figure 2.6 illustrates the working of federated identity and JWT:

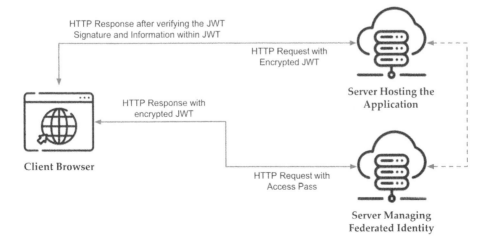

Figure 2.6: Federated identity and JWT

JWT consists of three parts separated by dots (**.**) and looks like **aaaaa.bbbbb.ccccc**:

- **Header:** It is a JSON array with two elements: type of token (here it is **jwt**) and type of hashing algorithm used (it can be HMAC SHA256 or RSA). It looks something like **{"alg": "HS256", "typ": "JWT"}**.

- **Payload:** It forms the core part of the information, again a JSON array, and is termed a claim. It can be marked additionally as registered, public or private. If the payload claim is public, the namespace of the JSON key must be adopted from the IAWA JSON Web Token Registry or URI with a collision-resistant namespace.

- **Signature:** JWT needs to be signed with a secret, and the resultant string is transmitted.

For fail-safe data handling, each JSON array must be encoded and decoded for fail-safe data handling with Base64. Broadly, the encryption of the JWT looks like the following:

HMACSHA256(base64UrlEncode(header) + "." + base64UrlEncode(payload), secret)

The website **jwt.io** provides a tool to encode and decode a JWT, as shown in *Figure 2.7*:

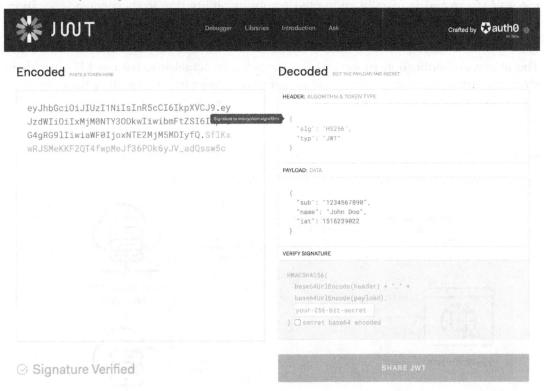

Figure 2.7: *JWT encoding and decoding*

As you can see, the information carried inside JWT may be viewed if the secret is known. As a security practice, it is advisable to encrypt confidential information before passing over a JWT.

Encryption

We discussed data security in storage, transit and processing in the previous chapter. One crucial aspect is encryption, where we encode the data value (encrypt), masking the value from unwanted eyes if exposed. In cryptography, the encryption process is of two types:

- **Symmetric encryption**

  Symmetric encryption is termed so because of the symmetric use of a single key for both encrypting and decrypting data. This symmetric key must be known to both parties and kept secret, establishing a shared, private method of communication. The data before encoding (**plaintext**) is converted into **ciphertext** (after encoding) with the help of a cryptographic key. We can always revert or decode (decrypt) and return our original value.

Figure 2.8 shows the process of encryption and decryption:

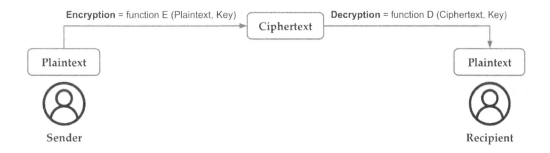

Figure 2.8: The process of symmetric encryption and decryption

Symmetric encryption is used for storing sensitive data in the database where the process needs to be fast. Please note that symmetric encryption is faster than asymmetric encryption, which we shall discuss next. Different algorithms are used for symmetric encryption; the popular one is AES.

- **Asymmetric encryption**

  Asymmetric encryption is named for its use of two distinct keys, creating an asymmetrical relationship between encryption and decryption processes. This approach utilizes a publicly shared key for encryption and a private key for decryption, thereby facilitating secure communications between parties who have not previously shared secret information.

As the process is slower due to the use of two keys and the nature of algorithms, it is mainly used for digital signatures and SSL certificates where a small amount of data is transferred, and there is a need for higher security.

Figure 2.9 illustrates the encryption and decryption of data when transferred from the sender to the recipient:

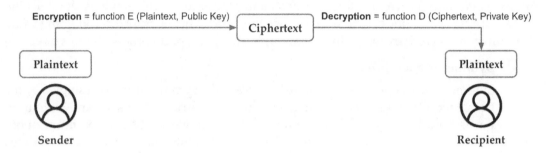

Figure 2.9: The process of asymmetric encryption and decryption

There are different asymmetric encryption algorithms available; the popular one is **Rivest-Shanir-Adleman (RSA)**.

An essential aspect of encryption is the management of the keys. While the encryption process creates the data in an unreadable form, the cryptographic key(s) exposure can diminish the advantage. Algorithms are open, but the keys need to be secured. Some advocate using unique keys for various tasks within an application, but using multiple keys increases more work in maintaining them; thus, the number of keys and their storage may be devised based on the use case.

Hashing differs fundamentally from symmetric and asymmetric encryption in that it is a one-way process. While encryption is about securing data for later retrieval in its original form, hashing is about verifying the integrity and authenticity of data without the need to revert to the original form. This irreversible nature is crucial for applications like secure password storage, where we need to validate input without actually storing the original sensitive information.

Let us focus on understanding the hash functions used to encrypt and decrypt data.

Hash function

A **hash** function provides a mechanism to create an irreversible string from the plaintext. The resulting string is called a **message digest** (or a **hash**). Hash is usually used for passwords, digital signatures and blockchains, etc. Two classes of algorithms are used for hashing:

- **md5** is available as a 128-bit hash and is still popularly used.

- **SHA 3** is available as 224, 256, 384 and 512-bit hashes and offers more robust encryption than md5.

Figure 2.10 illustrates the working of a hash function:

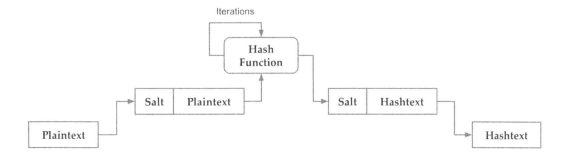

Figure 2.10: An illustration of hashing

The uniqueness of hash outputs is paramount. A hash collision, where two different inputs produce the same hash - could compromise the security and integrity of systems relying on hashing. For instance, in password verification, a collision might allow unauthorized access if two different passwords produce the same hash. Any attempt to compromise hash in this way is called a **hash attack**. Therefore, modern hash functions like SHA-3 are designed to minimize the risk of collisions, ensuring a nearly one-to-one correspondence between the original data and its hash value, it is achieved with multiple iterations of the hash function and addition of **salt**, a fixed-length random string is concatenated to the plaintext. This aspect is a cornerstone in maintaining the reliability and security of hash-based systems.

Public key infrastructure and secured socket layer

With a solid understanding of encryption and hashing, let us discuss the **Public Key Infrastructure (PKI)** and **Secured Socket Layer (SSL)**.

We already know the role of SSL in securing the data in transit (from the client browser to the server and vice versa). The PKI is managed by a **Certification Authority (CA)** that issues an SSL certificate for a uniquely **Distinguished Name (DN)** or domain name. There are many leading CAs, including GlobalSign (**globalsign.com**), Comodo (**comodosslstore.com**), let us encrypt (**letsencrypt.org**, which makes certificates available free), etc. Recently, the CA Setigo (**https://sectigo.com**).

> **Note: The Certification Authorities manage PKI for SSL certificates, digital signatures, and secure signing of codes, among other possible utilities.**

Figure 2.11 shows the SSL issue process in detail:

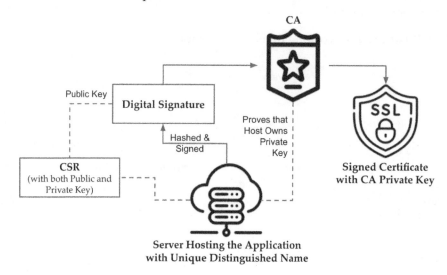

Figure 2.11: *The issuing process for an SSL certificate from CA*

Figure 2.12 shows the SSL information when we click the secure lock icon on the browser's address bar:

Figure 2.12: *A wildcard SSL issued on a domain name*

Microservices

Microservice is an independently running unit of an app. Such a modular approach has pushed for:

- **Smaller teams:** One to three developers can usually manage a microservice based on the complexities involved. The current practice of full-stack development greatly augments such efforts by aligning requisite technologies into human skills and pipeline automation.

- **Smaller iteration of sprint:** A microservice can run independently with requisite inputs though such inputs may come from other Microservices through API. With a small team and requirements to take care of, the Sprint cycle is relatively short.

Note: The Input/Output (I/O) is managed with the help of API. Microservice helps construct the app's business logic, UI components, or even both.

We maintain the list of microservices for our application in a dictionary or database called **service registry**. We must authenticate at the service registry to allow any microservice usage. This concept is vital to exposing the microservices outside the application through an API gateway.

Figure 2.13 illustrates how a microservice is stacked with a service registry and its ultimate use within an application:

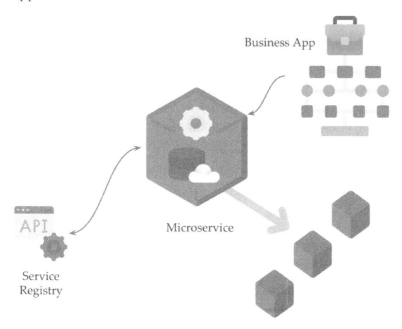

Figure 2.13: *Microservice, service registry and business application*

Microservice architecture is critical for scaling software applications. A microservice may use one dedicated database, multiple dedicated databases or a shared database as appropriate. Of course, a dedicated database for microservice will be a preferred option for its independence and simplicity of data management.

Let us now look at different ways of deploying a software application.

High availability deployment and multi-instance deployment

We have already discussed the infrastructure provisioning for a modern cloud-based software application in the section **Infrastructure Provisioning and Security** of the previous chapter. We shall discuss the two deployment models for an application with distinct objectives.

Figure 2.14 illustrates these two deployment models from the same repository:

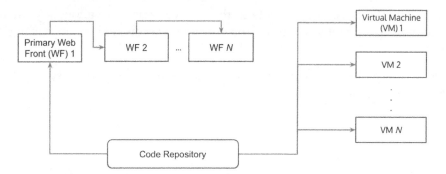

Figure 2.14*: Two different scenarios of two different deployment situations*

The left one depicts the deployment of an application to one server that is mirrored to multiple servers, and the right one depicts simultaneous deployment to multiple servers.

These two deployment models arise from different scenarios and challenges.

The high availability deployment requires multiple servers with replica hardware and software environments, and the application will be replicated on those. There is one primary server, and the others are mirror servers. When we make any change to the primary, the new version is reflected on each of the mirrored servers. During deployment, we must keep the following in mind:

- **Configuration file management:** In this deployment, the server operating system and application environment (technology stack) have the same configuration but can have different parameter values, like server login access details. There must be a way to preserve these values by avoiding replicating data from the primary to the mirror ones.

- **Database:** The database should also have a master-slave array of servers, but then we should do it separately. The database must not be located inside the web fronts - as discussed in the previous chapter.

- **File storage:** The file storage is kept separate from the web fronts, and an array of file servers is maintained to maintain data redundancy. If the file storage (user-generated data in the application) is kept to the web front, it will be disastrous. Let us understand this situation better. For example, we upload a file **F1.txt** while accessing a mirror web front **WF-N**. In such a case, the uploaded file will not be available when we access the application through other web fronts. It is because we only replicate the data from the primary server to all the mirror servers. In modern applications, we invariably store data files for web applications on cloud storage that adhere to such redundancy protocol; examples are AWS S3, Google Cloud Storage, etc. *Figure 2.15* describes the process of data transit where we use both cloud storage and primary data storage locally (local to the application):

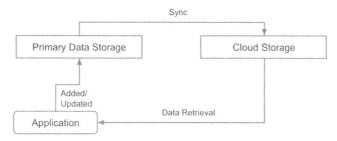

Figure 2.15*: Two different scenarios of two different deployment situations*

All the transactions are made over SSL, and the sync delay can be negligible. Of course, we must be aware of such a delay for certain mission-critical applications. The data from the application gets added or updated to the primary storage, which in turn is synced into the cloud storage (you may align this procedure into the mirror servers or **Content Delivery Networks (CDNs)**, as the case may be).

CDNs are a network of servers strategically distributed across various geographical locations, designed to deliver web content and services more efficiently to users. The primary objective of a CDN is to reduce latency by providing data from the server closest to the end-user. These are pivotal in enhancing the performance and speed of web services and applications. By caching content on multiple servers around the world, they minimize the distance between the server and the user, thus reducing latency and speeding up load times. This mechanism is not only crucial for delivering content quickly but also plays a role in handling high traffic loads and protecting against DDoS attacks. Furthermore, CDNs are dynamic in nature, meaning they can also serve personalized content based on the user's location, device, or other criteria.

Also, mirror servers are not merely backup servers. They serve the application to its users based on demand from the load balancer (We have discussed the concept of load balancer in the previous chapter). Thus, we must organize the data backup independent of the high availability configuration.

In contrast to the above, we may have a scenario where we want to deploy our application to multiple server locations - multi-instance deployment. Such a situation can be one or more:

First, different countries or economic regions have adopted their own digital data management acts. The reference can be for local data activities or even any activities involving people from the region. Two important examples are the GDPR by the European Union and the **California Privacy Rights and Enforcement Act (CCPA)**, which illustrate the varying geographies and the coverage of the acts. An increasing number of countries require that an application's data be stored within the geographic boundaries and even processed within. An enterprise wanting to deploy the same application in different geographies with a mandated need for localizing the data will go for the multi-instance deployment of the application. The application will be deployed in the respective local server environment even if the code repository is managed centrally.

The second possibility is when a vendor deploys their application for organizations requiring dedicated installations. The need entails the complete separation of data storage and processing. Such deployment can have a replica of the application deployed on different servers (on public cloud, private cloud or even traditional infrastructure). However, it becomes tricky if we have requirements for specific customizations concerning the following:

- Specific application features

- Natural language

- Integration with third-party software systems

The deployment can happen with just a vanilla codebase or the one bundled into a container. We shall discuss containers, their usages and their security in *Chapter 4, Containers and Security*.

Meanwhile, let us continue our discussion to understand the deployment environments further.

Serviceful and serverless

During our discussion of the microservice concept earlier in this chapter, we saw the significant architectural achievement is the independence of small functional units of the program that then work with other such programs (read microservices) through API to produce the full application. Thus, the code we write can be bundled into a microservice and brought to life within any application with the help of API. This is serviceful.

Major further advancement in a microservice architecture is towards building an application without worrying about server infrastructure is serverless computing.

While many enterprises raise concerns regarding the overall cost of use (development, deployment, migration and management), serverless computing is here to stay.

In fact, there has been widespread adoption of serverless computing, particularly for creating new applications. Some of the advantages of serverless computing are the following:

- Quick realization of **Minimum Viable Product** (**MVP**) of a new application, faster time to market

- Elimination of most of the system administration tasks

- Dynamic scalability based on workload demands from the users

Table 2.1 lists some of the important serverless computing facilities across cloud ecosystems:

Cloud ecosystem	Serverless Cloud services	Resource Link
AWS	Lambda, Fargate	**https://aws.amazon.com/serverless/**
Azure	Serverless functions, Serverless Kubernetes	**https://azure.microsoft.com/en-us/ solutions/serverless/**
GCP	Cloud Run, Cloud Functions	**https://cloud.google.com/serverless**

Table 2.1: *Serverless computing in Cloud ecosystems*

Serverless computing has rapidly evolved as a compelling alternative for developers, driven by advancements in serverless frameworks. These frameworks offer code scaffolding, which involves generating basic code structures from predefined templates, alongside essential configuration files and libraries. This approach significantly accelerates the development of serverless applications by reducing boilerplate coding tasks and allowing developers to focus on the unique aspects of their application. However, it's important to note that these frameworks still operate within serviceful configurations, where underlying services are fully managed and abstracted away by the cloud provider. In this context, microservice architecture often emerges as the preferred design pattern, aligning well with the distributed and scalable nature of serverless computing.

Refer to *Figure 2.16*:

The Seattle Times The Seattle Times uses AWS Lambda to resize images for viewing on different devices such as desktop computers, tablets, and smartphones. Read the case study »

Figure 2.16: *The most popular serverless cloud service has been AWS Lambda*

Putting all together: A security perspective

We have described the relevant concepts that constitute a modern application that is cloud native. We can choose whether we want to have a serverless app or a server-based app. In either option, the microservices constitute the application bundled in a container (a full-blown coverage is in *Chapter 4, Containers and Security*). *Figure 2.17* shows the modularization of the different assets in the cloud environment and how a business app stacks in it:

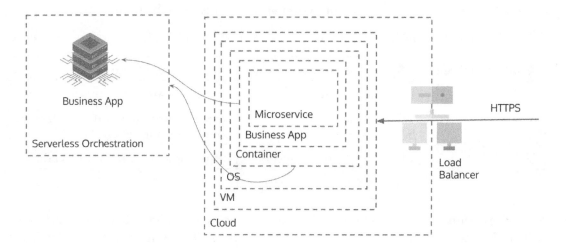

Figure 2.17: *Illustration of different levels of modularization*

In the above illustration, the server infrastructure with an **Operating System** (**OS**) and **Virtual Machine** (**VM**) is either visible to the developer or auto-managed by the cloud system. The data transaction between the cloud and the client browser is through HTTPS (secured HTTP), and the traffic is managed through the load balancer.

As discussed in the previous chapter, security is enforced at the transaction, storage and processing level. While SSL (which we shall discuss later in this chapter) ensures security during data transactions between the cloud and the client browser, the storage is protected through data encryption. Suppose there is a need for the processing of high-sensitive information. In that case, we can also opt for confidential computing (explained in the previous chapter) that involves hardware-level encryption to ensure data protection during processing.

CI /CD pipeline and security

During the DevSecOps cycle, the developers continually change the codebase. Instead of waiting for long period cycles of a traditional approach, tools and techniques around DevSecOps make it fast to incorporate (read integrate) the changes into the original codebase **Continual Integration (CI)** and to deploy the code so that it can be used, **Continual Deployment (CD)**.

As discussed in the section **Code Commit, Release and Security** of the previous chapter, the codebase is stored in a repository, and developers update their working copy through a pull request. Based on the tech stack and version control system, hooks can validate and monitor code quality and security aspects when the developer wants to commit the code to the repository. After the update, the repository goes through SAST scanning. It should be noted that the SAST process, though automated, has several dependencies:

- The programming language used

- Language framework used

- Any particular library or code practices

- Integration capability for your repository version control system and any other tools that you use

Many products are available in the market - some are free, some paid, and even some free and open source. You can see a comprehensive list of these tools at:

https://owasp.org/www-community/Source_Code_Analysis_Tools

While choosing the tool for your DevSecOps project, you must keep the above four things in mind.

There is another level of validation which can have far-reaching implications on compliance and security of the application, **Source Composition Analysis (SCA)**. These tools help analyze and track open-source components of the software. The advantages are the following:

- **Compliance advantage:** We spoke on technical liability regarding open-source software use. It can be the license terms and their compatibility with the overall application. With SCA tools, we track the open-source components, thereby feeding the digital asset tracking for compliance and determining the compatibility of the versions used.

- **Security advantage:** We do not intend in any way to any inherent weakness of open-source components. However, the maintenance, testing procedures and security measures in these components vary as these are managed by different developers' communities and as a community effort (not having the demand for the rigor of commercial compliance). It can safely be said that things vary from one to another. Thus, tracking the open-source components for dependencies and their versions for any inherent or introduced vulnerabilities is essential. CSA tools help us achieve that.

As a part of continuous deployment, the code from the repository makes its way to QA, staging or production environments. Please note that we use the name environment to incorporate scenarios like single server, high availability and serverless deployments.

DAST pertains to tracking and analyzing vulnerabilities when the application is in use. The organization may decide to invest in DAST in all environments or the production environment (a matter of criticality and economics).

> **Note: In a traditional security management method, a separate team (usually external) works on the vulnerability assessment and penetration testing. While this team use various scanners to assess the vulnerabilities and tools to collaborate with the developers to track and reconcile their findings, manual intervention may be wise to opt-out.**

We must draw our attention to other relevant categories of tools. One is **Interactive Application Security Testing (IAST)**. It combines some aspects of both SAST and DAST. The method requires installing an agent to track, analyze and alert the active attacks. Such an arrangement requires understanding the technology stack and the requirement for additional computing resources in our application environments. The major drawback is that it only handles active attacks, not potential vulnerabilities. The major products in this area are Synopsys (**synopsys.com**) and Acunetix (**acunetix.com**), etc.

Another category of tooling is **Runtime Application Self-Protection (RASP)**, where security analysis and monitoring are done for active vulnerabilities. IAST and RASP require resources from the application's host environment and only take care of active vulnerabilities. There are complexities in managing these; they can be adopted alongside SAST and DAST.

Web application firewall

While these tools help in ascertaining the vulnerabilities, alerting and possibly blocking suspicious user requests, there is a traffic regulating technology worth mentioning, the **Web Application Firewall (WAF)**. It works with the load balancer and is part of the network edge technology acting as an **Application Security Manager (ASM)**. It inspects all traffic coming to the web application or APIs and helps avoid cookie poisoning, SQL injection and denial attacks on the application.

The WAF comprises a set of rules that any incoming traffic needs to obey. In case of exception, the firewall software blocks the incoming traffic to the application. *Figure 2.18* illustrates the working of a WAF:

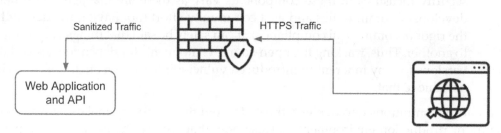

Figure 2.18: *Web application firewall in action*

WAF can be deployed in two forms:

- **Transparent bridge:** It only inspects traffic and is configured without any changes to the network devices or servers.

- **Reverse proxy**: It accepts incoming traffic to the server with a virtual IP address and reroutes it to the backend server.

We must be aware that WAF introduces a latency that must be accommodated into the application's overall performance. Moreover, specific user requests, even if they were genuine, may be flagged by WAF and must be manually reconciled by relaxing the rule or adding the exception. Blocking user IPs (when user requests are flagged suspicious particularly involving data update requests) is a common downside of using WAF, and whitelisting the IPs or IP ranges is the way to go. There are other weaknesses of WAF; it detects and blocks SQL injection attacks but does not resolve the issue in the code.

The WAF can be of two types. The first category is the **Host-Based WAF**. It stays within the server hosting the application.

Figure 2.19 shows different configuration points for ModSecurity. One of the most popular WAF software, which is also open source. It is usually deployed as a host-based or network firewall:

Figure 2.19: *ModSecurity, the open-source web application framework*

The second category is the **Cloud-Based WAF**. It is managed by the vendor, stays outside the private network of the application and is easier to deploy. The notable ones are mentioned in *Table 2.2*:

Cloud based WAF	Resource link
Cloudflare	**https://www.cloudflare.com/waf/**
AWS WAF	**https://aws.amazon.com/waf/**
Imperva	**https://www.imperva.com/products/web-application-fire-wall-waf/**
Stackpath	**https://www.stackpath.com/products/waf/**
Sophos firewall	**https://www.sophos.com/en-us/products/next-gen-firewall**
Akamai's Kona Site Defender	**https://www.akamai.com/products/kona-site-defender**
Signal Sciences (Fastly) Next-gen Firewall and Cloud WAF	**https://www.signalsciences.com/products/waf-web-applica-tion-firewall/ and https://www.signalsciences.com/products/cloud-waf/**

Table 2.2: Serverless computing in Cloud ecosystems

All modern servers or cloud infrastructures are also equipped with a network firewall. In particular, network and WAF may be used in combinations to be more effective.

Vulnerability DBs, automation and monitoring

With an increasing number of security vulnerabilities getting reported daily and thousands of security attacks every day, it becomes important to have an automated monitoring system and possible real-time counter-measures done by the system. It should be without human intervention as it may delay the process. Such efforts require building up an up-to-date database of vulnerabilities (**Vulnerability DB**) and automating the process of acting upon the system based on pre-defined criteria anytime.

The above processes of security information management and security event management broadly fall under a category called **Security Information and Event Management (SIEM)**. Sumo logic (**https://www.sumologic.com/solutions/cloud-siem-enterprise**) and Splunk (**splunk.com**) are two popular platforms for SIEM.

InfoSec as a service

As we discussed, the automation process of managing information security gives rise to tools that can manage and mitigate threats to the software application. Again, such a system (a piece of software) can be used on a SaaS model for the IT team to manage information security, and we call it InfoSec as a service.

Note: When mitigation is not achieved automatically, the system alerts the responsible party (humans) to intervene. We shall discuss the process and framework in *Chapter 6, Frameworks and Best Practices.*

The information security needs either monitoring or penetration and scanning of the application that may result in discovering the vulnerabilities (either active or possible ones as the objective entails) and a human-readable report with the list of findings (the issues that need remediation) and observations (the issues that may be kept in mind though remediation effort is not mandatory).

Figure 2.20 shows a typical screenshot of a report generated by an application security scanner:

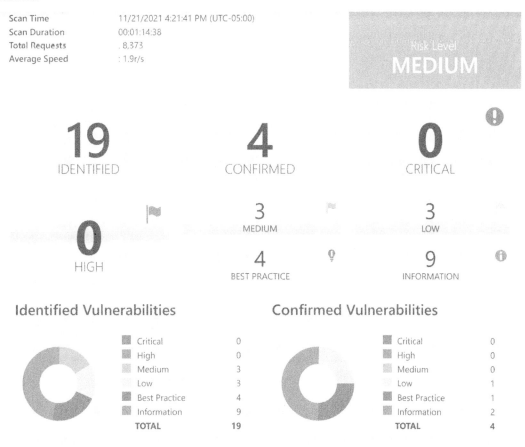

Figure 2.20: *A screenshot of a typical security scan on an application*

We then apply remediation measures by humans or machines (in the case of an automated process). Such measures get reviewed and validated against the findings and possible solutions. Approved findings get closed while we enter a new security review cycle for pending findings.

Figure 2.21 shows different steps in a security review cycle:

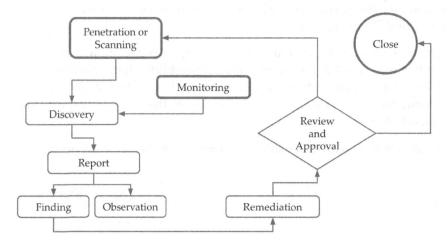

Figure 2.21 *Security review cycle*

While the trend of application security management looks forward to a complete automation of the whole cycle, there are complexities to handle. In practice, we use multiple tools for the purpose. While there are products like Aqua (**aquasec.com**) to manage multiple steps, we may also use security scanners to report the findings and audit workflow management software like Regstacker (**bcubeanalytics.com**) to manage the cycle.

Table 2.3 shows some of the popular products for security review test scanning:

Cloud-based WAF	Resource link
Invicti (Formerly Netsparker)	**https://www.invicti.com**
Nessus	**https://www.tenable.com/products/nessus**
Immuniweb	**https://www.immuniweb.com**
Metasploit	**https://www.metasploit.com**

Table 2.3: *Security review test scanners*

We shall discuss the CI/CD pipeline in detail in the next chapter. We shall cover the major ones like AWS, GCP and Azure while giving an alternative scenario using multiple tools. Now, let us discuss another set of important tools in the process of DevSecOps, the development platform and tools.

Low-Code, No-Code and RAD

Software engineering evolved from assembly languages to human readable code in the last century. The progress was further made in the previous three decades seeing language frameworks and sophisticated IDE with code generation facilities. These offered the ability for code scaffolding and methods to stick to the code best practices. However, the coder remains the king or queen to decide the fate of the program quality.

The last few years saw a rapid growth of cloud-based platforms, which offered the ability to generate code with no coding or writing the least amount of code, **Low Code, No Code (LCNC)**. While these platforms quickened the process of creating the application, some stuck to the usage-based commercial models without giving access to the source code, and others offered desktop-based tools (like a traditional IDE) to do GUI-based application development and push the code into the server. While later introducing the disadvantages like lack of access to source code (thus inflexibility and vendor-lockin) and transparency regarding security measures apart from the unfair game of cost.

On the other hand, **Rapid Application Development (RAD)** offered a way out of the dreaded situation of LCNC, improving flexibility and transparency. To capture the essence of a RAD platform, it provides low code and no code tools to develop whereas supporting a full-fledged DevSecOps pipeline for deployment and management of code. *Table 2.4* provide comparisons between the LCNC and RAD platforms:

	LCNC platform	**RAD platform**
Speed of code generation, Business Solution and Technology Solution	Fast though behind the scene code management by the platform	Fast while code management is transparent
Code documentation, adherence to coding best practices and security management	No transparency	Transparent
Flexibility to choose the deployment server or cloud environment	Not available	Available
Lowering cost of running digital asset	Lower cost for initial setup and usage phase, but cost increases exponentially with usage	Lower the overall cost

Table 2.4: Comparisons between the LCNC and RAD platforms

Let us now understand different solutions that will be feasible with this newest platform.

Business operation, workflow, and communication

Most applications businesses use broadly involve operational automation, collaboration, workflow management, and communications. These applications are available abundantly as ERP/CRM application stacks. While features are always a work in progress, broad architectural aspects are well understood and practiced in hundreds of thousands of enterprises. It is easy to find these components in the market. LCNC and RAD platforms use object-level components and microservices available to choose and customize in these areas.

Different techs and new ways of application development

The major tech development in recent years is using five technologies that will fundamentally change how we use digital technologies. They are as follows:

- **Artificial Intelligence (AI):** AI refers broadly to three subcategories: **Machine Learning (ML)**, **Natural Language Processing (NLP)** and **Computer Vision (CV)**.

- **Blockchain: Distributed Ledger Technology (DLT)** that proves critical for cryptocurrency and recording transactional data accurately.

- **IoT:** Small, low-powered devices equipped with sensors and transacting data with the cloud.

- **AR/VR: Augmented Reality (AR)** integrates virtual enhancements into the real world, and **Virtual Reality (VR)** creates a real-world-like environment within the virtual domain.

- **Analytics:** Interpreting data and identifying patterns therein using statistics.

The architecture demanded by these technologies also changes the way we develop applications. Whether it is **Decentralized apps (dApps)** or IoT data streaming and dashboarding, the way the data connection happens, and the data is used to serve the customer can be widely different. The new generations of platforms try to solve this problem by carving out the method of app building for one or more of these technologies.

We shall cover these technologies and application development using these technologies throughout the book with different relevant examples. However, comprehensive coverage will only be possible if each such thing becomes a book in itself.

Now, let us go back to the application's security and understand how best practices (guidelines) formulated by **Open Web Application Security Project (OWASP) (owasp. org)** mold our approach to defense and troubleshooting.

Application security

We have discussed a great deal about application security during our coverage of various architecture concepts in this chapter. It is important to remember three pillars of security in all our deliberations, the **Confidentiality, Integrity and Availability (CIA)** principles that we introduced in the previous chapter.

It is the foundational principle of DevSecOps that security must be considered from the very beginning of the application building, in fact, from the design phase. However, as we learnt in this section, security review deals with possible vulnerabilities and makes us try to mitigate these.

This section will discuss a prominent set of security standard guidelines for software applications, OWASP Top Ten (**https://owasp.org/www-project-top-ten/**). We shall also discuss another widely adopted set of guidelines for application security, SAN Top 25 (**https://www.sans.org/top25-software-errors/**). While OWASP Top 10 is geared towards cloud-based applications, SAN Top 25 extends its scope to desktop and network applications.

OWASP Top 10

OWASP Top 10 is a list of application security failures graded mainly from the risk standpoint they pose. It is an evolving list planned to be revised every few years. *Figure 2.22* shows how the items in the OWASP Top 10 have changed since 2017. The items move up and down in their order in the list; new items may appear, and old ones may go away:

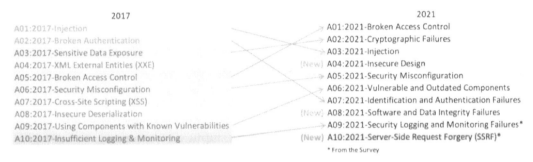

Figure 2.22: *A snapshot of the evolution of OWASP Top 10 since 2017*

Three new categories of vulnerabilities have been identified and included in the 2021 list:

- **A03:2021:** Insecure design

- **A08:2021:** Software and data integrity failures

- **A10:2021: Server-Side Request Forgery (SSRF)**

At the same time, items like A04:2017: **XML External Entities (XXE)**, A07:2017: **Cross-Site Scripting (XSS)** and A08:2017: Insecure decentralization did not find any place in the revised list in 2021.

Let us now discuss all the ten items in the 2021 list.

A01:2021 - Broken access control

The access control can be broken for many reasons, including violation of privilege (we shall discuss this more in *Chapter 6, Frameworks and Best Practices* when we discuss zero trust framework) or assigning inappropriate privilege to a user. It can happen for different reasons:

- Misconfiguration or exposing access to configuration (refer to A05:2021: Security misconfiguration)

- Access to user identity through sneaking into another user's session or JWT

- Gaining access to a privileged URL that was not accessible otherwise through cross-origin injection or simply with the open AJAX link with no privilege assigned

This category of vulnerabilities can be prevented by checking the access to configurations, checking privilege for each live URL and ensuring encryption and code for session or JWT management.

A02:2021 - Cryptographic failures

Cryptographic failures happen due to the choice of wrong cryptography or lack of the required data encryption level. We need to classify all datasets used in the application as per their encryption levels. We should also use secured protocols and ports for HTTP, FTP, SSH and SMTP.

A03:2021 - Injection

Injection is a wide area with different vulnerabilities. SQL injection is the most prominent one where the attacker can exploit the input in the SQL query, thereby doing things that are not intended. We prevent this by sanitizing the input. For example, we adopt **PHP Data Object (PDO)** in PHP language and parametrize the inputs to prevent SQL injection.

Another way is the injection of code on the URL (the same origin or cross-origin), which can alter the user requests, resulting in different results. It often happens at the GET requests. We should encrypt our URL query strings whenever possible and sanitize all GET inputs in the URL. It is critical as most API endpoints accept GET inputs.

A04:2021 - Insecure design

Insecure design is a crucial issue for any application to be vulnerable. The program and database architecture, microservice and API handling, coding practices and CI/CD pipelines are among many things we need to consider to design a secure application.

A05:2021 - Security misconfiguration

Misconfiguration at different levels of an application may introduce vulnerability. It can be the exposure of the cryptographic keys to the attacker by giving the privilege to access the configuration file or database storing the keys. It can be the configuration of the databases carrying user and system data. It can be the system configuration which is used for access control parameters. It can be a verbose message giving out confidential details due to the poorly conferred system or buggy codebase. These kinds of vulnerabilities are best addressed with a securely configured system where patching or upgrading the system's components is done regularly.

A06:2021 - Vulnerable and outdated components

Libraries and components (mainly from the open-source communities) in the system stay old and obsolete, giving opportunities for attackers to exploit the system. It can result in serious data loss.

We need to track the dependencies and patch/upgrade the libraries to reduce the possibility of exposing the system to exploitation.

A07:2021 - Identification and authentication failures

The vulnerabilities in identity and authentication come from weak session management, exposing secret strings in JWT, leaking cryptographic keys, etc. The prevention should follow the guidelines that we discussed earlier in this chapter in connection with encryption and hashing.

A08:2021 - Software and data integrity failures

The application depends on the host environment and components that may be managed by third parties. In many cases, all or part of the codebase may reside in CDNs. Loosening of the central control leads to scenarios where attackers exponent code assets used by the application. The prevention of such vulnerabilities can be done by:

- tracking and monitoring the dependencies against compromised code
- introducing hashing for compiled code if deployed in a public environment

A09:2021 - Security logging and monitoring failures

The attack surface of any modern application has grown due to distributed computing, a long software supply chain and data residing away from central control. It has given rise to the need for robust access log management and real-time monitoring of the application.

A10:2021 - Server-side request forgery

SSRF is the vulnerability due to non-validation or incorrect validation of the user request (user-supplied URL) for fetching a remote resource. The attack can compromise host files and the application's configuration.

We can prevent these by segregating the **Access Control List** (**ACL**) appropriately. A WAF helps in this direction.

For further details on each item of the OWASP Top 10, it is advisable to refer to the cheat sheet at:

https://cheatsheetseries.owasp.org/IndexTopTen.html

SAN Top 25

In comparison to the OWASP Top 10, SANs Top 25 (or precisely, CWE/SANS TOP 25 Most Dangerous Software Errors) are a comprehensive list of vulnerability categories ordered along the prevalence of these vulnerabilities (you may compare this with OWASP's). SANS Institute manages the guidelines.

Let us go back to our use case elaborated in the previous chapter and discuss how we should align our application architecture with DevSecOps.

Use case: Making a secure application

The central understanding that we gather in this chapter is devising a scalable and secured architecture for the application that will act as the IoT dashboard on the Cloud. The application will be the hub of data crunching from the ERP, the sensor network deployed on the factory floor, supplying the dashboard, information and alerts. *Figure 2.23* illustrates how different components stack up:

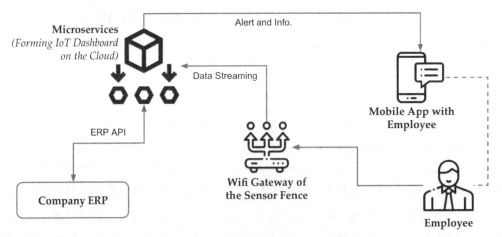

Figure 2.23: An illustration of application stack for the use case

The application (IoT dashboard on the Cloud) will consist of a few microservices:

- **ERP data connector:** This component will aggregate the requisite data from the company ERP and will cache with its expiry timestamp. The cached data will be used to verify employee details and attendance.

- **Sensor data aggregator:** The Microservice that will use the data pipeline on the **Google Cloud Platform** (**GCP**). We shall devise this in the next chapter when we discuss the use case again.

- **Dashboard widgets:** These build data reporting and visualization. In fact, each of these can be a separate microservice.

We shall also postpone building the CI/CD pipeline for the use case to the next chapter, when we discuss each cloud ecosystem and practical implementations.

Conclusion

In this chapter, we have comprehensively covered the concepts around modern cloud-native applications from the standpoint of DevSecOps. The concepts like microservices and their API architecture fundamentally change how we view an application and its security. We have seen how an application may be developed, deployed, scaled and managed. In our pursuit of automating the DevSecOps pipelines, we have discussed the security process in detail.

As we have built a strong foundation in understanding the security implications and best practices for modern applications, it's time to shift our focus to the backbone of these systems—the infrastructure. Knowing how to manage your cloud infrastructure effectively is just as crucial as understanding application security.

In the next chapter, we will delve deeper into **Infrastructure as Code (IaC)**, an approach that is pivotal for ensuring robust, scalable, and secure infrastructure. We will examine it from various perspectives and dissect its application within diverse cloud ecosystems. Moreover, we will explore methods and techniques for setting up and configuring deployment environments. This will amplify our understanding of DevSecOps and empower us with a comprehensive understanding of IaC as a critical tool in our DevSecOps arsenal.

Questions

1. How is a Cloud Service delivered over the network, and what does its software architecture look like?
2. What is virtualization, and how does it make the entire software delivery process a software-centric one?
3. What are the three special tools mandatory before accessing an app on the cloud?
4. What is the difference between user authentication and authorization?
5. What is MFA, and how is it implemented on an application?
6. What are the major parameters of concern during the metering and billing management?
7. How do provisioning and resource management work based on the cloud computing model?
8. What are the constituents of an app on the Cloud?
9. What is workflow are how is it implemented within an app?

10. What are the types of encryptions, and what are the use cases of these types?

11. What is hashing, how does it work, and where is it useful?

12. How do PKI and SSL work?

13. What is a microservice, and why is it so important for building an app?

14. What is a service registry in service-based application architecture?

15. What is the high availability and multi-instance deployment of an app?

16. Does the high availability deployment of the application serve as a mere backup?

17. What is serverless computing, and what are its advantages?

18. Can we include serverless components alongside server-based components in an application?

19. Which dependencies will a SAST tool have to incorporate?

20. What is SCA, and what are its advantages?

21. What is IAST, and what are its advantages and disadvantages?

22. What is RASP, and what are its advantages and disadvantages?

23. What is a WAF, and how does it work? What are the ways WAF can be deployed?

24. What are the disadvantages of WAF?

25. Will it be advisable to implement both WAF and network firewall, or should just one be adequate?

26. What are the different types of WAF?

27. How is vulnerability DB used for automating security management?

28. Can you describe a security review cycle?

29. What is InfoSec as a Service?

30. What is a LCNC platform?

31. What is a RAD platform, and how is it different from an LCNC Platform?

32. What is a SQL injection security issue, and how can it be mitigated?

33. What is a broken Authentication security issue, and how can it be mitigated?

34. What is SQL injection vulnerability, and how to mitigate it?

35. What is SSRF?

36. What are the differences between OWASP Top 10 and SANS Top 25 guidelines?

CHAPTER 3

Infrastructure as Code

Introduction

In the preceding chapter, we embarked on a journey to comprehend the anatomy of a cloud-based application, the intricate dynamics of CI/CD pipelines for application development, deployment, and audit, and the pivotal role of security within this entire orchestration. Our exploration revealed that any application, regardless of scale or complexity, requires a deployment environment: a conventional server-based infrastructure or a more contemporary serverless paradigm catering to development, staging, or production requirements.

As we venture into the realm of cloud ecosystems, we realize that the digital landscape of AWS, GCP, and Azure is evolving at an unprecedented pace. This rapid evolution has revolutionized the way we perceive deployment environments. Today, a server can be instantiated by a simple script that draws parameters from a text file. This paradigm shift has given rise to a new term: **Infrastructure as Code (IaC)**.

In this forthcoming chapter, we shall delve deeper into the concept of IaC in relation to the DevSecOps process. We shall examine it from various perspectives and dissect its application within diverse cloud ecosystems. We shall also explore various methods and techniques for setting up and configuring deployment environments, empowering us with a comprehensive understanding of IaC. It is time to transition from theory to practice as we navigate the fascinating intricacies of IaC. Let us embark on this enlightening journey.

Structure

In this chapter, we will discuss the following topics:

- Cloud infrastructure
- Benefits of IaC in DevSecOps
- IaC for DevSecOps in AWS
- IaC for DevSecOps in GCP
- IaC for DevSecOps in Azure
- IaC for DevSecOps in a hybrid environment
- IaC and DevSecOps with legacy system
- DevSecOps dashboard
- Use case: Setup software environment

Objectives

This chapter embarks on a journey to explore the diverse universe of cloud platforms and infrastructure management tools indispensable for the triumphant execution of a DevSecOps project. We delve into the intricate nuances of major cloud ecosystems, including AWS, GCP, and Azure, imparting valuable insights that guide us in selecting the most suitable tools tailored to specific usage scenarios.

We emphasize scalability, a cornerstone of modern IT systems, to address the complexities of multi-faceted and multi-region deployment. As we navigate through the labyrinth of building modern IT systems, we provide comprehensive coverage of how to manage and adapt to changes in infrastructure.

This chapter aims to introduce these concepts and paint a vivid picture of their interplay in the cloud environment. We strive to equip ourselves with a holistic understanding and practical knowledge, paving the way for us to successfully undertake and navigate our DevSecOps projects. So, let us embark on this enlightening expedition into the heart of cloud-based infrastructure management and DevSecOps.

Cloud infrastructure

As we discussed Cloud services and the constituents of a software application in *Chapter 2, Application Security*, it is paramount to understand the underlying concept of cloud infrastructure that makes all these happen. Automation is the key to orchestrating infrastructure, creating configurations, fast and smooth deployment, and validating infrastructure configuration. Again, it happens with a human creating the configuration file (through a text file edit or a UI tool); the system takes care of everything after that (except perhaps with the supervision of a human). We shall learn more about automation and auto-validation without human intervention in *Chapter 5, Automation and Integration*. However, let us focus on the tasks at hand.

IaC is the practice of managing and provisioning computing infrastructure with machine-readable definition files rather than physical hardware configuration or interactive configuration tools.

In other words, IaC involves writing code (in a high-level language) to manage configurations and automate the provisioning of infrastructure in addition to deployments. This might be for a virtual machine, a container, a piece of network equipment, a security policy, or even an entire data center.

This approach ensures that infrastructure deployment becomes reproducible and can be predictably standardized across environments. It can also help to avoid potential environmental drift in the development, staging, and production environments.

IaC brings to infrastructure the same versioning that DevSecOps practitioners are accustomed to with software source code. When changes are made, those changes are tracked and can be rolled back if they cause problems. This is a key principle of the DevSecOps movement.

Terraform is a key tool in the realm of IaC:

https://www.terraform.io

It is an open-source tool created by HashiCorp for building, changing, and versioning infrastructure safely and efficiently.

Terraform allows us to define and provide data center infrastructure using a **declarative configuration language**. This means we describe our desired state of infrastructure, and Terraform will figure out how to achieve that state. This contrasts with an imperative approach, where we must provide specific commands to reach the desired state.

Note: A declarative configuration language is a high-level language used in programming that expresses the logic of a computation without describing its control flow. In configuration management, a declarative language allows us to specify what the system should look like rather than providing explicit steps to reach that state.
The key characteristic of declarative configuration languages is focusing on the what rather than the how. This contrasts imperative languages, which require detailed instructions about steps to achieve the desired state.

Consider an example of a system where we want to ensure a particular software package, say, Package X, is installed.

In an imperative configuration language, we might have to check if the package is already installed. If not, install it. We define the exact steps to achieve our goal, such as:

```
if not exists(Package X) {
    install(Package X)
}
```

In a declarative configuration language, we simply state that Package X should be installed. The underlying system or tool is responsible for figuring out how to reach that state. For example:

```
ensure => package(Package X)
```

This difference makes declarative languages highly suitable for configuration management and IaC because they allow us to focus on the final state of the system, not the steps to get there. This makes configurations more straightforward to write and understand, reducing potential errors. Examples of declarative configuration languages are HashiCorp Configuration Language (HCL) used by Terraform and YAML or JSON used in Kubernetes or AWS CloudFormation templates.

For example, we might declare that we want a certain number of virtual machines of a certain type running in our infrastructure, along with a load balancer to distribute traffic between them. Terraform will then make the necessary API calls to our cloud provider (like AWS, GCP, Azure, etc.) to set up these resources and continuously monitor and adjust to maintain our desired state.

Here is an example of how we might use Terraform to define an AWS S3 bucket:

```
provider "aws" {
  region = "us-west-2"
}

resource "aws_s3_bucket" "bucket" {
  bucket = "my-bucket"
  acl    = "private"

  tags = {
    Name        = "My bucket"
    Environment = "Dev"
  }
}
```

In this example, the provider block configures the named provider, in this case, "aws". The resource block defines a resource of type **aws_s3_bucket**. The arguments inside the block (bucket, acl, tags) are configuration values for that resource.

When we run this code using the Terraform CLI, it will ensure that an S3 bucket named "**my-bucket**" exists, and if not, it will create it. If the bucket exists, Terraform will ensure it matches our provided configuration. If it does not, it will update it. This is the essence of IaC: defining the desired state of our infrastructure and using a tool to make reality match our desired state.

Terraform is cloud-agnostic and allows users to manage diverse service providers with the same workflow. This allows us to manage a multi-cloud environment with the same files, simplifying management and orchestration.

Overall, Terraform is a powerful tool that provides the benefits of IaC, immutability, and declarative configuration, making it a go-to choice for many DevSecOps professionals when managing infrastructure.

Several popular alternatives to Terraform for IaC exist. They each have their strengths and use cases. Here are a few of them:

- **AWS CloudFormation:** AWS CloudFormation provides a common language to describe and provision all the infrastructure resources in our cloud environment. It allows us to use JSON or YAML to model and provision all the resources needed for our applications across all regions and accounts in an automated and secure manner. Go to their website to learn more:

  https://aws.amazon.com/cloudformation

- **Azure Resource Manager (ARM) templates:** ARM is Azure's deployment and management service. It provides a management layer that enables us to create, update, and delete resources in our Azure account. We use management features like access control, locks, and tags to secure and organize our resources after deployment. Go to their website to learn more:

  https://learn.microsoft.com/en-us/azure/azure-resource-manager/templates/ overview

- **Google Cloud Deployment Manager:** Deployment Manager is an infrastructure deployment service that automates creating and managing Google Cloud resources. Write flexible templates and configuration files and use them to create deployments with various Google Cloud services, such as Cloud Storage, Compute Engine, and Cloud SQL, configured to work together. Go to their website to learn more:

  https://console.cloud.google.com/marketplace/product/google-cloud-platform/ cloud-deployment-manager

- **Pulumi:** It is an open-source infrastructure as a code tool for creating, deploying, and managing cloud infrastructure. Pulumi works with traditional infrastructure like VMs, networks, and databases and modern architectures, including containers, Kubernetes clusters, and serverless functions. It supports dozens of public, private, and hybrid cloud service providers. In fact, it stands out in the **Infrastructure as Code (IaC)** landscape by supporting general-purpose programming languages like JavaScript, TypeScript, Python, Go, and .NET, which offers several key advantages for developers. Firstly, it leverages the familiarity and extensive ecosystems of these languages, reducing the learning curve and allowing seamless integration into existing development workflows. Secondly, these languages provide greater expressive power and flexibility, enabling more complex and conditional infrastructure setups. This approach also facilitates cross-cloud compatibility, essential for multi-cloud strategies. Lastly, the robust communities around these languages drive continuous innovation and provide advanced tooling, such as strong typing and debugging, leading to more efficient and error-resistant infrastructure management. Go to their website to learn more:

  https://www.pulumi.com

- **Ansible:** Ansible is an open-source software provisioning, configuration management, and application-deployment tool enabling infrastructure as code. It runs on Unix-like systems and can configure Unix-like systems and Microsoft Windows. It includes its declarative language to describe system configuration. Go to their website to learn more:

  https://www.ansible.com

- **Chef, Puppet, SaltStack:** These configuration management tools are very useful for installing and managing software on existing servers. They are typically used to manage the state of servers and keep configuration consistent. The following are their links:

  o Chef website: **https://www.puppet.com**

  o Puppet website: **https://www.chef.io**

  o SaltStack website: **https://saltproject.io**

These tools are not directly interchangeable; each has strengths, weaknesses, and ideal use cases. The choice of tool depends on the specific needs of the project and the environment in which it will be used.

Benefits of IaC in DevSecOps

IaC and DevSecOps are closely related practices that offer many complementary benefits. Here are some key benefits and examples of how they work together:

- **Automation and consistency:** IaC allows us to automate infrastructure provisioning and management, ensuring a consistent and reproducible environment. This consistency is crucial in DevSecOps, where we need to ensure that security controls are uniformly applied. For example, by defining security groups and rules in an IaC script, we can ensure that these settings are consistently applied across all instances, reducing the chance of human error leading to a security vulnerability.

- **Speed and agility:** IaC allows rapid provisioning and de-provisioning of environments, which supports the agile methodologies used in DevSecOps. For example, developers can quickly spin up a replica of the production environment to reproduce and fix a security bug, then tear it down again when done, minimizing the cost and effort involved.

- **Version control and auditability:** With IaC, the infrastructure is defined in code and can be version controlled, just like application code. This provides a clear audit trail of what changes were made, when, and by whom, which is valuable for security audits and incident response. If a security incident occurs, we can easily review the infrastructure code to see what changed and potentially led to the incident.

- **Collaboration and communication:** IaC helps to break down silos between development, operations, and security teams by providing a common language and set of tools. This supports the core DevSecOps principle of fostering collaboration and shared responsibility for security. For instance, a security expert could review a Terraform script as part of a pull request, providing feedback directly in the developers' workflow.

- **Policy as code:** Just as IaC allows us to manage infrastructure as code, we can also manage security policies as code. This includes access controls, network policies, and compliance rules. By defining these policies as code, we can automate their enforcement and reduce non-compliance risk. For example, we could use a tool like Open Policy Agent to enforce policies, such as all S3 buckets must be private in our IaC scripts.

- **Early detection and remediation of issues:** By integrating IaC with CI/CD pipelines and automated testing, we can catch and fix security issues early in the development cycle, before they reach production. For example, we could use a tool like the following to learn more (as per the latest version) to automatically scan our IaC scripts for security issues as part of our CI/CD pipeline:

    o Checkov: **https://www.checkov.io**

    o Tfsec: **https://aquasecurity.github.io/tfsec/v1.28.1/**

These benefits make IaC a key DevSecOps enablers, helping automate security controls, improve auditability, and foster collaboration between teams.

IaC for DevSecOps in AWS

AWS, DevSecOps, and IaC form a powerful triad for modern, efficient, and secure software delivery. A DevSecOps team could use AWS CloudFormation (an IaC tool) to automatically deploy infrastructure for a new application. The team can write a CloudFormation template that describes the desired AWS resources (like EC2 instances, an RDS database, etc.) and their configuration. Then, they can use AWS CodePipeline and AWS CodeDeploy (part of the AWS suite of CI/CD tools) to automatically build, test, and deploy their application to this infrastructure. AWS security tools can automatically check for and report any security issues.

Let us now discuss the steps needed to implement IaC in alignment with DevSecOps principles on AWS. We shall use AWS CloudFormation, AWS's native IaC service, and other AWS services to create a DevSecOps environment.

Define our IaC with AWS CloudFormation

AWS CloudFormation allows us to model our entire infrastructure in a text file (YAML or JSON). This file serves as the single source of truth for our cloud environment. The file can be version-controlled, reviewed, and tested like any other code.

Figure 3.1 shows the screen for creating a new CloudFormation Stack:

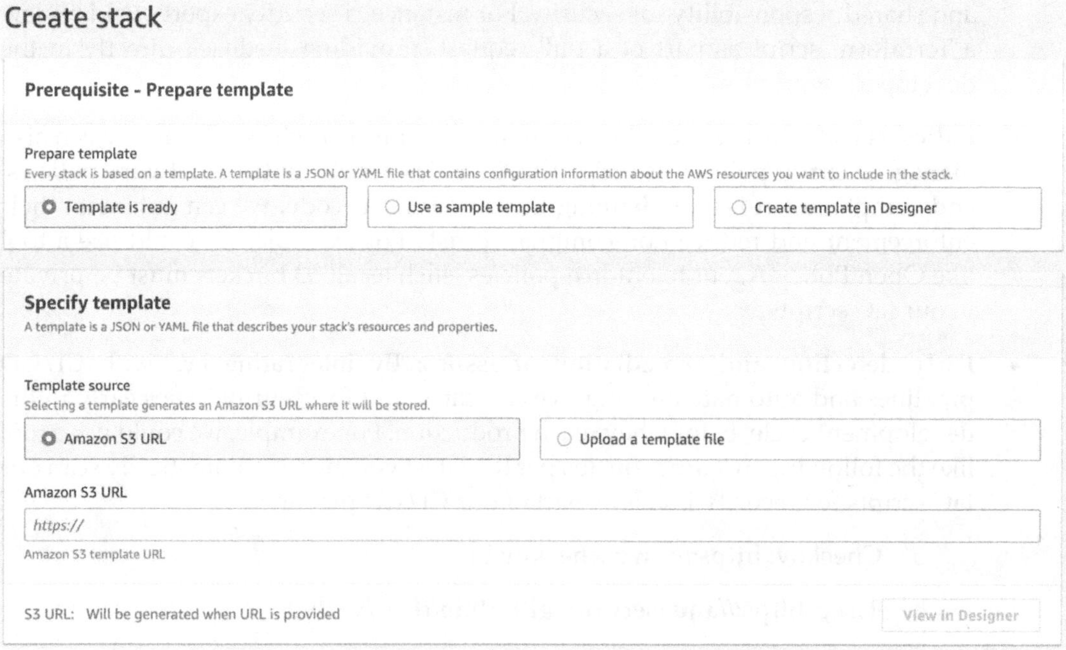

Create stack

Prerequisite - Prepare template

Prepare template
Every stack is based on a template. A template is a JSON or YAML file that contains configuration information about the AWS resources you want to include in the stack.

- ● Template is ready
- ○ Use a sample template
- ○ Create template in Designer

Specify template
A template is a JSON or YAML file that describes your stack's resources and properties.

Template source
Selecting a template generates an Amazon S3 URL where it will be stored.

- ● Amazon S3 URL
- ○ Upload a template file

Amazon S3 URL

https://

Amazon S3 template URL

S3 URL: Will be generated when URL is provided   View in Designer

Figure 3.1: *The first screen for creating a CloudFormation stack*

We might define an AWS CloudFormation template that includes EC2 instances for our application servers, an RDS instance for our database, and security groups with specific inbound and outbound rules.

Set up CI/CD pipeline

Setting up a **Continuous Integration/Continuous Deployment (CI/CD)** pipeline on AWS with IaC and DevSecOps involves several steps and AWS services. Here is a high-level overview of the process:

1. **Source Code Repository (AWS CodeCommit):** First, we need a repository for our source code. AWS CodeCommit is a fully managed source control service that allows teams to host secure and highly scalable Git repositories.

2. **Build (AWS CodeBuild):** After the source code is in the repository, the next step is to compile the code, run tests, and create deployable artifacts. AWS CodeBuild is a fully managed build service that compiles our source code, runs tests, and produces software packages ready to deploy.

3. **Security analysis:** As part of DevSecOps, we should integrate security checks at every stage of our pipeline. For example, we could use tools like AWS CodeStar, AWS CodeCommit, or third-party tools to scan our code for vulnerabilities during the build stage.

4. **Deploy (AWS CodeDeploy):** AWS CodeDeploy automates code deployments to any instance, including Amazon EC2 instances and servers running on-premises. AWS CodeDeploy makes it easier for us to rapidly release new features, helps avoid downtime during application deployment, and handles the complexity of updating our applications.

5. **Pipeline orchestration (AWS CodePipeline):** AWS CodePipeline is a fully managed continuous delivery service that helps us automate our release pipelines for fast and reliable application and infrastructure updates. CodePipeline orchestrates the build, test, and deploy stages of our release process every time a code changes based on the release model we define.

Figure 3.2 shows the options for creating a new project with either AWS CodeCommit or Git as the repository type:

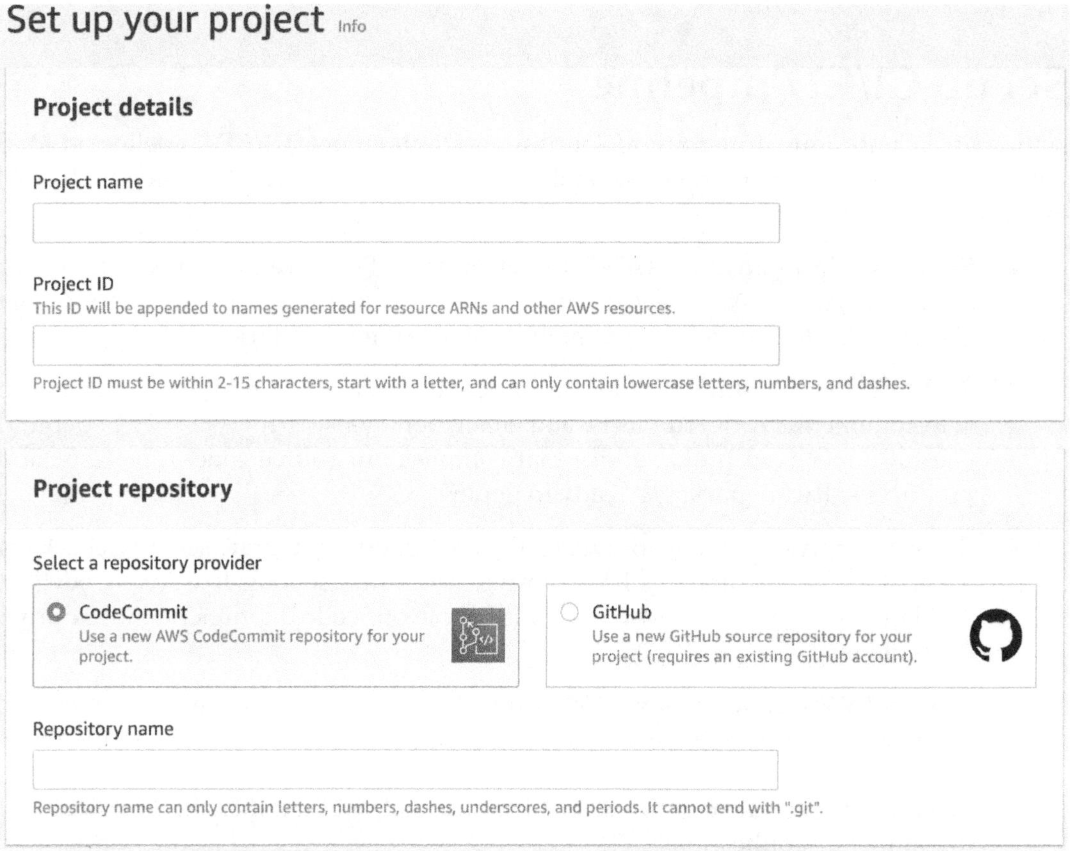

Figure 3.2: Creating a new project with either AWS CodeCommit or Git as the repository type

These services together form a robust CI/CD pipeline on AWS that includes IaC and DevSecOps principles. This pipeline can take code from commit to deployment in a secure and automated manner.

Incorporate security controls

In the CloudFormation templates, we can define various security controls. For example, we can restrict inbound traffic to our EC2 instances by allowing only specific IP ranges.

We can also use AWS **Identity and Access Management (IAM)** to control who can access and manage AWS resources. For instance, we might create IAM roles for our EC2 instances that limit what actions they can perform.

Use AWS Config for continuous compliance

AWS Config is a service that enables us to assess, audit, and evaluate the configurations of our AWS resources. We can use AWS Config to review resource changes and compare them against our desired configurations.

For example, we could create an AWS Config rule that checks whether our security groups allow unrestricted SSH access and alerts us if they do.

Automated testing

Integrate automated testing into our CI/CD pipeline. For instance, we can use AWS CodePipeline, a fully managed continuous delivery service, and AWS CodeBuild, a fully managed build service.

We can also use open-source tools like Checkov or tfsec to automatically scan our CloudFormation templates for security issues. These tools can be integrated into our CI/CD pipeline whenever we change our templates.

Incorporate monitoring and logging

We can use services like AWS CloudWatch for monitoring and alerting and AWS CloudTrail for logging API calls. These services can help us detect and respond to security incidents quickly.

For example, we could create a CloudWatch alarm that sends us an email notification if it detects an unusual amount of outbound traffic from our EC2 instances, which could indicate a security breach. AWS Security Hub gives us a comprehensive view of our high-priority security alerts and security status across our AWS accounts.

Use AWS Secrets Manager for managing secrets

For managing application secrets like database credentials, use AWS Secrets Manager. This prevents us from hardcoding sensitive information in our CloudFormation templates or application code.

By following these steps, we can implement IaC on AWS in a way that aligns with DevSecOps principles, automating security controls, incorporating continuous compliance, and fostering a culture of shared responsibility for security.

IaC for DevSecOps in GCP

Google Cloud Platform (GCP), DevSecOps, and IaC are key elements in modern application development and deployment. They form a powerful combination that enables fast, efficient, and secure software delivery.

These components create a secure and efficient application development and deployment pipeline when used together on GCP. Developers can use IaC tools to define and manage their infrastructure in GCP while incorporating security practices throughout the development and deployment processes (DevSecOps).

For example, we might use Cloud Deployment Manager to define and deploy our infrastructure on GCP. Then, using Google Cloud Build (GCP's CI/CD platform), we can automate the process of building, testing, and deploying our application to this infrastructure. Google's suite of security tools can be used to continuously monitor our application and infrastructure for security vulnerabilities and deviations from security best practices.

Let us now understand the steps of implementing IaC with respect to DevSecOps on the GCP. Here, we will focus on using Google Cloud Deployment Manager, which is GCP's native IaC service, and other Google Cloud services to create a DevSecOps environment:

Define our IaC with deployment manager

Google Cloud Deployment Manager allows us to specify all the resources needed for our application in a declarative format using YAML. This script serves as the single source of truth for our cloud environment. The script can be version-controlled, reviewed, and tested like any other code.

For instance, we might define a Deployment Manager template that includes computing engine instances for our application servers, a Cloud SQL instance for our database, and firewall rules with specific inbound and outbound settings.

CI/CD pipeline

Implementing a CI/CD pipeline in GCP typically involves using Google Cloud Build or other CI/CD tools like Jenkins. Here is a general approach to setting up a CI/CD pipeline using Cloud Build:

1. **Create a Google Cloud project:** First, create a new project in the Google Cloud Console if we do not have one already.

2. **Enable Google Cloud build API:** Navigate to **APIs & Services | Library**, search for Cloud Build API, and enable it for our project.

3. **Set up source repository:** Google Cloud Source Repositories is a single place for our team to store, manage, and track code. We can mirror code from GitHub or Bitbucket repositories to Cloud Source Repositories. To set it up, navigate to Source Repositories (see *Figure 3.3*) and start mirroring from our chosen repository:

Deploy in minutes

Built-in integrations with other GCP tools let you automatically build, test and deploy code within minutes.

Fast code search

Use regular expressions to search across multiple projects, files, and repositories to quickly review code.

Fully managed Git

Access fully featured, private Git repositories on Google Cloud. Bring in existing code from GitHub or Bitbucket repositories.

Unlimited private repositories

Create an unlimited number of private Git repositories to host and maintain your code.

Figure 3.3: Google Cloud Source Repository Service
(Source: **https://source.cloud.google.com/onboarding/welcome***)*

4. **Set up Google Cloud Build:** Create a **cloudbuild.yaml** or **cloudbuild.json** file, which specifies how Cloud Build should perform tasks based on changes that are committed to the source repository. This file should be placed at the root of our source code. Here is a basic example of a **cloudbuild.yaml**:

```
steps:
      name: 'gcr.io/cloud-builders/gcloud'
args: ['app', 'deploy']
timeout: '1600s'
```

In this example, Cloud Build uses the Google Cloud SDK (**gcr.io/cloud-builders/gcloud**) to deploy an app. The timeout field specifies that the operation should time out after 1600 seconds.

5. **Set up build triggers:** Navigate to Cloud Build | Triggers, then create a new trigger. Select our repository and specify the branch to watch for changes (we can use regex here). Also, specify the path to our **cloudbuild.yaml** or **cloudbuild.json** file.

6. **Push changes and monitor build:** Once our build trigger is set up, any changes pushed to the specified branch of the source code will automatically trigger the CI/CD pipeline. We can monitor the status of our builds within the Google Cloud Console under **Cloud Build | History**.

7. **Deploy:** The deployment step depends on the type of application and the environment where it will be deployed. Google Cloud Build supports deployments to App Engine, Cloud Functions, Cloud Run, GKE, Firebase, and more.

Remember always to ensure that the appropriate permissions are set for Cloud Build to be able to access and deploy to these resources.

While Cloud Build is a native GCP tool, we can also use other popular CI/CD tools like Jenkins, Spinnaker, GitLab CI/CD, and others in conjunction with GCP services to build our CI/CD pipelines.

Incorporate security controls

In the Deployment Manager templates, we can define various security controls. For example, we can restrict inbound traffic to our Compute Engine instances by allowing only specific IP ranges.

We can also use Cloud **Identity and Access Management (IAM)** to control who can access and manage Google Cloud resources. For instance, we might create IAM roles for our Compute Engine instances that limit what actions they can perform.

Use Google Cloud Asset Inventory for continuous compliance

Google Cloud Asset Inventory is a service that enables us to review and monitor our Google Cloud resources. We can use Cloud Asset Inventory to understand what resources we have and how they are configured.

For example, we could use Cloud Asset Inventory to ensure that our compute engine instances are using the correct machine type and are located in the desired region.

Automated testing

Integrate automated testing into our CI/CD pipeline. For instance, we can use Google Cloud Build, a fully managed CI/CD platform.

We can also use open-source tools like *Checkov* or *tfsec* to automatically scan our Deployment Manager templates for security issues. These tools can be integrated into our CI/CD pipeline so that they run every time we make a change to our templates.

Incorporate monitoring and logging

We can use services like Google Cloud Monitoring for monitoring and alerting and Google Cloud Logging for logging API calls. These services can help us detect and respond to security incidents quickly.

For example, we could create a Cloud Monitoring alert that sends us an email notification if it detects an unusual amount of outbound traffic from our Compute Engine instances, which could indicate a security breach.

Use Google Secret Manager for managing secrets

For managing application secrets like database credentials, use Google Secret Manager. This allows us to avoid hardcoding sensitive information in our Deployment Manager templates or application code.

By following these steps, we can implement IaC on GCP in a way that aligns with DevSecOps principles, automating security controls, incorporating continuous compliance, and fostering a culture of shared responsibility for security.

IaC for DevSecOps in Azure

Azure, DevSecOps, and IaC provide a robust foundation for building, deploying, and maintaining secure and scalable applications. When combined in Azure, these elements provide a powerful framework for developing, deploying, and managing applications. Azure provides the infrastructure and tooling, DevSecOps ensures security is considered at every stage of the development lifecycle, and IaC automates the process, making it more reliable and efficient.

A DevSecOps team can use ARM templates, which is Azure's native IaC service, to automatically deploy infrastructure for a new application. This template describes the desired Azure resources (like virtual machines, an Azure SQL database, etc.) and their configurations. Then, they can use Azure Pipelines (part of Azure DevOps) to automatically build, test, and deploy their application to this infrastructure. Azure security tools can be used to automatically check for and report any security issues.

ARM allows us to provision our applications using a declarative template. In a single template, we can deploy multiple services along with their dependencies. We use the same template to deploy our application during every lifecycle stage.

Here is a general process on how to implement IaC with Azure using ARM:

1. **Write an ARM template**: An ARM template is a JSON file that defines the infrastructure and configuration for our project. The template uses declarative syntax, which lets us state what we intend to deploy without having to write the sequence of programming commands to create it. For example, a simple ARM template to create a storage account might look like this:

```
{
  "$schema": "https://schema.management.azure.com/
schemas/2019-04-01/deploymentTemplate.json#",
  "contentVersion": "1.0.0.0",
  "resources": [
    {
      "type": "Microsoft.Storage/storageAccounts",
      "apiVersion": "2019-06-01",
```

```json
      "name": "[parameters(,storageAccountName')]",
      "location": "[parameters('location')]",
      "sku": {
        "name": "[parameters('storageAccountType')]"
      },
      "kind": "StorageV2",
      "properties": {}
    }
  ],
  "parameters": {
    "storageAccountType": {
      "type": "string",
      "defaultValue": "Standard_LRS",
      "allowedValues": [
        "Standard_LRS",
        "Standard_GRS",
        "Standard_ZRS",
        "Premium_LRS"
      ]
    },
    "location": {
      "type": "string",
      "defaultValue": "[resourceGroup().location]"
    },
    "storageAccountName": {
      "type": "string"
    }
  }
}
```

2. **Deploy the ARM template**: After we have created our ARM template, we can deploy it. We can deploy an ARM template using the Azure portal, Azure CLI, Azure PowerShell, or REST API. For example, with Azure CLI, we would use the following command:

```
az group deployment create --name ExampleDeployment --resource-group ExampleGroup --template-file ./storageaccount.json --parameters storageAccountName=examplestorage
```

3. **Manage deployments**: After deploying our resources, we can manage them by either updating the existing deployment or by deploying a new template. ARM provides features such as security and auditing, tagging, and concurrency control to help us manage our resources.

In addition to ARM, Azure also provides Azure **Command Line Interface** (**CLI**) and Azure SDKs for various programming languages to manage resources. We can also use third-party tools like Terraform for IaC on Azure.

For more complex scenarios, such as deploying a multi-tier application across multiple regions, we might break up the deployment into several templates, each representing a part of the deployment. Then, we use a main template to link all the templates together.

CI/CD pipeline

Implementing a CI/CD pipeline in Azure typically involves using Azure DevOps, which offers a suite of services, including Azure pipelines.

Below are the steps to create a CI/CD pipeline using Azure DevOps:

1. **Create a new project in Azure DevOps:** First, we shall need to create a new project in Azure DevOps. Navigate to Azure DevOps in our browser and select **New Project**. Provide a name and a description of our project.

2. **Connect our repository:** Azure Pipelines works with Git repositories hosted in Azure Repos, GitHub, GitHub Enterprise Server, Bitbucket Cloud, or a Subversion server. We will need to connect our repository to Azure Pipelines.

3. **Create a new pipeline:** In our project, navigate to **Pipelines** and select **New Pipeline**. We shall be asked to specify where our code is.

4. **Configure our pipeline:** Azure Pipelines will analyze our code and recommend a pipeline. If we are starting with a simple application, Azure Pipelines can automatically create a pipeline with jobs to build and deploy our app.

5. **Customizing YAML-defined pipeline:** We can customize our pipeline according to our needs. The pipeline is defined using YAML, and we can specify steps that run commands, tasks, or scripts. We can add tasks to our pipeline, such as build, testing, and deployment tasks.

6. **Run our pipeline:** Once we have created and configured our pipeline, we can run it. Every time we push changes to the connected repository, Azure Pipelines will automatically run the pipeline, building and testing our code.

7. **Deploy our application:** We can also use Azure Pipelines to deploy our application. We can create a CD pipeline to deploy our application to various stages, like staging and production. We can use different deployment strategies like rolling, blue-green, or canary deployments.

8. **Monitor our pipeline:** Azure Pipelines provides a rich set of features for monitoring our pipelines. We can check the progress and results of our runs, view logs, and troubleshoot failures.

Figure 3.4 shows the Azure DevOps Pipeline Home below:

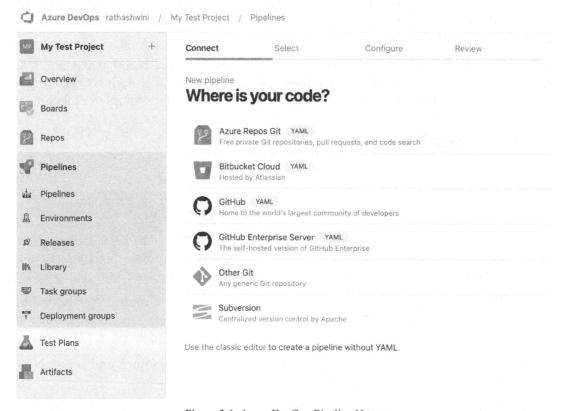

Figure 3.4: *Azure DevOps Pipeline Home*

By implementing a CI/CD pipeline in Azure, we can automate our build and release process, catch bugs sooner, and deliver value to our users more frequently and reliably.

Incorporate security controls

Incorporating security controls into our ARM templates is a key aspect of implementing a DevSecOps process. Here are a few steps to consider:

- **Network security:** We can define **Network Security Groups (NSGs)** in our ARM templates to control inbound and outbound network traffic to Azure resources such as **Virtual Machines (VMs)**. By doing this, we can limit access to our resources and reduce the surface area for potential attacks.

- **Azure Role-Based Access Control (RBAC):** With Azure RBAC, we can assign permissions to users, groups, and applications at a certain scope. We can define custom roles in our ARM templates to ensure the least privileged access, meaning users only have the access they need to perform their tasks and nothing more.

- **Azure Policy:** We can use Azure Policy to create, assign, and manage policies. These policies enforce different rules and effects on our resources, helping us manage compliance with corporate standards and regulatory requirements. Depending on our needs, we can assign these policies to different scopes, from a management group to a resource group.

- **Encryption and secrets management:** Use Azure Key Vault to store and manage secrets such as encryption keys, certificates, and API keys. Instead of embedding secrets in our ARM templates, reference them from Azure Key Vault. This not only enhances security but also aids in meeting regulatory compliance requirements.

- **Secure VMs and storage accounts:** For VMs, we can specify in our ARM templates that Azure Disk Encryption should be used. This service uses BitLocker for Windows and DM-Crypt for Linux to provide volume encryption for the OS and the data disks. For storage accounts, we should enable the secure transfer required, which enforces all requests to our storage account to be made over HTTPS.

- **Azure Security Center integration:** Azure Security Center provides unified security management and advanced threat protection. It can detect potential vulnerabilities in our ARM templates before deployment, helping us catch potential security issues before they become problems.

- **Regular audits and updates:** Regularly audit our ARM templates to ensure they follow best security practices. Update our templates as new security features become available in Azure.

Use Azure Policy for continuous compliance

Azure Policy is a service in Azure that we use to create, assign, and manage policies. These policies enforce different rules and effects over our resources so those resources stay compliant with our corporate standards and service level agreements.

Azure Policy does this by running evaluations of our resources and scanning for those not compliant with the policies we have created. These evaluations are run automatically every 24 hours, but we can also start them manually.

We can manage and prevent IT issues with policy effects. For example, we can prevent VMs from being deployed if they are exposed to a public IP address.

Now, to use Azure Policy for continuous compliance in DevSecOps, follow these steps:

1. **Define our policies:** We can define custom policies according to our organization's compliance requirements. A policy definition expresses what to evaluate and what action to take. For example, we can ensure that all NSGs deny traffic from a specific IP address.

2. **Assign policies:** Once we have defined our policies, we need to assign them. A policy assignment is a policy definition that has been assigned to take place within a specific scope. This scope could range from a management group to a resource group.

3. **Review and monitor compliance data:** We can monitor the compliance state of our Azure and non-Azure resources from the compliance dashboard in Azure Policy. This dashboard provides a snapshot of our resource compliance based on the assignment of our Azure policies.

4. **Remediate non-compliant resources:** Azure Policy not only provides details about how our resources are non-compliant but also provides a new capability to remediate those resources. For some types of policy rules, Azure Policy provides a managed capability for automatic remediation. For others, we can configure a remediation task.

5. **Use policy in Our CI/CD pipeline:** We can use Azure Policy in our CI/CD pipeline to catch compliance issues during development. The Azure Policy add-on for Azure DevOps allows us to evaluate our templates for compliance with a selected set of built-in or custom policies as part of our CI/CD pipeline.

By using Azure Policy in this way, we can ensure continuous compliance throughout our DevSecOps process, catching and remediating issues before they make it into our live environment.

Automated testing

Integrate automated testing into our CI/CD pipeline. For instance, we can use Azure Pipelines, part of Azure DevOps, for this purpose.

We can also use open-source tools like *Checkov* or *tfsec* to scan our ARM templates for security issues automatically. These tools can be integrated into our CI/CD pipeline so that they run every time we make a change to our templates.

Incorporate monitoring and logging

We can use services like Azure Monitor for monitoring and alerting and Azure Log Analytics for logging and analytics. These services can help us detect and respond to security incidents quickly.

For example, we could create an Azure Monitor alert that sends us an email notification if it detects an unusual amount of outbound traffic from our VMs, which could indicate a security breach.

Use Azure Key Vault for managing secrets

For managing application secrets like database credentials, use Azure Key Vault. This allows us to avoid hardcoding sensitive information in our ARM templates or application code.

By following these steps, we can implement Infrastructure as Code on Azure in a way that aligns with DevSecOps principles, automating security controls, incorporating continuous compliance, and fostering a culture of shared responsibility for security.

IaC for DevSecOps in a hybrid environment

Before we proceed to offer the steps for implementing IaC for DevSecOps in a hybrid environment, let us understand the key differences of such a process in AWS, GCP, and Azure.

Table 3.1 outlines the key differences in implementing IaC for DevSecOps across AWS, GCP, and Azure:

Feature	AWS	GCP	Azure
IaC services	AWS CloudFormation	Google Cloud Deployment Manager	ARM
Configuration language	YAML or JSON	YAML or Python	JSON
Template features	Creates and manages a collection of related AWS resources	Creates and manages a collection of related GCP resources	Creates and manages a collection of related Azure resources
Integration with CI/CD services	AWS CodePipeline, AWS CodeBuild, AWS CodeDeploy	Cloud Build, Cloud Source Repositories	Azure Pipelines
Security services	AWS Security Hub, AWS Config, AWS IAM	Google Cloud Security Command Center, Google Cloud IAM	Azure Security Center, Azure Policy, Azure Active Directory

Feature	AWS	GCP	Azure
Monitoring and logging	AWS CloudWatch, AWS CloudTrail	Google Cloud Operations Suite (formerly Stackdriver)	Azure Monitor, Azure Log Analytics
Scripting support	AWS SDKs and CLI	Google Cloud SDKs and CLI	Azure SDKs and PowerShell or Azure CLI
Third-partyIaC tool	Support Terraform, Pulumi, Ansible, Chef, Puppet	Terraform, Pulumi, Chef, Puppet	Terraform, Pulumi, Ansible, Chef, Puppet

Table 3.1: IaC for DevSecOps across AWS, GCP, and Azure, differences

Remember, the choice of a cloud provider should be influenced by our project's specific requirements and the features that align best with our use case.

Now, let us discuss the implementation of IaC in DevSecOps when we infrastructure that involves managing and coordinating resources across both on-premises and cloud environments, a hybrid environment. We often rely on third-party tools that can work across different platforms, such as Terraform, Ansible, and Chef, to handle this complexity.

Let us discuss the steps to implement IaC for DevSecOps in a hybrid environment.

Define our Infrastructure as Code

We can use a tool like Terraform to define our infrastructure declaratively. Terraform supports a wide range of providers, including AWS, Azure, GCP, and VMware, making it a good choice for hybrid environments. Our Terraform configurations can be version-controlled, reviewed, and tested just like any other code.

For example, we might have Terraform configurations that define AWS EC2 instances for our cloud-based application servers, VMware VMs for our on-premises database servers, and firewall rules for both environments.

CI/CD pipeline

Setting up a CI/CD pipeline is sometimes tricky if we go out of the trinity (AWS, GCP, and Azure). Let us discuss two scenarios, one for **Oracle Cloud Infrastructure (OCI)** and another for Beanstalk. The first is also a major cloud service provider offering a full suite of services, and the second just takes care of a part of the overall DevSecOps process.

OCI provides Resource Manager, a service that allows us to automate the provisioning and management of our OCI resources using the Terraform language. The first step in setting up a CI/CD pipeline is to have a source code repository where our code will be stored and versioned. We can use OCI's own **Source Code Management (SCM) service** or external Git repositories like GitHub or Bitbucket.

Once our source code is in the repository, it needs to be compiled, tested, and packaged into a deployable artifact. **OCI Developer Services** includes a build service that can compile the code, run tests, and produce deployable software packages.

Figure 3.5 shows the OCI Developer Services on their Cloud Control Panel:

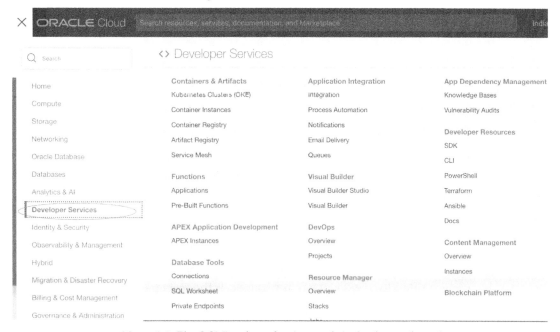

Figure 3.5: The OCI Developer Services on their cloud control panel

A key aspect of DevSecOps is integrating security checks into every stage of our pipeline. This includes scanning our code for vulnerabilities, checking our cloud resources for security compliance, and monitoring for threats. OCI provides various tools for this, such as **Oracle Cloud Guard** for threat detection and **Oracle Cloud Security Zone** for enforcing security best practices.

After the build process and security checks are complete, the next step is to deploy our application. This can be achieved with **Oracle's Deployment Pipeline**, which supports a range of deployment strategies and targets, including Oracle's own services and Kubernetes clusters (we shall discuss working with Kubernetes in *Chapter 4, Containers and Security*).

Once our application is deployed, it is crucial to have monitoring and logging in place to track application performance and identify any issues or threats. OCI provides logging and monitoring services for this purpose.

All these steps need to be orchestrated in a pipeline, where Oracle's Developer Services comes in. It provides the tools to create a full CI/CD pipeline, integrating our source control, build, test, and deploy steps into a single, streamlined process.

Remember, this is just a high-level overview, and the exact steps and tools we use may vary depending on our specific requirements and use cases.

On the other hand, Beanstalk is a simple, fast, and secure way to apply version control, collaborate, and deploy code. It supports both Git and Subversion repositories. While Beanstalk itself is not a **Continuous Integration (CI)** tool, it integrates well with many CI/CD tools to create a seamless deployment pipeline. Here are the general steps to create a CI/CD pipeline using Beanstalk:

1. **Create a repository:** Start by creating a repository in Beanstalk. We can choose either Git or Subversion as our version control system.

2. **Add our code:** Next, add our code to the repository. We can use any Git or Subversion client to do this.

3. **Set up automated deployments:** In Beanstalk, we can set up automated deployments to one or more servers whenever we make a commitment to a certain branch. To do this, go to the repository settings, then to the *Environment* section, and set up our deployment environment.

4. **Integrate with a CI/CD tool:** While Beanstalk does not provide built-in CI/CD capabilities, it integrates with popular CI/CD tools like Jenkins, TeamCity, and others. Set up our preferred CI/CD tool to automatically run our tests whenever code is committed to our Beanstalk repository. If the tests pass, the CI/CD tool can then push the code back to Beanstalk, triggering an automatic deployment.

5. **Collaborate and review code:** Beanstalk allows team members to review code, discuss changes, and collaborate effectively. Use these features to maintain high code quality and catch potential issues early.

6. **Monitor deployments:** Beanstalk provides notifications and a deployment history so we can monitor our deployments and quickly spot any problems.

Remember that Beanstalk is just one part of our CI/CD pipeline. We shall also need to consider how to manage our infrastructure, apply security controls, and monitor our applications once they are deployed. These tasks may involve other tools and services, depending on our specific needs and our cloud platform.

Incorporate security controls

In our IaC scripts, we can define various security controls for both our cloud and on-premises resources. For example, we can define firewall rules that restrict inbound traffic to our servers.

We can also use identity and access management controls to limit who can access and manage our resources. In AWS, we would use IAM roles, while in a VMware environment, we might use vCenter roles.

Continuous compliance

In a hybrid environment, ensuring continuous compliance can be more challenging due to the mix of different platforms and technologies. However, we can use tools like Chef InSpec or Open Policy Agent to define and enforce compliance rules across our environment.

For example, we might create an InSpec profile that checks whether our servers are configured according to our security guidelines and run this profile regularly to ensure continuous compliance.

Automated testing

Integrate automated testing into our CI/CD pipeline. For instance, we can use a tool like Jenkins or CircleCI to trigger tests whenever we make a change to our IaC scripts.

We can also use tools like Checkov or tfsec to automatically scan our Terraform scripts for security issues. These tools can be integrated into our CI/CD pipeline so that they run every time we make a change to our scripts.

Incorporate monitoring and logging

In a hybrid environment, we will likely need to use a mix of different monitoring and logging tools. For our cloud resources, we can use the cloud provider's native tools, such as AWS CloudWatch or Azure Monitor. For our on-premises resources, we might use a tool like Nagios or ELK Stack.

Secret management

For managing application secrets, we can use a tool like HashiCorp's Vault, which can manage and protect secrets across both cloud and on-premises environments. This allows us to avoid hardcoding sensitive information in our IaC scripts or application code.

By following these steps, we can implement Infrastructure as Code in a hybrid environment in a way that aligns with DevSecOps principles, automating security controls, incorporating continuous compliance, and fostering a culture of shared responsibility for security.

IaC and DevSecOps with legacy system

Legacy systems, which are older technologies, software, and hardware that are still in use, can present unique challenges when trying to implement modern practices like IaC and DevSecOps. These systems were often not designed with these practices in mind and may lack the necessary interfaces for integration. However, there are ways to work around these challenges and realize the benefits of IaC and DevSecOps, even in environments with legacy systems:

- **Efficiency and speed:** IaC can help manage legacy systems more efficiently, and DevSecOps can help ensure these systems are secure. By automating manual tasks, we can reduce errors and free up time for other activities.

- **Consistency:** IaC helps ensure that our infrastructure is consistent, which is especially important when dealing with legacy systems that might have been set up and configured manually.

- **Risk mitigation:** DevSecOps practices help reduce the risk associated with running legacy systems by integrating security into every phase of our software lifecycle.

- **Modernization:** When it is time to replace legacy systems, having IaC and DevSecOps practices in place can make the transition smoother. We can codify the configuration of the new system to match the legacy system as closely as possible, reducing the potential for errors or mismatches.

Implementing IaC and DevSecOps with legacy systems

There are challenges while implementing IaC in conjunction with a legacy system. Let us outline the broad points while implementing IaC in such scenarios:

- **Assess our legacy systems:** Not all legacy systems will be suitable for IaC or DevSecOps. Begin by assessing our systems to see which ones can be managed with IaC tools and where we can integrate DevSecOps practices.

- **Choose the right tools:** Some IaC tools are better suited to legacy systems than others. Ansible, for example, is a good choice because it is agentless and works well with a wide range of systems. For security, consider tools that can scan legacy code for vulnerabilities and integrate them into our existing systems.

- **Incremental changes:** Do not try to do everything at once. Start by automating a few simple tasks, then gradually increase our automation as we become more comfortable with the tools and processes.

- **Documentation and version control:** Legacy systems often lack comprehensive documentation. Make sure to document our IaC and DevSecOps processes and keep our code and configurations in a version control system.

- **Training:** Make sure our team has the necessary training to work with IaC and DevSecOps tools and practices. This may involve bringing in an external trainer or setting aside time for self-study.

- **Plan for modernization:** While we can make our legacy systems more efficient with IaC and DevSecOps, we should also plan for eventual modernization. When choosing tools and setting up processes, consider how they will work with newer systems.

Remember that implementing IaC and DevSecOps in an environment with legacy systems is a journey, not a destination. It requires ongoing effort, but the increased efficiency, security, and consistency are well worth it.

DevSecOps dashboard

A DevSecOps dashboard should provide a centralized view of our development, security, and operations data to allow teams to detect issues, respond quickly, and continuously improve their practices. Here are some essential elements of an effective DevSecOps dashboard:

- **Code commit activity:** This provides a summary of code changes in the repository, including the number of commits, branches, pull requests, and who made the changes. This helps in understanding the development pace and identifying any abnormal activity.

- **Build status:** This section provides real-time updates on the status of software builds, detailing whether they are passing or failing. It helps in identifying problems early in the software development lifecycle.

- **Deployment status:** Deployment status should provide insights into the number of deployments made, their success/failure rate, and where they were deployed. This helps in tracking the release velocity and understanding if there are any problems with the deployments.

- **Security alerts:** This section should show a summary of security threats or vulnerabilities detected, their severity, and the status of their remediation. This is critical for continuously monitoring the security health of our application.

- **Compliance status:** This shows the status of our application against defined compliance standards. It helps ensure that we are meeting the required regulatory standards.

- **Incident reports:** This section should provide a summary of operational incidents, their impact, and how long it took to resolve them. This helps in understanding the stability of our application and the efficiency of our incident response process.

- **Performance metrics:** Key performance metrics such as application response time, system resource utilization (CPU, memory, etc.), network latency, etc., should be included. This helps monitor our application's performance and proactively identify any performance bottlenecks.

- **Feedback and quality metrics:** Metrics related to application quality, such as the number of defects reported, defect density, and customer feedback scores, should also be present on the dashboard.

Remember, a good DevSecOps dashboard should be intuitive, real-time, customizable, and interactive. It should enable teams to understand data quickly, drill down for more details, and make data-driven decisions. Lastly, it is important that the dashboard aligns with the team's goals and supports the team's workflow.

Use case: Setup software environment

In our use case, the presence of IoT sensors and the IoT gateway creates unique challenges and opportunities for implementing IaC and CI/CD pipelines. IoT devices often have specific requirements and constraints, such as limited processing power, memory, and bandwidth, which can affect how we design and implement our infrastructure, security, and deployment processes.

IaC can be particularly beneficial for managing the infrastructure of IoT systems, which can involve a large number of devices spread out over multiple locations:

- **Device provisioning and configuration:** We can use IaC tools to automate the process of provisioning and configuring new IoT devices, including sensors and gateways. This can help to ensure that all devices are set up consistently and correctly.

- **Network configuration:** IaC can also be used to manage the network configurations of our IoT devices, ensuring that they can communicate effectively with each other and with our backend systems.

- **Resource management:** IaC can help to manage the resources that our IoT devices rely on, such as databases, data processing systems, and cloud storage.

Security is a crucial aspect of IoT systems, as these devices can often be vulnerable to attacks. Implementing DevSecOps practices can help to ensure that security is integrated into every stage of our IoT development and deployment processes:

- **Secure development practices:** Implement secure coding practices to minimize vulnerabilities in our IoT software. This could include regular code reviews, static and dynamic code analysis, and penetration testing.

- **Automated security testing:** As part of our CI/CD pipeline, implement automated security testing of our IoT software. This can help to catch any security issues before the software is deployed to our devices.

- **Security updates and patch management:** DevSecOps can help automate the process of deploying security updates and patches to our IoT devices, helping to keep them secure over time.

Continuous Integration and Continuous Deployment (CI/CD) can help to streamline the process of developing, testing, and deploying software to our IoT devices. Refer to the following points:

- **Automated testing:** As part of our CI/CD pipeline, implement automated testing of our IoT software. This can help to catch any bugs or issues before the software is deployed.

- **Staged deployment:** IoT deployments can be complex and risky. By using a staged deployment process, we can minimize the risk of issues affecting all of our devices at once.

- **Rollback capabilities:** If an issue does occur during deployment, having the ability to quickly roll back the changes can help to minimize the impact.

- **Device monitoring and feedback:** Once the software has been deployed, continuously monitor the performance and behavior of our IoT devices and feed this information back into our development process. This can help us identify and resolve any issues quickly and continually improve our software over time.

Remember, the key to effective IaC, DevSecOps, and CI/CD in our use case is to consider the specific requirements and constraints of our IoT devices and to tailor our processes and tools accordingly.

Conclusion

As we have journeyed through the vast landscape of IaC and DevSecOps, it is clear that the two are deeply intertwined, each enhancing and enabling the other in the continuous delivery of secure, high-quality software.

IaC, with its automated, repeatable processes, forms the backbone of any DevSecOps strategy. By codifying infrastructure, teams can quickly and consistently recreate environments, thereby eliminating work on machine problems and the potential security vulnerabilities that can accompany manual setups.

On the other hand, DevSecOps incorporates security at each step of the development process, a practice that IaC greatly facilitates. IaC scripts can be version-controlled and peer-reviewed, just like application code, to ensure that security best practices are being followed. Automated testing can validate that infrastructure changes do not introduce vulnerabilities, and monitoring can ensure that the running infrastructure remains secure and compliant.

Moreover, the combination of IaC and DevSecOps profoundly impacts the speed and reliability of software delivery. Changes can be rolled out more rapidly because both the application code and the infrastructure it runs on can be modified in tandem. The risks associated with these changes are minimized because they can be thoroughly tested before being applied.

In conclusion, the marriage of IaC and DevSecOps offers a clear pathway toward more secure, efficient, and reliable software delivery processes. By leveraging these practices, teams can not only respond more swiftly to business needs but also create an environment of continuous learning and improvement, where every change is an opportunity to increase quality and deliver value.

As we move on to the next chapter, we will delve into an essential component of this ecosystem: Container technologies. These technologies further augment the DevSecOps pipeline by offering a layer of consistency and security that complements the principles of IaC.

Questions

1. What is IaC? Can you explain it in your own words?

2. Can you name some benefits of using IaC?

3. What are some popular tools used for implementing IaC?

4. How does IaC contribute to the efficiency and consistency of infrastructure setup?

5. What is DevSecOps? How does it integrate into the software development lifecycle?

6. What are some benefits of implementing DevSecOps in an organization?

7. How does DevSecOps contribute to the early detection and resolution of security issues?

8. Can you explain what a CI/CD pipeline is and its importance in modern software development?

9. How does a CI/CD pipeline contribute to reducing downtime and early detection of issues in the software development process?

10. How will you implement IaC for DevSecOps on AWS?

11. How will you implement IaC for DevSecOps on GCP?

12. How will you implement IaC for DevSecOps on Azure?

13. What are the key differences while doing a setup of IaC for DevSecOps on AWS, GCP, and Azure?

14. How will you implement IaC for DevSecOps on OCI?

15. How can IaC, DevSecOps, and CI/CD be implemented in a hybrid environment?

16. How will you set up your CI/CD pipeline when you use Beanstalk?

17. What challenges might one face when implementing IaC, DevSecOps, and CI/CD in an environment with legacy systems, and how might these be overcome?

18. What are the key features of a DevSecOps Dashboard?

19. How will you implement a CI/CD pipeline when IoT devices are involved?

CHAPTER 4

Containers and Security

Introduction

In the previous chapter, we delved into the transformative concept of **Infrastructure as Code (IaC)** within DevSecOps. We explored its remarkable benefits, including consistency, efficiency, and scalability. We provided a detailed walkthrough on implementing it effectively on major cloud platforms such as AWS, GCP, and Azure.

As we continue our journey into the intricate landscape of DevSecOps, this new chapter will pivot our focus toward the increasingly critical role of container technologies in modern development pipelines. Though we mentioned containers in *Chapter 2, Application Security*, we have deferred the discussion to this chapter. Containers, with their promise of creating a consistent and reproducible environment across various stages of the development lifecycle, have become an integral component of efficient and secure software delivery processes.

In this chapter, we will consider two of the most widely adopted container technologies to provide a comprehensive understanding of their workings and a clear perspective on their associated security challenges. We will delve into common vulnerabilities, examining their potential impacts and the mitigation strategies essential for robust container security.

Further, we will investigate the ever-evolving landscape of fixes and patch management processes that are instrumental in addressing these vulnerabilities. To equip us with practical knowledge, we will also introduce and evaluate some of the best tools and techniques available to fortify our container environment against potential threats.

So, let us embark on this journey of exploring container security, understanding its complexities, and unraveling the strategies to navigate them effectively within a DevSecOps framework. It is time to delve deeper into the world where development, security, and operations seamlessly intertwine, enabling us to create functional, secure, and resilient software systems.

Structure

In this chapter, we will discuss the following topics:

- Introduction to containers
- Container technologies
- Role of containers in DevSecOps
- Container security basics
- Security in container lifecycle
- Container image security
- Runtime container security
- Network security for containers
- Secrets management in containers
- Best practices for container security in DevSecOps
- Case studies of container security in DevSecOps

Objectives

This chapter aims to provide an in-depth understanding of container technology and its crucial role in DevSecOps. We will begin by defining containers, outlining their key benefits, and distinguishing them from virtual machines. Next, we will delve into popular container technologies and their respective roles in DevSecOps. An emphasis will be placed on the security implications of using containers, focusing on identifying common vulnerabilities and exploring effective mitigation strategies. This chapter will also examine essential container security practices, including image scanning, runtime security, network policies, and secrets management. We aim to equip the reader with practical knowledge on integrating and securing containers within a DevSecOps pipeline, shedding light on the best tools and techniques to ensure robust container security. By the end of this chapter, readers will have gained a comprehensive understanding of how to navigate container security challenges within a DevSecOps context.

Introduction to containers

In the era of cloud computing and microservices, containers have emerged as a revolutionary technology, playing a pivotal role in shaping the landscape of modern software development and operations. Let us start by defining what exactly containers are.

Containers are lightweight, standalone, executable packages that encapsulate everything needed to run the software, including the code, a runtime, system tools, system libraries, and settings. In essence, a container is a portable, self-sufficient unit that provides a consistent and controlled environment for software to run, irrespective of the underlying host system. *Figure 4.1* illustrates this point:

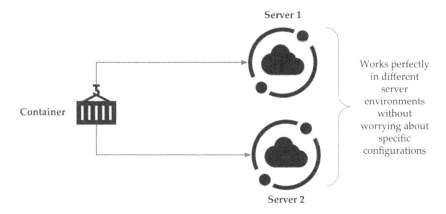

Figure 4.1: *Easy movement of containers through different server configurations*

The concept of containerization in computing is not new and has been contributed to by many companies and communities over the years. The idea took the ground as early as 1979 by introducing the chroot system call in Unix V7, which provided a way to isolate file system access. Introduced in 2000, FreeBSD Jails expanded on the idea of chroot to provide complete system virtualization by isolating not just the file system but also the process tree and network connections.

Linux-VServer and OpenVZ were early Linux-based containerization solutions that provided similar functionality to FreeBSD Jails. Introduced in 2008, LXC was the first, widely-used, Linux-based containerization solution built around the Linux kernel features like namespaces and cgroups.

Docker, introduced in 2013, popularized containerization by providing a high-level tool focusing on the developer experience. Docker made it easy to build, share, and deploy containerized applications. 2014 CoreOS introduced the **rkt** (pronounced **rocket**) container runtime as an alternative to Docker, focusing on simplicity and security.

Founded in 2015 by Docker, CoreOS, and other leaders in the container industry, the **Open Container Initiative (OCI)** established standard specifications for container formats and runtimes, promoting interoperability and avoiding vendor lock-in. Kubernetes is a container orchestration platform that automates containerized applications' deployment, scaling, and management. Google initially designed it, and the Cloud Native Computing Foundation maintains it.

Each of these contributors has played a role in the evolution of container technology, leading to the robust, flexible, and standardized container solutions we have today.

Natural fit for microservices

Microservices architecture (discussed in *Chapter 2, Application Security*) involves breaking an application down into small, independently deployable services. For example, an e-commerce application might have separate services for user management, inventory, payment processing, and so on.

Containers are ideal for this kind of architecture. Each microservice can be packaged into its container, allowing it to be developed, deployed, and scaled independently of the others. For instance, during a sales event, the inventory and payment processing services need to be scaled up to handle increased demand, and this can be done without affecting the other services.

In the following sections, we will explore container technologies, their role in DevSecOps, and how to secure them. This exploration will equip us with the knowledge to harness the power of containers effectively and safely.

Container technologies

In the world of containerization, a few technologies have risen to prominence due to their robust capabilities, strong community support, and widespread adoption. This section will explore Docker (**https://www.docker.com**) and Kubernetes (**https://kubernetes.io**), two of the most popular and influential container technologies. We will also touch upon other notable container orchestration tools.

Overview of Docker

Docker, introduced in 2013, has done more than any other tool to popularize container technology. Docker is an open-source platform designed to automate applications' deployment, scaling, and management by encapsulating them into containers. It uses resource isolation features of the Linux kernel, such as cgroups and kernel namespaces, and a union-capable file system, such as OverlayFS and others, to allow independent containers to run within a single Linux instance.

Docker provides a high-level, user-friendly interface to containerization, offering a standardized format for building, packaging, and distributing containers. This simplicity and standardization have contributed to Docker's wide adoption, making it the de facto standard for container runtime.

Introduction to Kubernetes

While Docker revolutionized how we package and distribute applications, it offered a partial solution for managing many containers across multiple machines. This is where Kubernetes comes in.

Kubernetes is an open-source container orchestration platform that automates containerized applications' deployment, scaling, and management. Originally designed by Google, Kubernetes is now maintained by the **Cloud Native Computing Foundation (CNCF)**.

Kubernetes provides a framework for running distributed systems resiliently. It handles scaling and failover for our applications, provides deployment patterns, and more. It groups containers that make up an application into logical units for easy management and discovery.

Docker and Kubernetes are both key components of containerization and are often used together, but they serve different roles in the system, as illustrated in *Table 4.1* below:

Feature	Docker	Kubernetes
Primary function	Containerization	Container orchestration
Scope	Handles individual containers	Handles clusters of containers
Networking	Uses single-host networking	Uses multi-host networking
Deployment	Docker Compose, Docker Swarm	Kubectl, YAML files
Load balancing	Manual intervention required	Automatic load balancing
Data volumes	Docker volumes	Persistent volumes
Autoscaling	Limited support (only with Docker Swarm)	Built-in support
Rollback function	Limited support	Provides version control and rollback

Table 4.1: Understanding the comparison of Docker and Kubernetes

Docker and Kubernetes are not competing technologies; they are rather complementary to each other. Docker provides the runtime environment for container applications, and Kubernetes provides the orchestration and cluster management for these containers. They are often used together to provide a complete containerization solution.

Note: We can use a drag-and-drop for Kubernetes on Docker using an extension like Harpoon (https://www.harpoon.io).

Other container orchestration tools

While Docker and Kubernetes are the most well-known container technologies, there are other notable tools in the ecosystem:

- **Docker Swarm:** Docker Swarm (**https://docs.docker.com/engine/swarm/**) is Docker's native clustering and scheduling tool. It is fully integrated into the Docker platform, making it simpler but less flexible and feature-rich than Kubernetes.

- **Apache Mesos:** Mesos (**https://mesos.apache.org**) is a powerful distributed systems kernel that provides resource isolation and sharing capabilities across distributed applications or frameworks.

- **Amazon Elastic Container Service (ECS):** ECS (**https://aws.amazon.com/ecs/**) is a fully managed container orchestration service provided by Amazon Web Services. It supports Docker containers and allows us to efficiently run applications on a managed cluster of Amazon EC2 instances.

- **OpenShift:** Developed by Red Hat, OpenShift (**https://www.redhat.com/en/technologies/cloud-computing/openshift**) is an open-source container platform that combines Docker and Kubernetes, adding developer and operations-centric tools on top of Kubernetes to enable rapid application development, easy deployment and scaling, and long-term lifecycle maintenance.

These tools and Docker and Kubernetes form the backbone of modern container-based infrastructures, playing a critical role in implementing DevSecOps pipelines.

Role of containers in DevSecOps

DevSecOps, a philosophy that integrates development, security, and operations into a unified process, is deeply intertwined with container technologies. Containers provide the necessary infrastructure to ensure a smooth, efficient, and secure DevSecOps workflow. Let us delve into how they contribute to various aspects of the DevSecOps paradigm.

Consistency and reproducibility

In a traditional development cycle, developers write code on their machines, which are then moved to different environments (like testing, staging, and production). However, differences in these environments can sometimes cause the code to behave differently. For instance, an application might work perfectly on a developer's machine but fail when deployed to the production environment due to differences in library versions or system configurations.

In a DevSecOps environment, code must behave the same way across different stages of the development pipeline and in different environments. With containers, the application and all its dependencies are bundled together. This means the environment remains consistent regardless of where the container is run. For example, a Python application might need a specific library version. In a container, that library version is bundled with the application, ensuring it is always available when it runs, regardless of the environment. This eliminates its work on my machine problem, leading to fewer bugs and higher productivity.

Isolation

Imagine two applications running on the same server, requiring different versions of the same library. In a traditional environment, this could lead to conflicts and potentially cause one or both applications to fail.

With containers, each application operates in its isolated environment with its dependencies. For example, one container could have version 1 of a library, and another container on the same server could have version 2 of the same library, which would not conflict.

Containers provide process-level isolation, meaning that each containerized application runs in its environment and does not interfere with other applications. This isolation allows developers to package their applications with specific versions of dependencies without worrying about conflicts. From a security perspective, this isolation is critical, as it limits the potential blast radius of an attack.

Scalability and efficiency

Online retail platforms must often scale their applications quickly during sales events to handle a sudden influx of users. With traditional virtual machines, spinning up new instances can take several minutes, leading to poor user experience and potential loss of sales.

Containers are lightweight and start quickly, allowing for rapid scaling based on demand. This characteristic is particularly important in a DevSecOps context, where the ability to iterate rapidly and scale applications can significantly enhance the agility and responsiveness of a team. In addition, containers can run efficiently on various infrastructure types, from bare-metal servers to virtual machines and cloud instances, providing flexibility and cost efficiency.

Immutable Infrastructure

Immutable infrastructure is an approach where servers are never modified after deployment. If a change is needed, new servers are built from a common image, and old servers are decommissioned. Containers lend themselves naturally to this approach, as they can be easily created, deployed, and destroyed. This makes the system more predictable, reliable, and easier to manage and aligns with the IaC principle.

With Docker, for instance, a Dockerfile can define everything that will go into a container, effectively becoming an executable specification for the environment. Kubernetes configuration files, meanwhile, can define complex application deployments involving many interconnected containers.

In sum, containers enable DevSecOps, providing consistency, isolation, and scalability while supporting critical practices such as immutable infrastructure and **Infrastructure as Code**. By properly leveraging these benefits, teams can build more robust, secure, and efficient systems.

Container security basics

Container security is a vast topic that involves securing container images, container runtime, and the underlying host system. As the usage of containers continues to grow, so does the importance of container security. In this section, we will look at some of the key aspects of container security.

Container security involves multiple layers, from the container images to the host operating system:

- Container images
- Container runtime
- Host system
- Orchestration and deployment

Let us explain each of these.

Container images

A container image can be considered as the blueprint from which containers are created. It bundles together the application code, runtime, libraries, environment variables, and configuration files the application needs to run. When we start a container from a container image, it is like creating an instance of a class in object-oriented programming. Here is an example using Docker:

```
docker run ubuntu:latest
```

This command tells Docker to run a container based on the **ubuntu:latest** image. If the image is unavailable locally, Docker will pull it from the Docker Hub, a public container image registry. *Figure 4.2* illustrates this process:

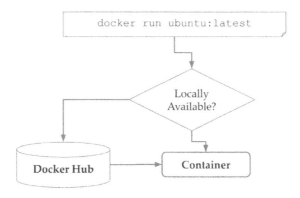

Figure 4.2: *The Process of creating a Docker container*

Security for container images is vital in a DevSecOps context because vulnerabilities in the container image can compromise the containers running from it. There are several aspects to securing container images. The most important is vulnerability scanning, which involves scanning the container image for known vulnerabilities. Several tools, such as Clair, Anchore, and Docker's scanning capabilities, can do this.

When constructing secure containerized applications, it is crucial to follow best practices to safeguard against potential vulnerabilities. One significant measure is to minimize the container's attack surface by only incorporating essential components. This not only keeps the container lightweight but also reduces potential entry points for malicious actors. Let us delve into a practical example of this.

Consider the following Dockerfile:

```
FROM alpine:latest
COPY . /app
WORKDIR /app
RUN apk add --no-cache python3 py3-pip && \ pip3 install --no-cache-dir -r
requirements.txt
CMD ["python3", "app.py"]
```

In this Dockerfile, we are intentionally using the minimalistic Alpine Linux as the base image, emphasizing our commitment to keeping things lean. By copying only the necessary application code and installing required Python packages without any caching, we are further reducing any superfluous data. Finally, the command set ensures that our application runs as intended when the container is started.

By adhering to these guidelines, we are ensuring a balance between functionality and security, demonstrating a proactive approach to reducing risks in our containerized applications.

Storing and distributing securely

Container images should be stored in a secure registry that supports access controls and audit logs. Images can also be signed to ensure their integrity. Docker Content Trust provides image signing capabilities.

A secure container image is a foundational step towards secure container deployments.

Container runtime

A container runtime is the software that is responsible for running containers. The runtime is responsible for several tasks, including image transfer and storage, container execution and supervision, low-level local storage, and network interface management. Popular examples include Docker, containerd, and CRI-O.

Let us take Docker as an example. When we run a Docker command like docker run nginx, the Docker daemon communicates with the containerd daemon, which manages the complete container lifecycle of its host system.

There are several aspects to consider for ensuring security at the runtime level. Let us discuss them.

Container isolation

Containers running on the same host should be isolated from each other and the host system. By default, Docker provides some isolation level using Linux namespaces and cgroups. For example, the PID namespace isolates the process ID number space, meaning processes in different containers can have the same PID. This isolates the processes running in different containers.

Least privilege

Containers should be run with the least necessary privileges. This can be achieved by not running processes as root inside the container, disabling inter-container communication, and using read-only filesystems when possible. An example command that embodies this principle is as follows:

```
docker run --user 1000 --network none --read-only ubuntu:latest
```

In executing this command, we are launching a container with several heightened security measures. The container is run using a non-root user (signified by UID 1000), its ability to communicate over the network is entirely disabled, and its filesystem is set to read-only mode, preventing unwanted modifications. This approach showcases a proactive stance in bolstering container security.

Security modules

Use **Linux Security Modules (LSM)** such as AppArmor (**https://apparmor.net**) or SELinux (**https://selinuxproject.org**), which provide an additional layer of security. Docker uses AppArmor by default but can be configured to use SELinux.

Runtime vulnerability scanning

Scan the runtime environment for vulnerabilities. Tools such as OpenSCAP (**https://www.open-scap.org**) can help with this. The security of the container runtime is critical, as it can directly affect all containers managed by the runtime.

Host system

The host system is the machine that runs the container runtime and the containers. As containers share the host system's kernel, ensuring the host system's security is paramount to the overall security of our containerized applications. A vulnerability in the host system can affect all containers running on it.

Here are some key aspects to consider for securing the host system:

- **Minimal installation:** The host system should only have the minimal software necessary to run our containers. The less software installed, the fewer potential vulnerabilities. We can use a minimal OS like CoreOS, RancherOS, or a stripped-down version of a common Linux distribution.

- **Regular updates and patching:** Keeping the host system updated with the latest patches is essential. This includes the OS, the container runtime, and any other software running on the host. Regularly check for updates and apply them as soon as possible.

- **Access control:** Set up proper user permissions and access controls on the host system. Only authorized personnel should have access to the host system, and they should only have the least necessary privileges. We can manage this with traditional Unix permissions or use more advanced systems like sudo rules or **Access Control Lists (ACLs)**.

- **Monitoring and auditing:** Monitor the host system for any suspicious activity. This includes monitoring system logs, network traffic, and resource usage.

The host system forms the basis on which our containers run. Therefore, ensuring its security is the first step toward secure container deployments.

Orchestration and deployment

Orchestration and deployment are the layers that manage containers at scale. The most popular tool for this is Kubernetes, but others like Docker Swarm and Apache Mesos are also used. These tools handle tasks such as rolling out updates, scaling in or out based on load, managing network communication between containers, and ensuring high availability.

Let us discuss some key aspects for securing our orchestration and deployment layer.

Role-based access control

RBAC lets us define who can do what within our Kubernetes cluster. For instance, we can specify that a specific user or group of users can only read information about Pods (a pod is the smallest deployable unit of computing that you can create and manage in Kubernetes: **https://kubernetes.io/docs/concepts/workloads/pods/**), but cannot modify them. As an example, consider the following manifest:

```
apiVersion: rbac.authorization.k8s.io/v1
kind: Role
metadata:
  namespace: default
  name: pod-reader
rules:
  - apiGroups: [""]
    resources: ["pods"]
    verbs: ["get", "watch", "list"]
```

This Kubernetes manifest defines a role named **pod-reader** that permits users to retrieve (**get**), observe (**watch**), and enumerate (**list**) pods, but only within the **default** namespace. It is a clear demonstration of how granular permissions can be set using RBAC in Kubernetes.

Securing the control plane

The Kubernetes control plane consists of several components that manage the state of the cluster, like the API server, etcd (**https://etcd.io**), and the controller manager. Securing the control plane involves ensuring these components are securely configured and updated.

Network policies

Ensuring proper networking boundaries within our Kubernetes cluster is pivotal to maintaining security and preventing unwanted access. Network policies serve as an integral tool in this pursuit, akin to firewalls, dictating how pods interact with each other and different network end-points. To illustrate, here is a concrete example.

```
apiVersion: networking.k8s.io/v1
kind: NetworkPolicy
```

```
metadata:
  name: deny-all
spec:
  podSelector: {}
  policyTypes:
  - Ingress
```

This Kubernetes manifest presents a **NetworkPolicy** named **deny-all**, specifically designed to block all incoming (Ingress) traffic targeting the pods. Implementing such stringent measures is paramount, particularly when juggling numerous containers in a microservices-driven setup.

Importance of container security in DevSecOps

In a DevSecOps culture, security is not an afterthought but is integrated into every step of the development pipeline. Containers, integral to modern deployment strategies, are critical to this security effort.

Here is why container security is essential:

- **Target for attackers:** Containers encapsulate the application and its dependencies. This makes them a likely target for attackers as a successful exploit can provide access to the application and possibly even sensitive data. For example, an attacker who exploits a vulnerability in a container running a database application could access all the data within that database.

- **Risk from misconfigurations or vulnerabilities:** Containers are complex pieces of software, and like any software, they can contain vulnerabilities. Misconfigurations can lead to security risks even without vulnerabilities in the container software. For instance, running containers with unnecessary root privileges could allow an attacker who compromises the container to escalate privileges and attack other system components.

- **Dynamic and ephemeral nature:** Containers are often dynamically scheduled and can be ephemeral, meaning they might only exist briefly. This introduces new security challenges as traditional security tools and processes may not be equipped to handle this. For example, by the time a security team identifies a vulnerability in a container, that container might no longer exist, having been replaced by a new instance.

Here is a code snippet demonstrating how a Docker container might be run with unnecessary root privileges:

```
docker run -d --privileged -p 80:80 my_web_application
```

In the above command, the **--privileged** flag gives the container nearly unrestricted access to the host OS, a significant security risk if the container is compromised. This risk highlights why focusing on container security is crucial in a DevSecOps approach.

The key point is that securing containers requires adapting traditional security practices for this new technology and integrating these practices into the DevSecOps pipeline. This might include automating vulnerability scanning for container images, using least privilege principles when configuring containers, and employing runtime security tools designed specifically for containers.

Challenges in container security

Container security can present several unique challenges, mainly because containers introduce a new technology layer with vulnerabilities and potential configuration pitfalls. Let us discuss some key challenges.

- **Image vulnerabilities**

  Containers are built from images, which include the application and its dependencies. If these images contain outdated or vulnerable software packages, attackers can exploit them. For example, consider a Node.js application that uses an old package version with known vulnerabilities. Even if the application code is secure, attackers can exploit the vulnerabilities in the outdated package.

  Here is an example of a Dockerfile that uses an outdated base image:

  ```
  FROM node:10
  WORKDIR /usr/src/app
  COPY package*.json ./
  RUN npm install
  COPY . .
  EXPOSE 8080
  CMD [ "node", "server.js" ]
  ```

  In the above Dockerfile, the base image node:10 is outdated, as Node.js 10 has reached its end of life and may contain unfixed vulnerabilities.

- **Runtime security**

  Containers might be configured to run with more privileges than needed, potentially allowing an attacker to access the host system or other containers. The principle of least privilege (to be elaborated on later in this chapter) should be adhered to when configuring containers.

- **Immutable infrastructure**

  With immutable infrastructure, any changes, including security patches, must be made to the container images, and new containers must be rolled out. We cannot patch the running containers. This requires a well-functioning CI/CD pipeline and container orchestration setup.

- **Orchestration complexity**

  Tools like Kubernetes add significant complexity and have a set of security considerations. Securing the control plane, setting up network policies, and managing service accounts are just a few security tasks involved in container orchestration.

- **Securing the CI/CD pipeline**

  The CI/CD pipeline builds and deploys containers. It is essential to use strong access controls and secret management practices to secure the pipeline. If an attacker gains access to the pipeline, they could inject malicious code into the containers or compromise the confidentiality and integrity of the application code.

Understanding and addressing these challenges is critical to maintaining security in a containerized environment. These challenges can be mitigated as part of a comprehensive DevSecOps strategy, turning potential weaknesses into strengths.

Security in container lifecycle

Implementing security in the container lifecycle is crucial to safeguard our applications and data. Security should be integrated into every phase of the lifecycle, from development to deployment and operations. Let us have a deeper look into each phase with specific steps and relevant examples.

Secure container development

Secure development primarily focuses on building secure container images. Here are some best practices to consider:

1. **Use trusted base images**

   Start with a minimal base image from a trusted source to reduce the attack surface and limit exposure to vulnerabilities. For example, in a Dockerfile, we would use a trusted and minimal base image like so:

   ```
   FROM debian:stretch-slim

   ...
   ```

2. **Scan for vulnerabilities**

   Incorporate automated tools to scan our container images for known vulnerabilities. This should be done when the image is built and whenever the image or its base image is updated. Tools like Clair or Anchore can be used for this purpose.

3. **Manage dependencies**

   Keep track of the dependencies in our container and ensure they are updated regularly. Tools like Dependabot can automatically check for updates and vulnerabilities in our dependencies.

4. **Do not store secrets in images**

   Never store secrets such as API keys or passwords within the container image. Use secure methods like Kubernetes Secrets or Docker secrets or inject environment variables at runtime.

Secure container deployment

Secure deployment practices involve securely running our containers. Here is how:

1. **Least privilege**

   Run containers with the least privilege necessary, avoiding running containers as root whenever possible. In Docker, this could look like the following in a Dockerfile:

   ```
   ...
   USER 1001
   ...
   ```

2. **Immutability**

   Containers should be immutable and disposable. Instead of patching running containers, update the image and roll out new containers.

3. **Use a secure orchestration platform**

   Platforms like Kubernetes offer strong security features, including **Role-Based Access Control (RBAC)**, network policies, and secrets management.

4. **Secure communications**

   Encrypt all communications between containers and between containers and users using protocols like TLS.

Secure container operations

Secure operations involve managing our containers securely over time. The following practices can bolster our operational security:

1. **Monitor and log:** Track our container behavior and employ tools to detect and alert suspicious behavior. Platforms like **Elasticsearch, Logstash, Kibana (ELK)**, or the **Elasticsearch, Fluentd, Kibana (EFK)** stack can be used for this purpose.

2. **Update and patch:** Regularly update our containers and host system to patch any security vulnerabilities. This includes updating the container runtime and orchestration software.

3. **Incident response:** Prepare an incident response plan to handle security incidents effectively. This includes understanding how to analyze, contain, and recover from an attack and learning from the incident to prevent future occurrences.

4. **Audit:** Regularly audit our container environment for any misconfigurations or vulnerabilities. Tools like kube-bench or kube-score can help check for common issues.

By integrating these security practices throughout the container lifecycle, we can significantly enhance the security of our container deployments, leading to more robust protection of our applications and data.

Container image security

Container images, the template from which containers are created, are crucial to container security. Ensuring these images are secure is foundational to the overall security posture of our applications.

Importance of secure container images

Securing container images is an essential part of container security strategy, with several key reasons emphasizing its significance:

- **Attack vector**

  When dealing with container deployments, one must be vigilant about the contents of the images being used. Vulnerabilities within these images can open up avenues for attackers, turning seemingly harmless images into potential threats. To elucidate, consider the Dockerfile below:

  ```
  # Dockerfile with vulnerable software
  FROM ubuntu:18.04
  RUN apt-get update && apt-get install -y openssl=1.1.0g-2ubuntu4
  ...
  ```

  This Dockerfile, while seemingly standard, intentionally installs an outdated version of OpenSSL that is known to be susceptible to the Heartbleed vulnerability. If this image is deployed, especially in a production setting, it stands as a ticking time bomb, awaiting exploitation by malicious entities.

- **Build once, run anywhere**

  One of the main advantages of containers is the ability to build once and run anywhere. However, this also implies that any vulnerabilities in the image can spread wherever the image is deployed. For instance, an insecure image built on a developer's local machine can end up running in production, bringing the same vulnerabilities with it.

- **Immutable infrastructure**

  Containers are often considered as part of an immutable infrastructure. Once they are up and running, they are not updated or patched. Therefore, ensuring the image is secure from the outset is crucial.

  ```
  # Dockerfile with secure practices
  FROM ubuntu:latest
  RUN apt-get update && apt-get upgrade -y && apt-get install -y
  openssl
  …
  ```

  In this updated Dockerfile, we use the latest version of Ubuntu and update all packages before installing OpenSSL, reducing the likelihood of including outdated or vulnerable software in the image.

Thus, using secure container images reduces potential attack vectors and upholds the principles of immutable infrastructure. Regular vulnerability scanning, updates, and adherence to best practices can help maintain the security of container images.

Vulnerabilities in container images

Container images should be thoroughly scanned for vulnerabilities at build time and whenever they are updated as part of a robust security practice. Automated tools can scan container images, compare included software packages against databases of known vulnerabilities, and provide detailed reports. Let us briefly discuss a few popular tools that we can use for vulnerability scanning.

Clair

Clair (**https://github.com/quay/clair**) is an open-source project for the static analysis of vulnerabilities in application containers. It scans each layer of our Docker to reveal any security weaknesses.

Here is an example of how to use Clair:

```
# pull the Clair image
docker pull quay.io/coreos/clair
# run Clair
docker run -d -p 6060:6060 -p 6061:6061 quay.io/coreos/clair
```

Anchore Engine

Anchore Engine (**https://anchore.com/blog/anchore-engine/**) is an open-source tool for deep image inspection and vulnerability scanning. It provides a centralized service for inspecting, analyzing, and certifying container images.

Here is how to use Anchore Engine:

```
# run Anchore Engine
docker run -d --name anchore_engine -v /var/run/docker.sock:/var/run/
docker.sock anchore/anchore-engine:latest
# add an image to Anchore for analysis
docker exec anchore_engine anchore-cli image add myrepo/myimage:latest
```

Docker Security Scanning

Docker Security Scanning is a security tool that scans images in private repositories to ensure they are free from known vulnerabilities or exposures. By enabling Docker Security Scanning, we can be sure that our images are free from known security risks, which can help to prevent data breaches and other security incidents.

To enable Docker Security Scanning, we can navigate to the Docker Hub repository (**hub. docker.com**), select the **Settings** tab, and then enable the **Security Scanning** option as in *Figure 4.3*:

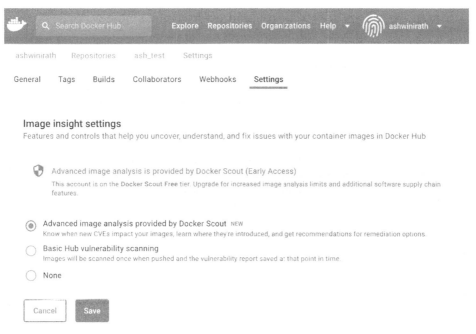

Figure 4.3: *Enabling security scanning option at the Docker Hub*

Regular audits of our images can ensure they are built according to best practices. This includes checking for non-root users, minimal base images, and appropriate handling of secrets. Automated tools like Docker Bench for security can provide these audit functionalities, checking for common best practices around deploying containers in production.

Remember, the goal of scanning and auditing container images for vulnerabilities is to uncover and fix issues before they can be exploited, thereby enhancing the overall security posture of our applications.

Signing and verifying container images

Signing container images is an essential part of ensuring their integrity and authenticity. Image signing can help prevent the use of unauthorized or tampered images in our environment. Several tools and processes can be used for signing and verifying images, such as **DCT** (**Docker Content Trust**), Notary, and Portieris.

Docker Content Trust

DCT (**https://docs.docker.com/engine/security/trust/**) is a feature in Docker that uses digital signatures to verify the authenticity of images. When enabled, DCT signs images automatically during the docker push command and verifies the signatures during the docker pull.

Here is an example of how to enable DCT and push a signed image:

```
# enable Docker Content Trust
export DOCKER_CONTENT_TRUST=1
# push a signed image
docker push myrepo/myimage:tag
```

When DCT is enabled, Docker will ask us to create a passphrase for the root and repository keys. These keys are used to sign the image.

Notary

Notary (**https://github.com/notaryproject/notary**) is an open-source project that provides a server for storing signed metadata and a client for creating and managing the signed metadata. It integrates with DCT but can also be used separately.

Here is an example of how to use a Notary to publish a signed collection:

```
# initialize a new collection
notary init myrepo/mycollection
```

```
# add and sign a file
notary add myrepo/mycollection myfile.txt
# publish the collection
notary publish myrepo/mycollection
```

Portieris

Portieris (**https://github.com/IBM/portieris**) is a Kubernetes admission controller for enforcing Content Trust. Portieris can be configured to prevent unsigned images or images signed by unauthorized keys from running.

We can install Portieris using Helm (the package manager for Kubernetes: **https://helm. sh**):

```
# add the Portieris Helm repo
helm repo add portieris https://raw.githubusercontent.com/IBM/portieris/
master/helm-repo/
# install Portieris
helm install portieris portieris/portieris --namespace portieris
```

These processes include signing images after they are built, verifying the signatures before an image is pulled and run, and configuring the system only to allow images to be run if they have a valid signature from a trusted source.

By following these steps, we can ensure the security of our container images, a key component of a secure container lifecycle and a vital part of the DevSecOps approach.

Runtime container security

Securing containers at runtime is just as important as securing the images from which they are instantiated. Ensuring the isolation of running containers, monitoring their activity, and promptly detecting and responding to any threats are key elements of runtime container security.

Container isolation mechanisms

Container isolation is vital to the security and functioning of containers. Let us dive into the three main kernel features that enforce this isolation: **Namespaces**, **Control Groups (cgroups)**, and **Capabilities**.

Namespaces

Namespaces partition the kernel resources so that each set of processes (or each container, in this context) sees a different set of resources. This provides an important isolation layer between containers.

In Linux, there are several types of namespaces, including PID (for process IDs), NET (for network resources), MNT (for mount points), and more. Docker, for instance, creates a new set of namespaces for each container.

Here is a basic example showing how we can create a new namespace using **unshare** command:

```
# create a new mount namespace
unshare --mount /bin/bash
```

After running the above command, we are in a new shell with a new mount namespace isolated from the original namespace.

Control groups

Control groups (cgroups) limit and prioritize the resources, CPU, memory, network bandwidth, etc. that a container can use. This prevents a single container from consuming all the host's resources and ensures fair sharing among multiple containers.

Here is how we can create a new cgroup and add a process to it:

```
# create a new cgroup and limit memory
echo "1000000" > /sys/fs/cgroup/memory/mygroup/memory.limit_in_bytes
# add a process to the cgroup
echo $$ > /sys/fs/cgroup/memory/mygroup/cgroup.procs
```

In this example, a new cgroup named **mygroup** is created, and its memory is limited to 1MB. Then, the current shell process is added to this cgroup.

Capabilities

Capabilities are a set of privileges that can be assigned to processes. They allow fine-grained control over what a container can and cannot do. Docker, for example, starts containers with a restricted set of capabilities and allows users to drop or add capabilities as needed.

Here is an example of running a Docker container with only the **CAP_NET_RAW** capability (required to use the **ping** command):

```
docker run --cap-drop all --cap-add net_raw myimage ping localhost
```

We can maintain a secure and efficient containerized environment by implementing these isolation mechanisms. It is essential to understand these mechanisms and their implications to take full advantage of the benefits of containerization and mitigate potential security risks.

Monitoring and auditing container activity

Monitoring and auditing container activity are critical aspects of maintaining a secure container environment. In order to set up a comprehensive monitoring system, let us consider a simple logging scenario using Fluentd and Elasticsearch with Kibana.

Monitoring container activity with Fluentd

Fluentd (**https://www.fluentd.org**) is an open-source data collector that unifies data collection and consumption for better use and understanding of data. Here is a basic example of using Fluentd to forward logs from a container.

First, install Fluentd on our host machine:

```
curl -L https://toolbelt.treasuredata.com/sh/install-ubuntu-bionic-td-agent3.sh | sh
```

Then, in our Docker container, set the: **log-driver** to **fluentd**:

```
docker run --log-driver=fluentd ubuntu echo 'Hello Fluentd!'
```

This will forward the logs from this container to Fluentd.

Log analysis with Elasticsearch and Kibana

Once we have logs being collected by Fluentd, we can forward them to a tool like Elasticsearch for analysis and storage and visualize them using Kibana (**https://www.elastic.co/kibana/**).

To set up Elasticsearch and Kibana, we can use Docker Compose. Here is a basic **docker-compose.yml** file:

```yaml
version: '3'
services:
  elasticsearch:
    image: docker.elastic.co/elasticsearch/elasticsearch:7.10.1
    ports:
      - 9200:9200
  kibana:
    image: docker.elastic.co/kibana/kibana:7.10.1
    ports:
      - 5601:5601
    depends_on:
      - elasticsearch
```

Then, run `docker-compose up` to start the services. Once they are running, we can visit `http://localhost:5601` in our browser to access Kibana and visualize our logs.

Auditing container activity with Auditd and Falco

Auditd (**https://www.redhat.com/sysadmin/configure-linux-auditing-auditd**) is a Linux auditing system that helps monitor, analyze, and record system activities. Here is a simple example of how to use auditd with Docker. Install auditd:

```
sudo apt-get install auditd audispd-plugins
```

Then start the auditd service:

```
sudo service auditd start
```

With auditd running, we can monitor system calls made by our containers.

Falco (**https://falco.org**) is a Kubernetes-native runtime security project. It is a rule-driven engine that observes and asserts the behavior of a system at runtime. An example of a Falco rule that alerts on any shell running in a container:

```
- rule: Terminal shell in container
  desc: A shell was used as an entrypoint/exec in a container.
  condition: container_started and shell_procs
  output: A shell was spawned in a container with an attached terminal
(user=%user.name container_id=%container.id container_name=%container.name
shell=%proc.name parent=%proc.pname cmdline=%proc.cmdline terminal=%proc.
tty)
  priority: WARNING
```

When the conditions in the rule are met, Falco will generate an alert. The Syslog mechanism can send these alerts to various destinations, including standard output, files, program pipes, and network services.

Monitoring and auditing are continuous processes. Regularly reviewing our log data and auditing our security controls is crucial for maintaining a secure container environment.

Detecting and responding to runtime threats

Detecting and addressing threats in real-time is crucial to the overall security of containerized applications. Even with stringent preventive measures in place, vulnerabilities may still appear, making runtime security solutions pivotal.

We may take some of the measures for detecting and responding to runtime threats in containers. Threat detection primarily involves monitoring container activities and identifying unusual behavior or anomalies. This process can be accomplished using various open-source tools like Prometheus (**https://prometheus.io**) for monitoring and Falco for anomaly detection.

Let us delve deeper into how one can ensure that containerized applications are not only secure at deployment but also during their lifecycle. A good starting point is understanding how to detect and respond to threats in real time, as illustrated in the following code snippets:

```
apiVersion: v1
kind: Pod
metadata:
  name: myapp-pod
  labels:
    app: myapp
spec:
  containers:
  - name: myapp
    image: myapp:1.0
  restartPolicy: Always
```

The Kubernetes pod definition given here provides an example of a self-healing mechanism; the **restartPolicy** set to Always ensures that Kubernetes is on the lookout and will take action by restarting the container should it fail.

Beyond just automated restarts, there are more comprehensive responses when addressing significant threats:

```
# Sysdig command to capture system state for later analysis
$ sudo sysdig -w /tmp/capture.scap
```

The above Sysdig command captures all the system's activity and saves it into a file. This file can be analyzed later to understand the nature of the security incident.

It is important to stress that maintaining a secure container environment is not a one-time effort but an ongoing process. It is essential to stay vigilant, keep systems up-to-date, and constantly monitor for potential threats. This approach is crucial for realizing the benefits of DevSecOps practices.

Network security for containers

Container networking, which is how containers communicate with each other and the outside world, introduces its set of security considerations. Ensuring secure networking is critical for protecting our containerized applications from network-based threats.

Container network models

The container network model we choose determines how our containers will communicate with each other and external networks. Let us discuss some examples of how we would set up and use each model in Docker.

Bridge networks

In a bridge network, each container gets its virtual network interface, with the host acting as a network bridge. Docker automatically creates a default bridge network for you, but you can also create your user-defined bridge networks.

To create a user-defined bridge network:

```
$ docker network create my-bridge-network
```

Then, to connect a container to this network when you run it:

```
$ docker run -d --network=my-bridge-network --name=my-container my-image
```

Host networks

In a host network model, containers share the network stack of the host and do not get their IP addresses. This means a container's network access is identical to that of the host's, which can be less secure because it does not provide network isolation.

To run a container with host networking:

```
$ docker run -d --network=host --name=my-container my-image
```

Overlay networks

An overlay network creates a virtual network that spans all the nodes in a Docker swarm, allowing containers on different hosts to communicate as if they are on the same host.

To create an overlay network:

```
$ docker network create -d overlay my-overlay-network
```

Then, to connect a service to this network:

```
$ docker service create --network=my-overlay-network --name=my-service my-image
```

The choice of network model will have security implications. For instance, using the host network provides the least isolation, while bridge and overlay networks offer better isolation but come with their complexities and considerations. It is essential to choose the model that best fits the needs of our application and aligns with our security policies.

Implementing network policies

Network policies in Kubernetes are a way to control the traffic in our cluster. They use labels to select pods and define rules that specify what traffic is allowed to the selected pods.

Here is an example of a network policy:

```
apiVersion: networking.k8s.io/v1
kind: NetworkPolicy
metadata:
  name: access-nginx
spec:
  podSelector:
    matchLabels:
      run: nginx
  policyTypes:
  - Ingress
  ingress:
  - from:
    - podSelector:
        matchLabels:
          access: "true"
```

In this example, the **NetworkPolicy** allows traffic to pods with the label **run: nginx**, but only from pods with the label **access: true**. The **policyTypes: Ingress** means that the policy will apply to inbound traffic (if you wanted it to apply to outbound traffic, you would use **Egress**).

You would save this YAML to a file (like **networkpolicy.yaml**), then apply it with **kubectl apply -f networkpolicy.yaml**.

However, note that defining NetworkPolicies is not enough. The network plugin you are using must support them. Some popular network plugins that support NetworkPolicies are Calico, Weave Net, and Romana.

Finally, it is a good practice to always define at least some network policies in your cluster to limit the potential impact of a compromised pod. For example, you might have a default network policy that denies all traffic, then define other network policies that allow specific traffic that you know needs to happen.

Secure service discovery and communication

Service discovery and secure communication between services are critical aspects of containerized applications, particularly in microservices architectures.

Consider the scenario where you have multiple services running in your Kubernetes cluster. These services need to be able to discover and communicate with each other securely.

Service discovery

In Kubernetes, services can be used to provide a reliable way for applications to discover other services within the cluster. Here is an example of a service that exposes a simple application on port 80:

```
apiVersion: v1
kind: Service
metadata:
  name: my-app-service
spec:
  selector:
    app: my-app
  ports:
    - protocol: TCP
      port: 80
      targetPort: 9376
```

In this example, the **my-app-service** service is created, which selects any pods with the label **app: my-app**. It listens on port 80 and forwards traffic to port 9376 of the pods it selects. Other services or pods can then communicate with this service by sending requests to **my-app-service**.

Secure communication

While service discovery enables services to find each other, it does not provide security features like encryption or **mutual TLS (mTLS)**. This is where a service mesh like Istio or Linkerd comes into play.

For instance, Istio automatically injects Envoy sidecar proxies into your pods, which intercepts all inbound and outbound network traffic. You can then enable mTLS on the service mesh to secure communication between services:

```
kubectl apply -f - <<EOF
apiVersion: "security.istio.io/v1beta1"
```

```
kind: "PeerAuthentication"
metadata:
  name: "default"
  namespace: "foo"
spec:
  mtls:
    mode: STRICT
EOF
```

This **PeerAuthentication** policy enforces mTLS for all services in the **foo** namespace.

Additionally, service mesh solutions often provide features for traffic management (like intelligent routing and load balancing), observability (like tracing and monitoring), and resilience (like circuit breaking and rate limiting), making them a valuable tool in microservices architectures.

Remember that network security is a crucial aspect of container security. It is not just about securing the container images and the runtime but also how these containers communicate. Implementing secure service discovery and communication can greatly enhance the overall security posture of your containerized applications.

Secrets management in containers

Managing secrets like API keys, passwords, and certificates is important to container security. Secrets should never be included in a container image or source code but should be securely provided to the container at runtime.

Challenges of managing secrets in containers

Managing secrets is fundamental to maintaining secure applications, especially in a containerized environment. Here, we will highlight the challenges mentioned with examples and propose solutions using tools like Kubernetes Secrets and HashiCorp Vault.

Ephemeral nature of containers

In containerized environments, security and confidentiality are paramount, especially when dealing with sensitive information like database credentials. When an application residing in such an environment needs to connect to a database, exposing its credentials directly in the configuration can pose a security risk. The following Kubernetes pod definition demonstrates a secure way to handle this challenge:

```
apiVersion: v1
kind: Pod
metadata:
```

```
  name: myapp-pod
spec:
  containers:
  - name: myapp-container
    image: myapp
    env:
      - name: DB_CONN_STRING
        value: "jdbc:mysql://db.example.com:3306/mydb"
      - name: DB_USER
        valueFrom:
          secretKeyRef:
            name: db-user
            key: username
    - name: DB_PASS
      valueFrom:
        secretKeyRef:
          name: db-pass
          key: password
```

In this Kubernetes pod definition, the **DB_USER** and **DB_PASS** are fetched from Kubernetes Secrets named **db-user** and **db-pass**, respectively. This addresses the problem of delivering secrets to ephemeral containers at the right time.

Scale

When you have many services, each needing its own set of secrets, managing them can be daunting. A centralized secrets management solution like HashiCorp Vault can help scale this process.

Vault provides a unified interface to any secret while providing tight access control and recording a detailed audit log. A secret is anything that you want to tightly control access to, such as API keys, passwords, or certificates. Vault can write secrets into, read secrets from, or use secrets with many systems.

Immutable infrastructure

Containers should be treated as immutable; thus, secrets should be provided when the container starts. For instance, you can use Kubernetes Secrets to store and manage sensitive information. The Secrets can then be mounted as data volumes or exposed as environment variables to be used by a Pod. Changes to the Secret are distributed dynamically.

However, remember, Kubernetes Secrets do not provide a strong guarantee of confidentiality. By default, they are only base64 encoded. Using an encryption solution like Vault or Sealed Secrets can enhance the security of your Kubernetes Secrets.

Embracing the philosophy of immutable infrastructure, containers should always be initiated with the necessary configuration and secrets to operate without requiring changes during their lifecycle. One of the mechanisms that Kubernetes offers for managing sensitive information is through its Secrets API. While beneficial, it is crucial to understand its nuances and limitations to employ it securely:

```
# create a secret
kubectl create secret generic db-user-pass --from-literal=username=myuser
--from-literal=password=mypass


# use the secret in a pod
apiVersion: v1
kind: Pod
metadata:
  name: myapp-pod
spec:
  containers:
  - name: myapp-container
    image: myapp
    env:
      - name: DB_USERNAME
        valueFrom:
          secretKeyRef:
            name: db-user-pass
            key: username
      - name: DB_PASSWORD
        valueFrom:
          secretKeyRef:
            name: db-user-pass
            key: password
```

In this example, we first create a Secret **db-user-pass** with two key-value pairs. Then, we reference this secret in the pod definition for **myapp-container**. This addresses the challenge of managing secrets in an immutable infrastructure.

In summary, managing secrets in a containerized environment can be complex, but it can be effectively managed with the proper practices and tools.

Secure strategies for storing and accessing secrets

Handling secrets securely involves properly storing and accessing these sensitive data. This includes using environment variables, secrets volumes, or even dedicated secrets management services. Let us take a look at each of these strategies.

Environment variables

In Docker, you can provide secrets as environment variables when starting a container. However, care must be taken to prevent logging or leaking these variables.

Here is an example using Docker:

```
docker run -d -e "API_KEY=123456" myapp:latest
```

In this command, we are starting a new container using the **myapp:latest** image and setting the **API_KEY** environment variable.

Secrets volume

In Kubernetes, you can store and manage sensitive information using a Secrets object. The Secrets can then be mounted as data volumes or exposed as environment variables to be used by a Pod. Here is an example of creating a Secret and using it in a Pod:

```
# create a secret
kubectl create secret generic db-secret --from-literal=DB_USER=myuser
--from-literal=DB_PASS=mypass
# use the secret in a pod
apiVersion: v1
kind: Pod
metadata:
  name: myapp-pod
spec:
  containers:
  - name: myapp-container
    image: myapp
    volumeMounts:
    - name: db-creds
      mountPath: "/etc/creds"
  volumes:
  - name: db-creds
    secret:
      secretName: db-secret
```

In this example, we first create a Secret named **db-secret** with two key-value pairs. Then, we reference this Secret in the Pod definition for **myapp-container**. The Secret is mounted as a volume at the path **/etc/creds**.

Secrets management service

Various services like HashiCorp Vault, AWS Secrets Manager, Azure Key Vault, or Google Secret Manager provide secure, auditable, and automated secrets management capabilities. They can be integrated with containers to provide secrets securely.

Here is an example of how to read a secret from Vault using the **vault kv get** command:

```
# read a secret from vault
vault kv get secret/myapp
```

This command retrieves the **myapp** secret stored in Vault. It can be run as part of a startup script in a container, or Vault can be integrated with Kubernetes to automatically inject secrets into Pods.

In summary, how you store and access secrets will depend on your specific needs and the environment you are working in. Whichever method you choose, ensure it is done in a secure and controlled manner.

Tools for secrets management in containers

Managing secrets in a containerized environment can be facilitated with various tools. Let us discuss examples of using some popular options.

Docker secrets

Docker Swarm includes a secrets management tool called Docker secrets. You can easily create, update, and rotate secrets with Docker secrets. Secrets are stored in a distributed and encrypted state and are available only to services running in the swarm that have been granted explicit access.

Here is an example of how to create a Docker secret:

```
echo "my_secret" | docker secret create my_secret -
```

Here is how to use that secret in a service:

```
docker service create --name my_service --secret my_secret my_image
```

Kubernetes Secrets

Kubernetes has a built-in object called Secrets that can store and manage sensitive data. Here is an example of creating a Secret and using it in a Pod:

```
# Create a secret
```

```
kubectl create secret generic db-secret --from-literal=DB_USER=myuser
--from-literal=DB_PASS=mypass
# Use the secret in a pod
apiVersion: v1
kind: Pod
metadata:
  name: myapp-pod
spec:
  containers:
  - name: myapp-container
    image: myapp
    env:
      - name: DB_USER
        valueFrom:
          secretKeyRef:
            name: db-secret
            key: DB_USER
      - name: DB_PASS
        valueFrom:
          secretKeyRef:
            name: db-secret
            key: DB_PASS
```

In this example, we first create a Secret named **db-secret**. Then, we reference this Secret in the Pod definition for **myapp-container**. The Secret is exposed as environment variables **DB_USER** and **DB_PASS**.

Vault by HashiCorp

Vault is a widely used secret management tool that can handle various use cases. Here is a basic example of writing and reading a secret in Vault:

```
# Write a secret to Vault
vault kv put secret/myapp password="my_password"
# Read the secret from Vault
vault kv get secret/myapp
```

Cloud secrets management services

Cloud providers like AWS, Azure, and Google Cloud have their secrets management services. Here is an example of creating a secret in AWS Secrets Manager:

```
aws secretsmanager create-secret --name MyTestDatabaseSecret --secret-
string '{"username":"testuser","password":"testpassword"}'
```

This command creates a new secret with the specified username and password. The secret can then be accessed by services running in AWS.

While handling secrets can pose challenges in a containerized environment, it is possible to manage them securely with the right tools and strategies. Always ensure that you follow best practices for managing secrets to maintain the security of your applications.

Best practices for container security in DevSecOps

Securing containers in a DevSecOps context is more than just using the right tools. It requires adopting a set of best practices built around the core principles of DevSecOps: automation, continuous improvement, and a shared responsibility for security.

Following the principle of least privilege

The **Principle of Least Privilege (PoLP)** is a computer security concept in which users are given the minimum access levels necessary to complete their job functions. Applying the PoLP can significantly reduce the attack surface and potential damage from breaches in the context of container security. To illustrate the implementation of this principle with containers, let us understand some examples.

Running containers as non-root user

By default, Docker containers run as root, which means that if an attacker breaks out of the container, they can get root access to the host machine. This can be avoided by running containers as a non-root user.

Here is an example Dockerfile instruction to create a non-root user and switch to that user:

```
FROM ubuntu:18.04
RUN useradd -m myuser
USER myuser
```

In this example, **RUN useradd -m myuser** creates a new user named **myuser**, and the **USER myuser** switches to that user. The instructions following **USER myuser** will be run as the **myuser** user, not as root.

Limiting container capabilities

Linux capabilities is a kernel feature that allows dividing the privileges of the root user into distinct units, which can be independently enabled or disabled. Docker starts containers with limited capabilities, but we can further limit this set based on our application needs.

We can drop all capabilities and add only those necessary for our application with the following:

```
docker run --cap-drop all --cap-add NET_BIND_SERVICE --cap-add CHOWN
myimage
```

In this example, **--cap-drop all** drops all capabilities, **--cap-add NET_BIND_SERVICE** adds the capability to bind to network ports below 1024, and **--cap-add CHOWN** allows the container to change file ownership.

Implementing fine-grained access control

Kubernetes provides RBAC, which can be used to set fine-grained access permissions. The following is an example of a Role that only allows listing and getting Pods in a specific namespace:

```
kind: Role
apiVersion: rbac.authorization.k8s.io/v1
metadata:
  namespace: default
  name: pod-reader
rules:
- apiGroups: [""]
  resources: ["pods"]
  verbs: ["get", "watch", "list"]
```

A RoleBinding that binds the role to a specific user:

```
kind: RoleBinding
apiVersion: rbac.authorization.k8s.io/v1
metadata:
  name: read-pods
  namespace: default
subjects:
- kind: User
  name: myuser
  apiGroup: rbac.authorization.k8s.io
roleRef:
  kind: Role
```

```
name: pod-reader
apiGroup: rbac.authorization.k8s.io
```

In this example, **myuser** will only be able to list and get Pods in the **default** namespace and will not be able to create, delete, or update Pods or access other resources or namespaces.

Implementing the PoLP will help limit the potential damage if a container is compromised and is a best practice for secure container deployment.

Regularly updating and patching containers

Keeping containers up to date with the latest security patches is critical to maintaining a secure container environment. Let us understand this concept with a few examples.

Updating container images

Consider a Dockerfile for a Node.js application that uses the latest LTS version:

```
FROM node:lts
WORKDIR /app
COPY package*.json ./
RUN npm install
COPY . .
CMD [ "node", "app.js" ]
```

In this Dockerfile, **FROM node:lts** uses the latest **Long Term Support** (**LTS**) version of Node.js as the base image. However, the latest is only as of the time the image is built. So, if a new Node.js LTS version is released with important security patches, your image will not have them until it is rebuilt.

Regularly rebuilding your images ensures they have the latest base image and any updates to your application. You could do this manually, but automating this process is more efficient and reliable. For example, you could set up a CI/CD pipeline that rebuilds and tests your image whenever changes are pushed to your application repository or on a schedule.

Deploying updated containers

Once you have an updated image, you need to deploy new containers from this image and remove the old ones. In a container orchestration system like Kubernetes, this can be done by updating the image in your deployment and applying the updated deployment:

```
kubectl set image deployment/my-app my-app=my-repo/my-app:latest
kubectl rollout status deployment/my-app
```

In this example, `kubectl set image deployment/my-app my-app=my-repo/my-app:latest` updates the image used in the **my-app** deployment, and `kubectl rollout status deployment/my-app` watches the status of the rollout to make sure it succeeds.

Again, this process should be automated as much as possible. A CI/CD pipeline can handle not just building images but also deploying them.

Monitoring for vulnerabilities

Even with regular updates, new vulnerabilities can be discovered in your containers' software. Therefore, it is important to regularly scan your images for vulnerabilities. Tools like Clair, Anchore, or Docker's security scanning can be integrated into your pipeline to scan images during the build process. When new vulnerabilities are found, these tools can alert you, and you can update your images accordingly.

Regularly updating your containers and monitoring for vulnerabilities ensures that your container environment is as secure as possible.

Using immutable containers

Containers should be immutable, meaning once they are running, they do not change. Instead of updating a running container, we should build a new image and replace the running container with a new one. This simplifies rollbacks, reduces inconsistencies between environments, and improves security by reducing the attack surface.

Automated security scanning and remediation

Automated security scanning and remediation involves detecting vulnerabilities in your containers as early as possible and addressing these issues promptly to reduce security risks. Let us illustrate this concept with some examples.

Automated security scanning during build

While building a Docker image, you can use tools like Trivy (**https://www.aquasec.com/products/trivy/**) to scan the image for any known vulnerabilities (you may use Clair, too).

For instance, here is an example of using Trivy in a CI/CD pipeline using GitLab CI:

```
trivy:
  image: aquasec/trivy:latest
  script:
    - trivy image --severity HIGH,CRITICAL $CI_REGISTRY_IMAGE:$CI_COMMIT_
REF_SLUG
```

In this example, Trivy scans the Docker image built in the pipeline for high and critical vulnerabilities.

Continuous scanning

Even after the images have been deployed as containers, you should periodically scan them to uncover any new vulnerabilities discovered since the last scan. Tools like Sysdig Falco, Anchore, or Prisma Cloud can monitor running containers for anomalies and security issues.

Automated remediation

Once a vulnerability is detected, the next step is to remediate it. This often involves updating the software package with the vulnerability to a patched version.

For example, if your scanning tool detects a high-severity vulnerability in the version of a package used in your Docker image, your CI/CD pipeline could automatically trigger a new build to update the package:

```
RUN apt-get update && apt-get upgrade -y
```

Once the new image is built and tested, your pipeline can deploy the updated containers and retire the old ones, effectively remediating the vulnerability.

Alerts and manual intervention

While automated remediation can handle most issues, some will require manual intervention. For example, a vulnerability might require a significant software upgrade that could break your application, or you might need to update your application code to fix a security issue. In such cases, your scanning tool should alert you to the issue. This could involve sending an email or Slack message, creating a Jira ticket, or opening a GitHub issue.

With automated security scanning and remediation, you can catch and fix issues early, reducing the security risks for your container environment.

Integrating security into the CI/CD pipeline

Integrating security into the CI/CD pipeline allows teams to automate, ensuring the container images are safe, compliant, and without known vulnerabilities. Let us illustrate this with some examples.

Image scanning during build

You can integrate image scanning into the CI/CD pipeline, as discussed. For instance, using the open-source tool Clair, the pipeline could be configured to fail the build if any high-severity vulnerabilities are found:

```
stages:
  - build
  - scan
build:
  stage: build
  script:
    - docker build -t my-image .
    - docker save my-image | gzip > my-image.tar.gz
  artifacts:
    paths:
      - my-image.tar.gz
scan:
  stage: scan
  script:
    - docker load < my-image.tar.gz
    - docker run --rm -v /var/run/docker.sock:/var/run/docker.sock -v
$PWD:/root/result/ arminc/clair-scanner my-image
  allow_failure: false
```

In the example above, the build stage creates the Docker image and saves it as an artifact. The scan stage then loads the image and uses Clair to scan it for vulnerabilities. If any are found, the job fails, preventing vulnerable images from being pushed to production.

Static code analysis

You can use static code analysis tools like SonarQube, FindSecBugs, or Checkmarx to analyze your application's source code for security vulnerabilities during the build process. This can be integrated into the CI/CD pipeline to automate the process and catch issues early.

In the realm of DevSecOps, integrating static code analysis into the CI/CD pipeline is paramount to ensure the early detection of vulnerabilities. Here is an illustrative example using the popular SonarQube tool:

```
stages:
  - test

sonarqube_check:
  stage: test
  script:
    - sonar-scanner -Dsonar.projectKey=my_project -Dsonar.sources=.
-Dsonar.host.url=http://my-sonarqube.com
```

In this configuration snippet, the source code is examined by SonarQube during the `test` phase of the build pipeline. Employing such strategies bolsters security and accelerates feedback loops, enabling developers to address potential threats promptly.

Security policy enforcement

You can also enforce security policies as part of your deployment process. Tools like Open Policy Agent can define policies that must be satisfied for a deployment to proceed.

For example, you might have a policy that disallows deployments on Fridays to avoid weekend incidents. When a deployment is triggered, the pipeline will use Open Policy Agent (**https://www.openpolicyagent.org**) to check whether the current day is Friday and, if so, halt the deployment.

Integrating security into your CI/CD pipeline ensures that security checks and balances are an inherent part of your development process rather than an afterthought. This approach aligns with the DevSecOps philosophy of shifting security left, incorporating security early in the development lifecycle.

These best practices form the foundation of a secure approach to using containers in a DevSecOps context. By adopting these practices, we can significantly improve the security of our containerized applications.

Case studies of container security in DevSecOps

Seeing real-world examples can help solidify container security's importance in a DevSecOps context. Here, we will explore two case studies illustrating how some organizations have successfully integrated security into their container-based deployments.

Case study: Adobe

Adobe is a global software company that provides a wide range of products and services, including Adobe Creative Cloud, Adobe Experience Cloud, and Adobe Document Cloud. Adobe has used containers for several years to improve its software development and delivery processes' speed, agility, and security.

In 2015, Adobe adopted a DevSecOps approach to software development. This approach integrates security into all phases of the software development lifecycle, from design and development to testing and deployment. Containers are crucial in Adobe's DevSecOps approach by providing a consistent and secure software development and deployment environment.

Adobe uses Docker containers to build, deploy, and manage its software. Docker containers are lightweight, portable, and secure, making them ideal for DevSecOps. Adobe has developed many tools and processes to help ensure the security of its Docker containers. These tools and processes include:

- A security scanner that scans Docker images for known vulnerabilities
- A policy that requires all Docker images to be scanned before they are deployed
- A process for remediating vulnerabilities that are found in Docker images

Adobe's use of containers and DevSecOps has helped the company improve its software development and delivery processes' speed, agility, and security. As a result, Adobe has been able to deliver new features and updates to its customers more quickly and securely. In fact, the DevSecOps journey with containers by Adobe is still on. You may refer to the blog at **https://blog.developer.adobe.com/how-ethos-powers-a-cloud-native-transformation-at-adobe-16c1a2e2f67a** for further reading.

Case study: Shopify

Shopify is a global e-commerce platform that helps businesses of all sizes sell online. The company has been using containers for several years to deploy its applications, and it has recently adopted DevSecOps practices to improve the security of its containerized infrastructure.

Shopify's use of containers began in 2014 when the company was looking for a way to improve the scalability and reliability of its applications. Containers provide a lightweight, portable way to package and deploy applications, and they can be easily scaled up or down as needed. This made them a good fit for Shopify's needs, as the company's traffic can vary significantly depending on the time of year and other factors.

In 2017, Shopify began to adopt DevSecOps practices. Shopify has implemented various security scanning tools to identify vulnerabilities in its containerized infrastructure. This ensures that vulnerabilities are identified and addressed before they can be exploited.

Shopify's use of containers and DevSecOps practices have helped the company improve its containerized infrastructure's security. The company has seen a significant decrease in security vulnerabilities; it has improved its applications' scalability and reliability.

The above case studies represent the successful application of container security practices within a DevSecOps context. They illustrate how automation, secure defaults, access control, secure communication, and secrets management can be effectively implemented for container security.

Conclusion

In this chapter, we learned that securing containers within a DevSecOps framework is a nuanced endeavor underlined by the pressing need to comprehend container technologies and their inherent security challenges. This discourse highlighted the merits of container technology over virtual machines and emphasized the pivotal roles of consistency, reproducibility, and scalability in a DevSecOps context. We discussed different aspects of container security, from image security to network concerns and secret management. Crucial best practices were elucidated, such as least privilege principles, consistent updates, and the significance of immutable containers in the DevSecOps paradigm. As we look ahead, the evolution of container security is evident, with emerging technologies paving new avenues and challenges.

The forthcoming chapter explores overarching security strategies for expansive enterprise systems, spotlighting tools like CWPP, CSPM, CASB, and CNAPP. Through this learning trajectory, readers are equipped with insights and anticipations to navigate the evolving domain of container security in DevSecOps efficiently.

Questions

1. What are the primary purposes of using containers in a DevSecOps context?

2. What is the primary function of Docker and Kubernetes? How do they differ?

3. How does Docker handle networking compared to Kubernetes?

4. Discuss the role of Docker volumes and Kubernetes Persistent Volumes. How are they different?

5. How do Docker and Kubernetes handle autoscaling? What are the key differences?

6. What is Docker Swarm, and how does it compare to Kubernetes regarding features and usability?

7. Discuss other notable container orchestration tools such as Apache Mesos, Amazon ECS, and OpenShift. How do they compare to Docker and Kubernetes?

8. In what ways do Docker and Kubernetes complement each other in a DevSecOps environment?

9. How do containers contribute to consistency and reproducibility in a DevSecOps environment?

10. Discuss the role of container isolation in improving security in a DevSecOps environment.

11. How do containers support the principle of immutable infrastructure in DevSecOps? Give an example with Docker and Kubernetes.

12. Discuss how containers enable rapid scaling in DevSecOps and its importance.

13. Discuss how the use of containers can lead to higher efficiency and flexibility in managing various types of infrastructure in a DevSecOps context.

14. How do containers contribute to consistency and reproducibility in DevSecOps?

15. Why is container security important in the context of DevSecOps, and what are some of its challenges?

16. What are some best practices for ensuring security in each phase of the container lifecycle: development, deployment, and operations?

17. Why is it important to scan and audit container images for vulnerabilities, and what does signing a container image mean?

18. How can container isolation mechanisms improve security, and what threats can be detected during runtime?

19. What are some key considerations for implementing network policies in containerized environments?

20. What are the challenges of managing secrets in containers, and what tools can be used effectively?

21. What does the principle of least privilege mean in the context of containers, and why is integrating security into the CI/CD pipeline important?

22. Can you provide an example of how a real-world company has successfully implemented container security within a DevSecOps context?

Join our book's Discord space

Join the book's Discord Workspace for Latest updates, Offers, Tech happenings around the world, New Release and Sessions with the Authors:

https://discord.bpbonline.com

CHAPTER 5

Automation and Integration

Introduction

In the preceding chapter, we navigated the intricate world of containers and delved into their security aspects within the DevSecOps landscape. We uncovered the numerous benefits of containerization and demonstrated its effective implementation across various scenarios. The transformation from traditional methodologies to agile practices, and now to DevOps, has brought significant changes in the software development world. However, this rapid pace of development and deployment necessitates an even greater focus on security, thereby giving rise to DevSecOps.

As we venture further into this new chapter, we shall discuss various platforms and tools necessary for holistic security management within enterprise systems and large-scale software applications that inherently come with expansive attack surfaces. In DevSecOps, we will discover how security is not an afterthought or a final gatekeeper but an integral part of the entire software development lifecycle.

Our journey will take us deeper into cloud security, exploring key solutions such as **Cloud Workload Protection Platforms (CWPP)**, **Cloud Security Posture Management (CSPM)**, **Cloud Access Security Brokers (CASB)**, and **Cloud-Native Application Protection Platforms (CNAPP)**. We will explore automation and integration, two core elements of DevSecOps that primarily focus on automating routine tasks and integrating various tools, platforms, and teams to enable seamless collaboration.

By automating tasks and integrating security practices into every step of the development process, we can develop, deploy, and maintain secure and high-quality software efficiently and swiftly. Furthermore, we will delve into a practical use case, showing how effective integrations can yield significant advantages in the DevSecOps environment. So, without further ado, let us embark on this insightful journey into *Automation and Integration* in DevSecOps.

Structure

In this chapter, we will discuss the following topics:

- Automating integration workflows
- Policy as code
- Monitoring as code
- Security as code
- Cloud security solutions
- Supply chain and risks
- Automating integration workflows challenges and best practices
- Use case: Integrations

Objectives

The primary objective of this chapter is to provide a comprehensive overview of various platforms and tools crucial for robust security management within enterprise systems and large-scale software applications, which inherently possess vast attack surfaces. Our exploration will encompass a range of cloud security solutions, including CWPP, CSPM, CASB, and CNAPP. These solutions form the backbone of cloud security, protecting applications and data residing in the cloud and ensuring compliance with regulatory standards.

In the context of our previous discussions on DevSecOps, we aim to demonstrate the profound influence of automation and integration in enhancing the security posture. By weaving security into every facet of the software development lifecycle, we can ensure the delivery of secure, high-quality software. We will delve into a practical use case to illuminate how effective integrations can yield significant advantages in a DevSecOps environment. By the conclusion of this chapter, the reader will have a solid understanding of how to leverage automation and integration in implementing and enhancing DevSecOps practices.

Automating integration workflows

Automating integrations is about managing the integration of different systems or platforms in an automated and code-controlled way, using APIs and other methods of inter-system communication. This approach can streamline and improve the consistency of operations within complex, multi-system environments. It can remove a significant amount of manual effort in setting up and maintaining system integrations and enhance the reliability and accuracy of data exchange between systems.

Figure 5.1 generically illustrates the concept of automated integration workflow in DevSecOps:

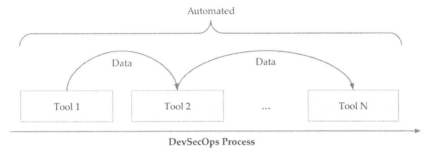

Figure 5.1: *Conceptual illustration of automated integration workflows*

Automated integration workflows serve as critical components in establishing automation and seamless integration within the DevSecOps model, thus improving the overall efficacy and efficiency of the development process.

An integral aspect of these workflows is their natural compatibility with **Continuous Integration/Continuous Delivery (CI/CD)** pipelines. When new code is committed, it initiates an automated process that compiles the code, runs tests, checks for security issues, and deploys it to a staging or production environment. Facilitating these steps requires efficient integration between various tools such as source control like Git, build tools such as Jenkins, security tools, and deployment platforms like Kubernetes. Automated integration workflows step in to manage these integrations and drive automation.

Moreover, these workflows also extend their functionality to automated testing. For example, when a new feature is slated for testing, the workflow facilitates the automatic creation of a replica of the production environment. The new feature is then deployed to this environment, tested automatically, and the environment is dismantled after completion. This makes the testing process systematic and efficient.

Automated integration workflows also contribute significantly to enforcing security compliance. In organizations where an API gateway applies specific security rules to all incoming traffic, these workflows can manage the integration between this gateway and other systems. This assures consistent enforcement of security policies without the need for manual intervention.

Data synchronization is another essential application of automated integration workflows. These workflows can expedite and streamline the process of harmonizing data between different systems, enhancing operational efficiency.

To illustrate this, let us consider a typical company that utilizes a **Customer Relationship Management (CRM)** system to record customer interactions and an **Enterprise Resource Planning (ERP)** system for managing orders. In such an environment, an automated integration workflow can be instituted to seamlessly synchronize data between these systems. This means that each time a new customer is recorded in the CRM, the automated workflow triggers an update in the ERP system to reflect the same data.

While rooted in business operations, this example mirrors how data synchronization can be applied within the DevSecOps framework. DevSecOps tools can also share and synchronize data through automated integration workflows, similar to how the CRM and ERP systems exchange data. This ensures a more coherent and unified development, security, and operations pipeline, boosting productivity and efficiency.

Furthermore, automated integration workflows assist in handling errors and the recovery process. If a system fails or encounters an error during data exchange, the workflow can be programmed to try to rectify the error automatically. It can alert the relevant team members and, if necessary, revert to a previous state to maintain system stability.

In the grand scheme, the most substantial benefit of automated integration workflows in DevSecOps is the reduced manual effort. This not only saves time but also reduces the risk of human error. By managing system integrations through automated workflows, teams can ensure that their integrations are reliable, repeatable, and auditable, leading to a highly effective DevSecOps process.

Let us now discuss a few concepts like **policy as code (PaC)** and **monitoring as code (MaC)** before deliberating about **security as code (SaC)**.

Policy as Code

PaC is a foundational pillar in the realm of DevSecOps. As a subset of **Infrastructure as code (IaC)**, PaC employs automation to enforce and monitor policy adherence throughout the infrastructure landscape. This methodology entails encoding organizational or security policies within the very fabric of our codebase.

PaC can be applied across many levels of a tech stack:

- **Application level:** PaC can enforce specific rules in our application code, like not using deprecated libraries, maintaining a particular code structure, and so on. Tools like ESLint (**eslint.org**), StyleCop (**https://github.com/StyleCop/StyleCop**), or SonarQube (**https://www.sonarsource.com/products/sonarqube/**) can be used for this purpose.

- **Infrastructure level:** At the infrastructure level, PaC can enforce rules like certain ports being closed, ensuring encryption is enabled, or a specific set of allowed instance types. Tools like Chef, Puppet, and Ansible, or cloud-native services like AWS Config, can be used for this purpose.

- **Platform level:** At the platform level, PaC can enforce governance and operational excellence policies, like ensuring all cloud resources have a specific set of tags or restricting the creation of resources in certain regions. Tools like **Open Policy Agent (OPA)**, HashiCorp Sentinel (**hashicorp.com/sentinel**), or cloud-native services like AWS Organizations can be used for this purpose.

PaC tools are crucial in creating, enforcing, and auditing policies across the infrastructure. These tools are endowed with several capabilities that facilitate effective policy management.

PaC tools offer avenues for encoding policies, enabling easy creation and modification. One such capability involves the definition of policies as code. This improves precision and promotes consistency across different stages of the infrastructure.

In addition to defining policies, PaC tools also equip us with mechanisms for policy enforcement. This can occur at different points, such as during the execution of CI/CD pipelines or during runtime. This feature allows preventive action by checking policy adherence during the CI/CD pipelines. Simultaneously, it provides detective controls monitoring policy compliance during runtime, ensuring discrepancies are caught and addressed promptly.

Moreover, PaC tools offer the ability to audit compliance, a feature indispensable for robust policy management. They can generate comprehensive reports or create intuitive dashboards that display the current compliance status across the infrastructure. This capability allows for a clear overview of policy adherence, highlighting areas of excellence and those requiring attention. As such, PaC tools not only strengthen policy enforcement but also promote transparency and accountability.

Table 5.1 lists some popular PaC tools:

PaC Tool	Website	Description
Cedar	**cedarpolicy.com**	A cloud-based solution to create, store, and manage policies and procedures. It is open-source, too.
OPA	**openpolicyagent.org**	An open-source, general-purpose policy engine that unifies policy enforcement across the stack. OPA provides a high-level declarative language that lets us specify policy as code and simple APIs to offload policy decision-making from our software.

PaC Tool	Website	Description
HashiCorp Sentinel	**hashicorp.com/sentinel**	An embedded policy-as-code framework integrated with the HashiCorp Enterprise products. It enables fine-grained, logic-based policy decisions and can be extended to use information from external sources.
Chef InSpec	**github.com/inspec/in-spec**	An open-source, language-based framework for creating and managing tests. It allows us to describe compliance rules and policies in human-readable language.
AWS IAM	**aws.amazon.com/iam/**	Not a traditional PaC tool. It allows us to define policies in JSON format that specify who can access which AWS resources. We can version control these policies and apply them programmatically.
Google Cloud IAM	**cloud.google.com/iam**	Let us administrators authorize who can take action on specific resources, giving us complete control and visibility to manage Google Cloud resources centrally. Policies are defined in a JSON format.
Azure Policy	**azure.microsoft.com/en-us/products/azure-poli-cy**	A service in Azure that we use to create, assign, and manage policies. These policies enforce different rules and effects over our resources so those resources stay compliant with our corporate standards and service level agreements.

Table 5.1: A list of some popular PaC tools, their websites, and descriptions

Each tool has its strengths and is suited to different use cases. It is recommended to evaluate different options and choose the one that fits the best with our requirements.

A PaC tool significantly contributes to enforcing and maintaining policies across infrastructure programmatically and automatically. Its strategic importance cannot be overstated, given its many benefits.

One of the primary benefits of employing a PaC tool is the assurance of consistency. It ensures policies are uniformly applied across the entire infrastructure, minimizing human errors and configuration drift risk. This consistency fosters a more reliable and predictable operational environment.

A notable advantage of these tools is the facilitation of compliance. It becomes considerably simpler to adhere to industry standards, regulations, and internal best practices when the checking and enforcing of policies are automated. This also minimizes the likelihood of overlooked non-compliance issues.

Additionally, the auditability of a PaC tool aids in transparency and accountability. The tool generates logs and reports useful for auditing, making demonstrating compliance to stakeholders and regulatory bodies easier.

Further, PaC tools enable policy management in version control systems, like Git, alongside infrastructure and application code. This integration offers a clear history of policy changes, greatly easing the tasks of tracking and auditing.

Another significant benefit lies in the immediate feedback these tools provide. By integrating PaC tools into CI/CD pipelines, developers are promptly notified about policy violations, allowing for early resolution and reducing the chance of deploying non-compliant infrastructure.

Increased efficiency is another clear advantage of using PaC tools. Automation of policy enforcement decreases manual efforts, freeing up teams to focus on more strategic tasks and reducing deployment delays due to policy violations.

Moreover, these tools foster improved team collaboration, including security, operations, and development. This is achieved by easing the definition, sharing, and enforcement of policies across the organization.

Scalability is also an inherent benefit of PaC tools. They can be effortlessly integrated with IaC tools, like Terraform or CloudFormation, enabling us to manage and enforce policies at scale as our infrastructure expands.

Lastly, PaC tools enhance visibility into the current state of policy compliance across the infrastructure. This visibility enables the prompt identification and remediation of policy violations or security gaps.

Figure 5.2 shows the benefits of PaC tools while working with DevSecOps:

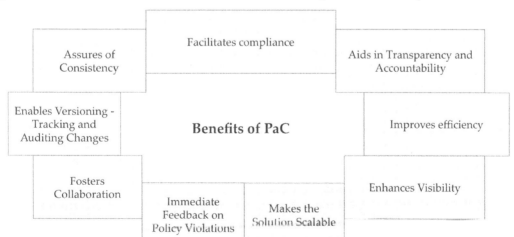

Figure 5.2: *Benefits of PaC tools*

PaC contributes to various improvements, including consistency, efficiency, and security across IT infrastructures. By enabling uniform policy enforcement, reducing human error, streamlining compliance processes, simplifying auditing, promoting collaboration, offering scalability, and providing visibility into policy compliance, PaC is a strategic asset for any organization aiming for robust security, persistent compliance, and operational efficiency.

Monitoring as code

The principle of MaC, an integral component of the DevSecOps philosophy, advocates for treating monitoring configurations and processes similarly to code. It enables teams to employ the same strategies used for application code, such as version control, code review, and automated testing and deployment, for monitoring systems.

In the context of DevSecOps, MaC significantly contributes to automation and integration. The foremost advantage is the ease of setup and consistency. Monitoring configurations can be written, deployed, and updated as code, ensuring uniformity across environments and simplifying new environment setups.

Similar to application code, monitoring configurations can be placed under version control. This facilitates tracking changes and, if needed, rolling back to a previous state. This becomes especially crucial in a DevSecOps environment with rapid iterations and frequent changes.

Automation, a key component of DevSecOps, aligns perfectly with MaC. Automating monitoring setups not only reduces manual effort but also bolsters efficiency. This includes automating the deployment of monitoring agents, alerts, and more.

With monitoring setup coded, scalability becomes an easier task. The setup can be scaled up or down based on requirements, which is critical for cloud-based DevSecOps environments that must be responsive to changing demand.

Furthermore, MaC can be seamlessly integrated with other DevSecOps tools and processes. For instance, alerts generated from the monitoring system can be incorporated with incident response tools. Similarly, monitoring can be integrated into CI/CD pipelines for identifying issues during the build and deployment process.

MaC also promotes collaboration and visibility. Making the monitoring setup visible in the code simplifies team collaboration and comprehension. It fosters shared ownership of monitoring and system health among developers, security, and operations.

From a security perspective, MaC enables teams to establish proactive monitoring for security threats. It allows quick identification and resolution of deviations from the norm, reducing the likelihood of security breaches.

In essence, MaC applies the proven principles of IaC to monitoring setup, ensuring it is an integral part of the DevSecOps process rather than an afterthought. It enhances monitoring efficiency, consistency, and effectiveness in a DevSecOps environment.

Table 5.2 lists some popular MaC tools:

MaC Tool	Website	Description
Prometheus	**prometheus.io**	An open-source monitoring solution that supports a multi-dimensional data model with time series data identified by metric name and key/value pairs.
Grafana	**grafana.com**	A multi-platform open-source analytics and interactive visualization web application that provides charts, graphs, and alerts for the web when connected to supported data sources.
Datadog	**datadoghq.com**	A monitoring service for cloud-scale applications, providing monitoring of servers, databases, tools, and services through a SaaS-based data analytics platform.
New Relic	**newrelic.com**	A software analytics product that helps software-driven businesses innovate faster by showing them how their applications perform in real-time.
Elastic (ELK) stack	**elastic.co**	A group of open-source products from Elastic designed to help users take data from any source and in any format and search, analyze, and visualize that data in real-time.
Splunk	**splunk.com/en_us/ products/observ- ability.html**	A software platform to search, analyze, and visualize the machine-generated data gathered from the websites, applications, sensors, devices, and so on., which make up our IT infrastructure and business.

Table 5.2: *A list of some popular MaC tools, their websites, and descriptions*

To optimize the utility of MaC tools, it is essential to adhere to a set of best practices. At the forefront, monitoring requirements should be identified early and incorporated into the application and infrastructure design process. This allows for a comprehensive, fine-grained approach that covers all crucial elements, aiding in creating detailed and actionable alerts. Secondly, use version control for all monitoring configurations. This practice ensures traceability and simplifies rollback in case of errors. Consistent naming conventions and clear documentation are also key to making the configuration more understandable and manageable.

Automation should be at the heart of the monitoring setup, automated deployment of monitoring agents, alerting rules, and dashboards can significantly reduce manual effort and increase efficiency. Alerts should be meaningful and actionable to avoid alert fatigue, and they should be integrated with the incident response system to ensure quick remediation. It is also vital to regularly review and update the monitoring setup to reflect system architecture or application behavior changes.

Emphasise creating a culture where developers, operations, and security teams share ownership of monitoring. This collaboration promotes transparency and shared responsibility, leading to a more effective response to incidents. Lastly, always ensure the scalability of our monitoring setup. As our system grows or changes, our monitoring tools and configurations should be able to adapt accordingly. Following these best practices will ensure we can fully leverage the potential of MaC tools in our DevSecOps workflow.

Security as code

Security as code is a philosophy and practice that involves integrating security practices into the DevSecOps process. It is an approach to building security into the tools and techniques part of the software delivery lifecycle. In other words, it is about making security an integral part of the CI/CD pipeline.

Traditionally, security practices have been somewhat separate from the development process. They were often seen as a separate phase in the software delivery lifecycle, typically towards the end. This could lead to problems, such as finding critical security issues late in the development process, which could delay a release.

With security as code, the goal is to integrate security considerations and practices into every part of the development process. Let us discuss the practices this could involve.

Automated security checks

Automated security checks are a crucial part of the security as code approach, aiming to catch vulnerabilities early in the development cycle when they are easiest to and cheapest resolve. Two primary types of tools are used:

- **Static Application Security Testing (SAST):** SAST tools analyze source code to identify and report potential security vulnerabilities. They examine the code at rest, hence the term **static**. SAST tools check the code against predefined rules or patterns often aligning with common coding best practices and known vulnerability patterns.

  For example, a SAST tool may flag when user-provided input is directly used in a SQL query, as this can open the door to SQL Injection attacks. It also warns about using insecure functions, such as certain hash functions no longer considered secure.

  Table 5.3 lists some popular SAST tools:

SAST tool	Website	Description
SonarQube	sonarsource.com/products/sonarqube	An open-source platform used for continuous inspection of code quality, including security. It supports multiple languages and integrates with CI/CD pipelines.
Fortify	microfocus.com/en-us/cyberres/application-security/static-code-analyzer	A commercial product from Micro Focus, Fortify offers end-to-end application security with SAST, DAST, and other features.
Checkmarx	checkmarx.com/cxsast-source-code-scanning/	An enterprise-level SAST software, named a leader in the 2023 Gartner's Magic Quadrant for Application Security Testing
Synopsys	synopsys.com/software-integrity/info/fast-static.html	A user-friendly, cloud-native SAST solution meticulously optimized for integration within a DevSecOps framework.

Table 5.3: A list of some popular SAST tools, their websites and descriptions

- **Dynamic Application Security Testing (DAST):** DAST tools, on the other hand, analyze the application in its running state, hence **dynamic**. These tools interact with the application, like an attacker might, looking for exploitable vulnerabilities.

  For example, a DAST tool might attempt various input attacks on form fields to see if the application responds in a way that suggests a vulnerability.

  Table 5.4 lists some popular DAST tools:

SAST tool	Website	Description
OWASP ZAP (Zed Attack Proxy)	owasp.org/www-project-zap/	An open-source web application security scanner. It can be used manually for penetration testing or integrated into CI/CD pipelines for automated scans.
Nessus	tenable.com/products/nessus	A widely-used commercial vulnerability scanner from Tenable. It can identify vulnerabilities in web applications and other network services.

Table 5.4: A list of some popular DAST tools, their websites and descriptions

Both SAST and DAST have their strengths and limitations. SAST can find issues earlier in the development cycle and pinpoint the exact location of a vulnerability in the code, but it may produce false positives or negatives. DAST can find issues only apparent when the application runs and can better emulate an attacker's perspective, but it cannot point directly to the problematic code.

A combination of SAST and DAST tools is often recommended for a thorough security check, sometimes supplemented with additional security practices like manual code reviews or penetration testing.

Table 5.5 presents a comparison of SAST and DAST tools:

	SAST	DAST
When it is used	Early in the development cycle, it is often integrated into the developer's IDE or the CI/CD pipeline.	Later in the development cycle, often after an application has been fully integrated and deployed to a test environment.
What it tests	Source code, byte code, or binary code.	Running applications in their operational environment.
How it works	Analyses code against a set of predefined rules to identify potential security issues.	Interacts with the running application, sending inputs and analyzing responses to identify potential security issues.
Strengths	Identifies issues early in the development cycle when they are often easier to fix. Can pinpoint the exact location of a vulnerability in the code.	Finds issues that only become apparent when the application is running. It can emulate an attacker's perspective.
Limitations	It may produce false positives or negatives. It may not find issues that only become apparent when the application runs.	Cannot point directly to the problematic code. It may not find issues that are only apparent in the code itself.

Table 5.5: *A comparison of SAST and DAST tools*

Remember, this is a simplified comparison. The right approach for a given application will depend on various factors, including the nature of the application, the development process, and the threat model. It is often recommended to use a combination of SAST and DAST, supplemented by other security practices, for a comprehensive approach to application security.

Infrastructure security

Infrastructure security encompasses integrating security practices directly into the management process of our infrastructure. We can bake security into our infrastructure templates by leveraging IaC tools, ensuring a secure foundation for our applications and data. Let us delve into this with some practical examples and implementation strategies.

One of the most popular IaC tools is Terraform by HashiCorp. Terraform scripts, or templates, allow developers to define and provide data center infrastructure using a declarative configuration language. This means we describe our desired state of infrastructure, and the IaC tool (Terraform in this case) would make it so.

By integrating security into these templates, we create a form of security as code. For instance, we could create a Terraform template that sets up a secure **Virtual Private Cloud (VPC)** in AWS, complete with necessary subnets, gateways, route tables, and security groups. Our security group rules could be configured only to allow necessary ports and block all unnecessary inbound traffic.

Once this template is written, it can be stored in a version control system like Git. Storing the template in version control means it can be code-reviewed for security best practices, just like any other piece of software. Security teams can examine the infrastructure code to ensure it follows best practices, such as least privilege access, encryption of data at rest and in transit, and appropriate logging and monitoring configurations.

Furthermore, automated checks can be implemented to ensure that the deployed infrastructure meets security standards. This is often achieved through PaC tools.

For example, Chef InSpec allows us to write **controls**, which are essentially code tests for checking that certain security standards are met. An InSpec control could check that all security groups in our AWS VPC disallow inbound traffic on a specific port or that encryption is enabled for a particular resource.

These controls can then be executed as part of a CI/CD pipeline or regularly on a schedule to continuously monitor our infrastructure for compliance with our defined security standards. Any deviations from the standards are flagged, allowing us to quickly remediate any issues and maintain a strong security posture.

Security as code takes the principles of IaC and applies a security-focused lens. By defining secure infrastructure templates, utilizing version control and code reviews, and implementing automated checks with policy as code tools, we can ensure that our infrastructure is secure from the ground up. This proactive approach to infrastructure security allows us to catch potential vulnerabilities earlier, reduces the chance of human error, and makes security an integral part of our development process.

Secure defaults

Secure defaults form a fundamental principle of security as code, ensuring that the applications and services are secure from their inception. This is all about setting up tools, libraries, and even infrastructure components in such a way that they adhere to security best practices by default. In doing so, the reliance on the individual security expertise of developers is reduced, and a baseline level of security is established throughout the development process. Let us explore this concept in more depth with some practical examples and strategies for implementation:

- **Choice of libraries and frameworks:** One of the first steps in ensuring secure defaults involves choosing the correct libraries and frameworks for our application.

Prioritize those widely recognized for their security features and consistently updated to address potential vulnerabilities. For instance, frameworks like Django for Python or Ruby on Rails for Ruby are known for their emphasis on secure defaults, such as built-in protection against common web application vulnerabilities like **Cross-Site Scripting (XSS)** and **Cross-Site Request Forgery (CSRF)**.

- **Configuration management:** Many security breaches occur due to misconfigurations. Adopt tools that enforce secure configurations by default. For instance, AWS Config continuously monitors and records our AWS resource configurations, enabling us to automate the evaluation of recorded configurations against desired configurations.

- **Secure coding practices:** Implement secure coding practices across our development teams. This includes practices such as input validation, parameterized queries, and proper error handling. Tools such as linters and static code analyzers can be integrated into our development process to enforce these practices automatically.

- **Security in CI/CD pipelines:** Integrate security checks into our CI/CD pipelines. Tools like OWASP Dependency-Check can be used to check our codebase for the usage of out-of-date libraries with known security issues. Similarly, SAST and DAST tools can be incorporated into our CI/CD pipeline to automatically detect potential security vulnerabilities in our code.

- **Least privilege access:** Implement the principle of least privilege across our infrastructure. This means giving a user or service only the permissions necessary to perform its intended function and no more. Cloud platforms like AWS, Azure, and GCP all have robust **Identity and Access Management (IAM)** systems that allow for fine-grained control over permissions.

- **Encryption by default:** Data should be encrypted at rest and in transit by default. Most cloud providers offer automatic encryption for data at rest in their storage services, and HTTPS should be used for all web communication.

- **Container security:** If we use containerization technologies like Docker or Kubernetes, we need to ensure that we follow best practices for container security. This could include using minimal base images, scanning our images for vulnerabilities, and ensuring our containers run with the least necessary privileges.

By adhering to the principle of secure defaults, we can ensure that our applications and services are secure from the outset. This approach reduces the reliance on individual developers' security knowledge and creates a secure foundation that is easier to maintain and build. Therefore, adopting secure defaults is essential to the security as code paradigm.

Authentication and authorization

Authentication and authorization form the bedrock of security in cloud environments. We have already delved into these two concepts in detail in *Chapter 2, Application Security*. As we shift towards a DevSecOps model, automating and integrating these aspects into the development lifecycle becomes crucial to maintaining robust security.

In a DevSecOps model, the lines between development, operations, and security blur, making it crucial to ensure that only authenticated and authorized entities can access and manipulate applications and data. The rapid pace of CI/CD pipelines makes manual checks untenable, necessitating automated authentication and authorization checks.

There are numerous strategies and methods for managing authentication and authorization in the cloud. Let us discuss them.

Identity and access management tools

AWS IAM allows us to control access to AWS services and resources securely. For example, we might create an IAM role with the necessary permissions to read files from an S3 bucket and then assign this role to an EC2 instance. This way, the applications running on the EC2 instance can access the files in the bucket.

In AWS, the process of creating and assigning IAM roles programmatically is seamless, thanks to the Boto3 library for Python. Let us delve into a practical example. Below, we will utilize the Boto3 library to set up an IAM role named **'S3ReadAccessRole'**. This role is endowed with permissions to read from an S3 bucket. Subsequently, we will associate the role with a predefined AWS policy granting read-only access to Amazon S3. Here is how we can achieve this:

```python
import boto3
iam = boto3.client('iam')
response = iam.create_role(
    RoleName='S3ReadAccessRole',
    AssumeRolePolicyDocument='...',  # This would be the policy document
that specifies who can assume the role
)
iam.attach_role_policy(
    RoleName='S3ReadAccessRole',
    PolicyArn='arn:aws:iam::aws:policy/AmazonS3ReadOnlyAccess',
)
```

Multi-factor authentication

MFA significantly improves the security of user accounts. For example, after entering our password, an application might require a fingerprint or a code from an authenticator app on our phone.

Single sign-on

With **Single Sign-On (SSO)**, users can sign in once and access multiple applications without needing to sign in to each one separately. This is often used in corporate environments, where users can access various internal and third-party applications using their corporate credentials.

Identity federation

Federation allows users to authenticate with an external **identity provider (IdP)** and access AWS services without an IAM identity. For example, we might allow users to authenticate with a SAML IdP and then assume an IAM role based on their SAML attributes.

Secrets management

In DevSecOps, managing sensitive information such as database credentials remains a paramount concern. HashiCorp's Vault emerges as a powerful tool for this purpose, offering a secure way to store and access secrets. To illustrate its capabilities, let us consider a scenario where we want to safeguard a database password. The following is a demonstration of how we can store this password in Vault and subsequently retrieve it for our application:

```
# Store the secret
vault kv put secret/myapp/db password="db-password"
# Retrieve the secret
vault kv get secret/myapp/db
```

Automation and integration are key to effectively managing authentication and authorization in DevSecOps. Automation helps to eliminate human errors and streamlines the process, while integration ensures that every stage of the development lifecycle incorporates these checks. This might include integrating IAM tools into the CI/CD pipeline, automating the rotation of secrets, or using automated policy checks to enforce the principle of least privilege.

AWS Secrets Manager, for instance, offers functionalities that can be harnessed to rotate secrets periodically, thereby enhancing security. Let us walk through how we can achieve this rotation with a simple command:

```
aws secretsmanager rotate-secret --secret-id mysecretARN
```

For example, we might use a tool like Open Policy Agent to enforce IAM policies as part of our CI/CD pipeline. If a proposed IAM change violates a policy, the pipeline will fail and prevent the change from being made.

Strong authentication and authorization are fundamental to securing cloud environments. By integrating and automating these processes in a DevSecOps model, organizations can ensure that access control is robust, efficient, and scalable, bolstering their overall security posture.

Cloud security solutions

Cloud security solutions form a critical layer of protection in the cloud-based infrastructure of modern businesses. As more and more applications are delivered as services over the internet, the importance of robust cloud security mechanisms cannot be overstated. In this context, several solutions have emerged, including CWPP, CSPM, CASB, and CNAPP. Let us delve into each of these.

Cloud workload protection platforms

CWPPs focus on securing workloads in the cloud, including **Virtual Machines** (**VMs**), containers, and serverless workloads. They offer protection against common threats to these environments, such as vulnerabilities, malware, and unauthorized access. Examples of CWPP providers include Palo Alto's Prisma Cloud, Symantec's Cloud Workload Protection, and McAfee's Cloud Workload Security.

For example, Prisma Cloud offers a variety of protection features, including:

- **Vulnerability management:** Identifies vulnerabilities in our images, functions, and hosts.

- **Compliance:** Validates our workloads against regulatory standards and best practices.

- **Runtime defence:** Detects and prevents anomalous behaviors during runtime.

Cloud security posture management

CSPM solutions help organizations fully use the security controls offered by their cloud providers. These tools continually monitor and manage security posture across multiple cloud platforms, ensuring compliance with internal policies and external regulations. CSPM tools typically focus on configuration management, visibility, and compliance assessment. Examples of CSPM solutions include Check Point's CloudGuard, McAfee's MVISION Cloud, and Sophos' Cloud Optix.

For instance, McAfee's MVISION Cloud offers:

- **Risk discovery:** Identifies risky configurations and security threats across cloud services.

- **Compliance monitoring:** Monitors and assesses our cloud configurations for compliance with external regulations and internal policies.

- **Threat protection:** Identifies and protects against insider threats, compromised accounts, and privileged access misuse.

Cloud access security brokers

CASBs act as gatekeepers, facilitating the enforcement of enterprise security policies when accessing cloud-based resources. They bridge the gap between cloud service consumers and providers, ensuring visibility, compliance, data security, and threat protection. Some prominent CASBs are McAfee's MVISION Cloud, Symantec's CloudSOC, and Microsoft's Cloud App Security. For instance, Microsoft's Cloud App Security is designed to detect cloud applications and services utilized by an organization, control cloud data through granular policy settings, and identify high-risk usage and security incidents.

On the other hand, CNAPP is a terminology coined by Gartner to represent the progression of CWPP and CSPM tools. CNAPPs broaden the capabilities of CWPPs and CSPMs by encompassing all facets of an application deployed in a cloud-native setting, including the application code and the underlying infrastructure. Emerging CNAPPs include the Sysdig Secure DevOps Platform and Prisma Cloud by Palo Alto Networks. For example, the Sysdig Secure DevOps Platform offers vulnerability and misconfiguration scanning to report on risk posture, checks configurations and activity against compliance standards. It identifies suspicious activities that signal a threat.

Each playing a unique role, these cloud security solutions significantly contribute to managing security risks and bolstering an organization's security posture in cloud environments. When these tools are incorporated into a comprehensive security strategy, organizations are equipped to enhance the protection of their cloud assets, ensure compliance with regulations, and promptly respond to threats.

Table 5.6 is a comparison table that categorizes the main functions of each type of cloud security solution:

	CWPP	CSPM	CASB	CNAPP
What it protects	Cloud workloads (VMs, containers, serverless)	Cloud infrastructure	Cloud applications	Cloud-native applications (code + underlying infrastructure)

	CWPP	**CSPM**	**CASB**	**CNAPP**
Key features	Vulnerability management, runtime defense	Risk discovery, compliance monitoring, configuration management	Discovery, data protection, threat protection	Risk reporting, compliance, threat detection
Examples	Prisma Cloud, Symantec Cloud Workload Protection, McAfee Cloud Workload Security	Check Point CloudGuard, McAfee MVISION Cloud, Sophos Cloud Optix	McAfee MVISION Cloud, Symantec CloudSOC, Microsoft Cloud App Security	Sysdig Secure DevOps Platform, Prisma Cloud

Table 5.6: A visual summary of the main differences between CWPPs, CSPMs, CASBs, and CNAPPs

Please note that while these categories can help understand the general use cases for each solution, many vendors offer products that span multiple categories or offer features that might not be outlined in this table. Always consider our specific needs and constraints when selecting a solution.

Table 5.7 illustrates the integrability of various Cloud security solution vendors with DevSecOps tools, Cloud providers, and identity providers. This comparison provides an understanding of the flexibility and compatibility of different solutions in a DevSecOps environment:

Vendor	**Product(s)**	**Integration with DevSecOps tools**	**Integration with cloud providers**	**Integration with identity providers**
Microsoft	Azure Security Center	Azure DevOps, GitHub	Azure	Azure AD
McAfee	MVISION Cloud	Jenkins, Jira	AWS, Azure, Google Cloud	SAML, OIDC
Symantec	CloudSOC CASB	Not specified	AWS, Azure, Google Cloud	SAML, OIDC
Palo Alto Networks	Prisma Cloud	Jenkins, CircleCI, GitLab, GitHub, Bitbucket, Jira	AWS, Azure, Google Cloud, Oracle Cloud, Alibaba Cloud	SAML, OIDC

Vendor	Product(s)	Integration with DevSecOps tools	Integration with cloud providers	Integration with identity providers
Check Point	CloudGuard	Jenkins, CircleCI, GitLab, GitHub, Bitbucket	AWS, Azure, Google Cloud	SAML, OIDC
Sophos	Cloud Optix	Jenkins, Jira	AWS, Azure, Google Cloud	SAML, OIDC
Sysdig	Secure DevOps Platform	Jenkins, CircleCI, GitLab, GitHub, Bitbucket, Jira	AWS, Azure, Google Cloud, Oracle Cloud, Alibaba Cloud	SAML, OIDC

Table 5.7: An illustration of the integrability of various cloud security solution

Palo Alto Networks' Prisma Cloud, McAfee's MVISION Cloud, Check Point's CloudGuard, and Sysdig's Secure DevOps Platform stand out due to their extensive integrations. They integrate with multiple popular DevSecOps tools such as Jenkins, CircleCI, GitLab, GitHub, Bitbucket, and Jira, facilitating seamless security checks and remediation in the CI/CD pipeline. They also support a range of Cloud providers, including AWS, Azure, Google Cloud, Oracle Cloud, and Alibaba Cloud, providing flexibility to organizations utilizing multi-cloud environments. SAML and OIDC support ensure that they can integrate with various identity providers.

Microsoft's Azure Security Center is tailored specifically for the Azure environment. It integrates well with Azure DevOps and Azure AD, making it a strong choice for organizations heavily invested in the Microsoft ecosystem.

Sophos's Cloud Optix offers integrations with Jenkins, Jira, AWS, Azure, and Google Cloud, along with SAML and OIDC support for identity providers. Similarly, Symantec's CloudSOC CASB also provides a range of integrations, although specific DevOps tools are not specified.

This comparison underscores the importance of choosing a Cloud security solution that aligns with an organization's existing tools and platforms. Each of these solutions offers a unique set of features, and their effectiveness would ultimately depend on an organization's specific needs and infrastructure.

Supply chain and risks

The software supply chain encompasses everything constituting our software and its origin, including source code, libraries, container images, and IaC. With the inherent complexity of modern application development, the software supply chain is often a mosaic of various components from different sources. While this enhances development efficiency, it simultaneously introduces numerous security risks.

Potential vulnerabilities

Modern applications typically depend heavily on open-source or third-party libraries and frameworks. Take, for example, a common Node.js application that utilizes express. js for routing and middleware, mongoose for MongoDB object modeling, and passport.js for authentication. Although these components expedite development, they can also be a source of vulnerabilities if they need to be regularly updated or correctly configured.

Malicious or compromised components introduce another layer of risk within the software supply chain. If an attacker taints a popular open-source library, like what transpired with the event stream in 2018, the security of numerous applications and their data could be threatened.

Additionally, vulnerabilities can be introduced through insecure development practices or a lack of robust security within the development environment. These vulnerabilities can occur from using insecure functions, overlooking input validation, or incorrectly managing errors, all of which can be exploited by threat actors.

Finally, the build and CI/CD infrastructure, integral to the software supply chain, presents its security challenges. This infrastructure can become an attractive attack surface for hackers who, upon breaching these systems, could insert malicious code or gain access to sensitive information.

Possible exploits

Numerous potential threats exist within software supply chain vulnerabilities, but the most prominent is the supply chain attack. In such an attack, an intruder compromises one component intending to impact systems further down the chain. A few of these significant supply chain attacks are worth discussing.

In the infamous SolarWinds Orion breach of 2020 (**https://www.cisa.gov/news-events/ alerts/2021/01/07/supply-chain-compromise**), advanced threat actors compromised the build system of SolarWinds' Orion software, a well-known network management tool. The attackers inserted a malicious backdoor into a software update, distributed to global customers (**https://www.solarwinds.com/sa-overview/securityadvisory**). When the infected update was installed, many organizations inadvertently allowed the attackers access to their networks. The incident resulted in substantial data breaches across various government agencies and large corporations.

A different example occurred in 2017 with Avast (**https://blog.talosintelligence.com/avast- distributes-malware/**), the creators of the popular system cleaning software CCleaner. Avast announced that their download servers had been compromised by hackers who replaced the legitimate CCleaner software with a malware-infected version. With 2.27 million users downloading the infected CCleaner, the compromise was extensive. This attack demonstrated the far-reaching effects of compromising a single link in the supply chain.

The 2017 NotPetya ransomware event also created worldwide chaos (**https://www.wired. com/story/notpetya-cyberattack-ukraine-russia-code-crashed-the-world/**). The initial infection stemmed from a popular Ukrainian tax software known as M.E.Doc. In this case, attackers compromised M.E.Doc's update servers, releasing the NotPetya malware disguised as a software update. Using the EternalBlue exploit, NotPetya spread rapidly across networks, encrypting files and demanding a ransom. The attack affected many organizations and led to billions of dollars in damages.

The Event-Stream incident 2018 presents a notable case of a supply chain attack within the Node.js ecosystem (**https://github.com/dominictarr/event-stream/issues/116**). A malicious actor managed to gain control of a popular Node.js package, Event-Stream, which was downloaded millions of times each week. The actor introduced a harmful dependency that aimed to steal Bitcoin from users' wallets of a specific Bitcoin wallet application.

These examples underpin the potential severity and widespread impact of supply chain attacks. They highlight the importance of ensuring the security of every part of the software supply chain, from the code and its dependencies to the build and distribution systems.

Mitigation strategies

Despite these potential risks, several strategies can help mitigate software supply chain vulnerabilities:

- **Adherence to secure coding practices:** Developers should follow secure coding practices and utilize tools like static code analyzers or security linters to identify possible security issues. For instance, using tools such as SonarQube or Coverity can help identify potential vulnerabilities early in development.

- **Software Composition Analysis (SCA):** SCA tools, like Black Duck or WhiteSource, help identify vulnerabilities within a project's open-source components. They check for outdated libraries and alert the team of known vulnerabilities in current dependencies.

- **Regular updates and patching:** All third-party components should be updated regularly. This practice ensures that known security vulnerabilities are patched, thereby reducing exposure. A patch management tool like ManageEngine Patch Manager Plus or Ivanti Security Controls can help automate this process.

- **Securing the CI/CD pipeline:** Securing the CI/CD pipeline is crucial. This includes controlling access, auditing actions, and regularly scanning for vulnerabilities. For instance, tools like Jenkins or CircleCI offer robust access control and auditing capabilities.

- **Vendor risk management:** Suppliers should be assessed for their security posture, including their history of security incidents, security policies, and approach to vulnerability management. Vendor risk management platforms such as UpGuard or SecurityScorecard can help streamline this process.

- **Container security:** Containers are integral to many software supply chains. Container images should be scanned for vulnerabilities, and security should be enforced at runtime. Access to containers should also be tightly controlled. Solutions like Aqua Security or Sysdig provide these capabilities.

To sum up, while presenting multiple security risks, the software supply chain can be effectively secured with diligent management, risk assessment, and robust security measures. DevSecOps principles advocate for **shifting left**, meaning integrating security early in the development lifecycle. This mindset is equally crucial when managing the software supply chain to ensure comprehensive security coverage.

Automating integration workflows challenges and best practices

DevSecOps involves a multitude of tools, teams, and processes, and effectively integrating these elements can be complex. For instance, integrating security tools with CI/CD pipelines necessitates understanding how these tools function and how they can operate together.

Consider a scenario where our team uses Jenkins for CI/CD, SonarQube for code analysis, and JFrog Xray for vulnerability scanning. Each of these tools possesses its set of APIs and configurations. Ensuring these tools operate harmoniously can be both intricate and time-consuming.

As a project expands, the required integrations can grow, complicating management. Scaling our DevSecOps practices to accommodate an expanding codebase, a growing list of tools, or a larger team can pose difficulties. As our application grows, we may integrate additional tools into our pipeline, such as Docker for containerization, Kubernetes for orchestration, and Terraform for infrastructure management. Each tool contributes an additional layer of complexity to our DevSecOps practices.

The process of integrating multiple tools and systems can also introduce security risks. If not adequately secured, APIs used for integration could become a potential target for attackers. Moreover, data transmitted between integrated systems could be intercepted or manipulated.

Suppose we have integrated our CI/CD pipeline with a third-party code analysis tool using APIs. If these APIs lack appropriate security measures, an attacker could exploit them to gain unauthorized access to our codebase or insert malicious code.

The following represent best practices for automating integration workflows in DevSecOps:

- **Use standard APIs and protocols:** Adhere to standard APIs and protocols to simplify integration and guarantee tool compatibility. When possible, prefer RESTful APIs over HTTP(S), which are widely understood and supported.

- **Embrace automation:** Automation is a fundamental principle of DevSecOps. Automating integrations can help to decrease human error, streamline processes, and enhance consistency. Automate pushing code changes to a repository, triggering a build in our CI/CD pipeline, running tests, performing code analysis, scanning for vulnerabilities, and deploying to production. Each of these steps can be automated through integrations between our tools.

- **Secure our integrations:** Employ encryption for data in transit between systems, ensure APIs are secured, and restrict access to integration points. Consider using a secret management system to securely handle API keys and other sensitive data. Use HTTPS for any API calls between systems to guarantee encrypted data in transit. Securely store API keys using a tool like HashiCorp Vault or AWS Secrets Manager, and utilize these keys only when necessary to authenticate API calls.

- **Monitor our integrations:** Continuously monitor our integrations to ensure they function correctly and detect any unusual activity that could indicate a security issue. Logging and monitoring tools can assist in this endeavor. Use a monitoring tool like Prometheus or Datadog to oversee the activity and performance of our CI/CD pipeline. Set up alerts to inform us of any failures or significant events.

- **Regularly review and update our integrations:** Our integrations may need to adapt as tools and practices evolve. Regularly review our integrations to ensure they remain necessary, effective, and secure. As part of our periodic security audits, scrutinize our tool integrations. Verify that API keys remain valid, data is correctly transferred between systems, and there are no new security vulnerabilities.

Automating our DevSecOps tool integration can provide substantial benefits, but it is crucial to manage this process attentively to avoid introducing new complexities or security risks. By adhering to these best practices, we can successfully implement automation of integration workflows in our DevSecOps practices.

Use case: Integrations

We discussed the security of our IoT application in *Chapter 2, Application Security* and orchestrated infrastructure in *Chapter 3, Infrastructure as Code*. We also discussed containerizing the application in *Chapter 4, Containers and Security*. Let us now understand how we should automate integration workflows and enforce security for our IoT application.

The following are the five steps for automating integration workflows for the IoT application use case in a DevSecOps environment.

Step 1: Defining the DevSecOps workflow

We shall start by defining the DevSecOps workflow to visualize how different components will integrate. This involves identifying the tools, tasks, and dependencies involved in the project. Let us list every tool we plan to use, such as Jenkins for CI/CD, SonarQube for code analysis, and JFrog Xray for vulnerability scanning. Let us identify each tool's tasks and understand how these tools can work together.

We have already automated the Sensor Network Creation using Terraform. This has involved specifying the number of sensors, their positioning, and the data they will collect. We have also used Terraform to automate the provisioning and management of the cloud infrastructure. This has also included the creation of the data pipeline for streaming data into the cloud.

Step 2: Building dashboards

We shall utilize Grafana to automate the creation of dashboards. These dashboards will display real-time data about the location and activities of the workers on the factory floor.

Let us begin by signing up with Grafana. Next, let us configure Grafana to connect with the data source. In our case, let us choose a time-series database, InfluxDB, where sensor and ERP data are being streamed (in fact, Grafana provides options for connecting to various databases). The connection setup will include specifying the data source URL, database name, credentials, and other necessary information.

Now, it is time to create the dashboards. Grafana offers a rich array of visualization options such as graphs, heatmaps, tables, and so on. We shall create a new dashboard and add panels for each data metric we want to visualize.

Figure 5.3 shows the screen for creating an InfluxDB data source (please note that Grafana ships with built-in support for InfluxDB):

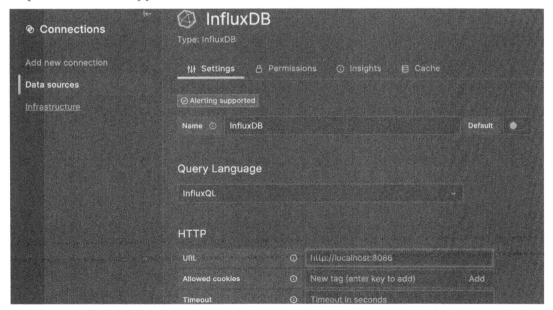

Figure 5.3: *A screenshot showing the creation of an InfluxDB data source on Grafana*

For example, we might want a panel showing the real-time location of each worker. Another panel could be a heatmap showing the frequency of workers entering unsafe areas. We can customize these panels with data queries, visualization types, labels, colors, and other options.

Grafana provides a feature to export dashboards as JSON files to automate dashboard creation. We can create a dashboard manually, export it as JSON, and then use this JSON file to recreate the dashboard automatically on another instance of Grafana.

Lastly, we might want to set up alerts for critical situations, such as a worker entering an unsafe area. Grafana allows us to define alert rules based on our data queries. Grafana can send notifications via email, Slack, or other communication channels when the alert condition is met.

Step 3: Integrating the ERP system

Our focus here is to automate the integration of the ERP attendance management module with the application. This can be done using APIs provided by the ERP system and should allow the application to access the data of workers entering and exiting the factory floor.

Figure 5.4 shows the steps to integrate the organization's API with the new IoT application:

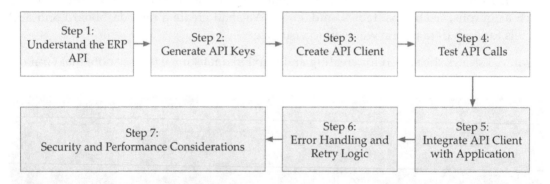

Figure 5.4: *Seven steps to integrate the organization's API with the new IoT application*

Let us understand the structure of the API, including the endpoints, the request and response formats, and the authentication requirements. We assume that our ERP has ReST API. Accessing an ERP system's API will require authentication through API keys or tokens. Follow the ERP system's process to generate these keys, following best security practices. Store these keys securely, ideally using a secrets management system like HashiCorp Vault or AWS Secrets Manager.

Next, let us create an API client to interact with the ERP system's API in our application. This client will send requests to the API and process the responses. We shall use HTTP libraries available in our programming language of choice to create this client.

We need to test the API calls before integrating the API client into our application. We shall use Postman for testing. We shall verify that we can retrieve the necessary data from the ERP system, like worker entry and exit times, and that the data is in the expected format.

We shall integrate it with our application once we have verified that the API client is working correctly. This involves writing the code to call the API client and handling the returned data. For example, when our application needs to know if a worker has entered the factory floor, it should call the appropriate method in the API client, which requests the ERP system's API.

Error handling and retry logic step focuses on building resilience in the application's interaction with the ERP system's API. Effective error handling ensures that any issues, such as network interruptions or data format errors, are gracefully managed, with user-friendly notifications or alternative actions. Concurrently, implementing retry logic is vital, where the application intelligently retries failed requests, using strategies like exponential backoff and setting sensible limits on retry attempts. This not only enhances stability but also minimizes potential disruptions in operations.

The final integration aspect revolves around maintaining the security of data exchanges and optimizing the system's performance. Security measures should include encrypted data transmissions, stringent management of access credentials, and regular monitoring for any unusual access patterns. On the performance front, efficient data handling, such as minimizing unnecessary data retrieval and caching frequently requested data, ensures swift and effective application responses. Additionally, being mindful of the ERP system's load by implementing request throttling or rate limiting can help maintain overall system performance and reliability.

Including robust error handling and retry logic in our application is important. If a call to the ERP system's API fails, our application should be able to handle that gracefully. This could mean showing an appropriate error message, attempting the request again after a delay, or taking corrective action.

Step 4: Securing the application

Implement security measures to protect the application and its data. This can include encryption of data in transit, secure storage of API keys, and use of HTTPS for API calls. Automated security testing and scanning for vulnerabilities should also be integrated into the CI/CD pipeline.

We shall also limit the rate of requests to avoid hitting API rate limits and ensure sensitive data is handled securely.

Step 5: Monitoring and managing the application

Now, we shall implement automated monitoring and alerting using Prometheus. This should provide visibility into the application's performance and alert the team to any issues or anomalies. Also, we shall use a configuration management tool to manage the application's settings and ensure consistency across different environments.

It is a mandatory consideration that we regularly review and update the application and its integrations to ensure they remain effective and secure. This would include checking that API keys are still valid, data is being transferred correctly, and there are no new security vulnerabilities.

Conclusion

Throughout this comprehensive exploration, we have discussed a variety of platforms and tools vital for robust security management in enterprise systems and large-scale software applications. Considering the extensive attack surfaces inherent to such systems, the importance of diligent and comprehensive security management cannot be overstated.

One of the main themes of this chapter is the exploration of cloud security solutions like CWPP, CSPM, CASB, and CNAPP. These solutions are essential in cloud security, safeguarding applications and data in the cloud and maintaining compliance with relevant regulatory standards.

In addition, we have explored the role of integration and automation in the DevSecOps model, particularly emphasizing the integration of various tools and platforms. As we have seen through several case studies, successful implementation of such integration strategies can considerably bolster security practices.

Furthermore, we have examined the challenges associated with software supply chains in the DevSecOps context. With an understanding of potential vulnerabilities, possible exploits, and mitigation strategies, we can better secure our software supply chains against the growing threat of supply chain attacks.

In the next chapter, we will delve into different leading security frameworks and their management in the DevSecOps process. We will prioritize audit and compliance management while offering an in-depth understanding of reporting, visualization, and workflows.

Questions

1. What does the term PaC mean in DevSecOps?

2. How does PaC benefit an organization's security posture?

3. Provide an example of how PaC can be implemented.

4. What is MaC? Give some example tools.

5. What are the benefits of implementing MaC tool?

6. Explain the security as code concept and its role in the DevSecOps lifecycle.

7. What tools are commonly used to implement security as code, and how do they work?

8. How does security as code contribute to continuous integration and continuous deployment?

9. Why are both authentication and authorization important in a DevSecOps model?

10. What are CWPP, CSPM, CASB, and CNAPP, and how do they help manage security risks in cloud environments?

11. How can these security solutions enhance an organization's overall security posture?

12. Compare and contrast these solutions and provide examples of where each would be appropriate.

13. What are some of the risks associated with software supply chains in a DevSecOps context?

14. Explain the concept of a supply chain attack and provide an example.

15. What are some strategies to mitigate the risks associated with software supply chains?

16. What are some common challenges faced when implementing integration as Code in DevSecOps?

17. Describe a few best practices for successful implementation of integration as Code in DevSecOps.

18. How does Integration as Code contribute to the DevSecOps goals of automation and continuous integration/deployment?

19. Based on the case studies discussed, how have organizations successfully implemented integration as Code in a DevSecOps context?

20. What challenges did these organizations face, and how did they overcome them?

21. What were the benefits of implementing integration as code in these case studies?

Join our book's Discord space

Join the book's Discord Workspace for Latest updates, Offers, Tech happenings around the world, New Release and Sessions with the Authors:

https://discord.bpbonline.com

Frameworks and Best Practices

Introduction

In our previous chapter, we dove deep into the expansive world of security as code, shedding light on various platforms and tools crucial in securing enterprise systems and large-scale software applications with wide-ranging attack surfaces. In the journey, we will explore the labyrinth of leading security frameworks and their alignment with the DevSecOps process. With the fast-paced evolution of the digital landscape, compliance and auditing have emerged as vital aspects of security management. We will examine these elements in detail, exploring the nuances of reporting, visualization, and workflows that enable effective management of these processes. We will also focus on the complex yet critical realm of threat modeling, introducing its various types and their role in an organization's security posture. Let us begin.

Structure

In this chapter, we will discuss the following topics:

- Risks and compliance
- Overview of security frameworks
- Compliance as code and its importance

- Understanding security audit workflows

- Threat modeling

- CSA's six pillars of DevSecOps

- Compliance and risk management for our IoT application

Objectives

This chapter aims to offer an exhaustive understanding of how leading security frameworks dovetail with the DevSecOps process. Audit and compliance management plays a significant role in the ever-evolving digital landscape. To that end, we delve into the mechanisms of reporting, visualization techniques, and the workflows involved in compliance management. We conclude our discourse with an introduction to the vital field of threat modeling, breaking down its different types and their role within the DevSecOps context. Our focus is to provide a comprehensive understanding of these critical elements, empowering us with the knowledge and tools to effectively manage security within a DevSecOps framework.

Risks and compliance

The digital landscape is filled with potential threats and vulnerabilities. Implementing risk management and compliance measures is crucial for any organization, especially in a digital context. Adopting DevSecOps methodologies allows for seamless integration of these measures within the development lifecycle. Risk management allows an organization to:

- Identify and evaluate these risks in terms of their likelihood and potential impact.

- Develop strategies to mitigate, transfer, accept, or avoid them.

- Continuously monitor and reassess these risks as the organization's digital infrastructure evolves.

It protects the organization from potential harm, helps maintain stakeholder trust, and even provides a competitive advantage. There are two concepts concerning risk management: risk assessment and risk treatment. In DevSecOps, risk assessment is an integral part of the security lifecycle. It identifies potential vulnerabilities or threats in a system, analyzes their likelihood of occurrence and impact, and prioritizes them for treatment.

Table 6.1 illustrates different phases of risk assessment as an integral part of the security lifecycle:

Phase	To-do	Description
1.	Risk identification	Identification of potential vulnerabilities in the system, which could range from software or hardware issues to data breaches or system failures.
2.	Risk analysis	Examine identified risks based on their likelihood of occurrence and the potential impact should they materialize.
3.	Risk evaluation	Comparing the risk analysis results against the organization's risk criteria to determine which risks must be addressed.

***Table 6.1**: Different phases of risk assessment as an integral part of the security lifecycle*

Once risks have been assessed, they must be managed or treated. It can involve one or more of the following:

- **Risk mitigation:** Implementing measures to reduce the likelihood or impact of the risk. In a DevSecOps environment, this could include using better security tools or improving code quality.

- **Risk transfer:** Shifting risk to a different party, for example, purchasing cyber insurance to cover potential losses from a cyberattack.

- **Risk acceptance:** Sometimes, accepting the risk and preparing a contingency plan might be more cost-effective and preferred rather than attempting to mitigate or transfer it.

- **Risk avoidance:** Changing business practices or technology to avoid the risk altogether.

In a DevSecOps environment, these steps are integrated into the development and operations processes. It can be achieved by using tools that enable the automation of risk management activities, such as automated vulnerability scanners or **Security Incident and Event Management (SIEM)** systems.

For example, in the risk identification phase, automated tools can be integrated into the CI/CD pipeline to scan for security issues in the code as it is being developed. When a potential issue is identified, the development team can be alerted immediately, allowing them to remediate it before the code is deployed to production.

In the risk mitigation phase, automated security controls can be implemented to help protect against identified risks. For example, a **Web Application Firewall (WAF)** could be implemented to help protect against web-based attacks such as SQL injection or cross-site scripting.

By integrating risk management into the DevSecOps process, organizations can ensure that they are taking a proactive approach to managing security risks and that security considerations are being taken into account throughout the development lifecycle.

Now, let us discuss **compliance**. There are a host of regulatory standards, laws, and best practices that govern data security and privacy. Non-compliance can lead to:

- Legal penalties, such as fines or sanctions.

- Damage to the organization's reputation.

- Loss of customer trust.

Therefore, compliance is a regulatory requirement and crucial for maintaining an organization's brand image and customer relationships. This is achieved through audits - both internally (within the organization) and externally (performed by external auditors). Auditing is necessary to achieve compliance. An audit is a systematic, documented, and independent process for obtaining and evaluating evidence objectively to determine the extent to which pre-defined criteria are fulfilled. In DevSecOps, audits can be used to verify that security controls are being correctly implemented and are effective. In this context, we need to know the following two items:

- **Gap analysis:** It is a method for comparing the current state of our system or process with a desired or future state. In the context of DevSecOps, it can be used to identify gaps in security measures and compliance with established standards or regulations.

- **Remediation:** Remediation involves rectifying identified gaps, vulnerabilities, or non-compliance issues. In a DevSecOps context, this could include fixing code vulnerabilities, improving security controls, or altering processes to ensure regulatory compliance.

The operationalization of risk management and compliance within a DevSecOps framework allows organizations to protect their digital assets, comply with regulatory standards, and build a culture of security, all while maintaining the agility and efficiency that DevSecOps is known for. Let us now discuss a few popular security frameworks used as risk management and compliance standards.

Security frameworks

Security frameworks serve as the foundational structure that outlines the processes, policies, and controls needed to secure an organization's digital environment. These frameworks act as a guide, offering best practices, standards, and comprehensive strategies to ensure robust security measures are in place.

Let us now explore some leading security frameworks widely adopted within the industry for **Information Security Management Systems (ISMS)** and understand their salient features and use cases.

Note: An ISMS is a management framework of policies, procedures, and controls designed to manage information security risks within an organization. An ISMS aims to safeguard the confidentiality, integrity, and availability of information through a risk management process and deliver assurance to interested stakeholders.

ISO/IEC 27001

ISO/IEC 27001 is a popular standard adopted for planning, implementing, maintaining, and continually improving an ISMS. It encompasses people, processes, and IT systems. It aligns well with the DevSecOps approach, which integrates people, processes, and technologies in a continuous development cycle, security, and operations.

ISO/IEC 27001 outlines requirements for an ISMS and includes details for planning, establishing, implementing, operating, monitoring, reviewing, maintaining, and improving an ISMS. It systematically manages information security risks, considering the organization's exposure to risks and its treatment approach. ISO/IEC 27001 applies to all types and sizes of organizations, including public and private companies, government entities, and not-for-profit organizations.

There are several challenges to the implementation of ISO/IEC 27001. Defining the scope of the ISMS can take time and effort. Secondly, the process requires substantial time, human resources, and cost. Lastly, adopting ISO/IEC 27001 necessitates shifting towards a security-oriented operational culture, encountering resistance from stakeholders.

Despite these challenges, the advantages of implementing ISO/IEC 27001 are noteworthy. One of the main benefits is that it promotes a risk-based approach. This strategy guides organizations to make decisions based on systematic identification, evaluation, and mitigation of risks, focusing on areas with the highest security risks. Doing so helps organizations better protect their information assets, reduce the likelihood of security breaches, and manage threats effectively.

Furthermore, achieving ISO/IEC 27001 certification signals customers, stakeholders, and business partners that the organization is deeply committed to information security, enhancing their trust and confidence.

We usually follow these steps for implementing ISO/IEC 27001:

1. **Scope definition:** Begin by defining the ISMS scope. It involves identifying the information that needs protection and the systems, processes, and locations interacting with it.

2. **Risk assessment:** Conduct a comprehensive risk assessment within the defined scope. It involves identifying assets, threats, vulnerabilities, and their impacts.

3. **Risk treatment:** Develop a risk treatment plan based on the risk assessment. This plan may encompass risk mitigation strategies, risk transfer, risk acceptance, or risk avoidance tactics.

4. **Implement controls:** Following the risk treatment plan, implement security controls. These controls should address identified risks and be selected from Annex A of the ISO/IEC 27001 standard.

5. **Monitor and review:** Regularly monitor and review the ISMS to ensure effectiveness and identify improvement areas. This step includes conducting periodic risk assessments and audits.

6. **Continual improvement:** ISO/IEC 27001 is not a one-off project but demands continuous improvement. The ISMS should be continually refined and enhanced based on regular reviews and audits.

ISO/IEC 27001 is a comprehensive and holistic standard. In the context of DevSecOps, it can help ensure that security is integrated into all stages of the software lifecycle, from initial development through to ongoing operation and maintenance. By understanding the challenges, benefits, and steps discussed above, organizations can effectively leverage ISO/IEC 27001 to enhance their information security posture and build a resilient ISMS.

National Institute of Standards and Technology Cybersecurity Framework

The **National Institute of Standards and Technology (NIST)** Cybersecurity Framework is a comprehensive and voluntary tool designed to assist organizations, particularly those in the critical infrastructure sector, in managing and reduce cybersecurity risks. This adaptable framework is based on existing standards, guidelines, and practices and has proven beneficial even to non-critical infrastructure organizations, including those outside the United States.

In a DevSecOps environment, the NIST Cybersecurity Framework provides an ideal foundation for ensuring the incorporation of security principles throughout all phases of the software development lifecycle, echoing the key tenets of DevSecOps. The framework has three distinct parts:

- **The core:** Outlines crucial cybersecurity outcomes that an organization identifies as necessary based on its unique needs.

- **The profile:** Reflects the alignment of the framework core's functionalities with an organization's business requirements, risk tolerance levels, and resources.

- **The implementation tiers:** Help define the extent to which an organization's cybersecurity risk management practices exhibit the characteristics detailed in the Framework.

Implementing the framework, however, has its challenges. Given the comprehensive nature of the NIST Cybersecurity Framework, stakeholders may need considerable time to comprehend its structure and various components fully. While the framework is designed to be flexible and adaptable, aligning it with specific business needs and risk environments may prove challenging for some organizations. Also, the initial stages of implementing the framework can require substantial investment in time and resources.

Yet, the advantages of adopting the NIST Cybersecurity Framework are significant. The framework can be adapted to suit a wide range of sectors and organizations of varying sizes. It offers a holistic approach to managing cybersecurity risks, encompassing every aspect, from risk identification to recovery from cybersecurity incidents. Moreover, by adopting this framework, organizations can identify and prioritize actions to reduce cybersecurity risks and align risk management activities with business requirements, risk tolerances, and available resources.

To effectively implement the NIST Cybersecurity Framework, organizations may follow these steps:

1. **Prioritize and scope:** Identify business or mission objectives and strategic priorities. Based on these, identify systems, assets, regulatory requirements, and risk appetite to assess business risk.

2. **Orient:** Recognize related systems and assets, regulatory requirements, and the overall risk approach. The organization should also identify threats and vulnerabilities affecting those systems and assets.

3. **Create a current profile:** Develop a profile representing the outcomes chosen from the framework categories and subcategories, which reflect the organization's business needs.

4. **Conduct a risk assessment:** Undertake a risk assessment, which could be guided by the risk management process as often as required.

5. **Create a target profile:** Design a target profile to assess the framework categories and subcategories that describe the organization's desired cybersecurity outcomes.

6. **Determine, analyze, and prioritize gaps:** Compare the current and target profiles to identify gaps, then formulate a prioritized action plan to address those gaps.

7. **Implement action plan:** Act according to the plan, monitor its progress, and use collected information for process improvement, potentially leading back to the beginning of the Cybersecurity Framework Implementation process.

Integrating the NIST Cybersecurity Framework with DevSecOps can promote a more proactive and process-oriented approach to managing cybersecurity risks, marking it as an essential tool in any organization's security toolkit.

Center for Internet Security Controls

The **Center for Internet Security (CIS)** Controls represent a prioritized sequence of actions that offer a defense-in-depth set of best practices to thwart the most common attacks on systems and networks. These controls are crafted by a consortium of IT experts utilizing their first-hand experience as cybersecurity defenders to produce these globally recognized security best practices. The CIS Controls' principles dovetail with DevSecOps, enhancing security throughout the software development lifecycle.

Comprising 20 critical security controls, the CIS Controls are partitioned into three categories:

- **Basic controls (1-6):** Lay the groundwork for essential cybersecurity defense readiness, applicable across all organizations.

- **Foundational controls (7-16):** Offer technical best practices that confer clear security advantages, fitting organizations with moderate resources to boost their cyber defense.

- **Organizational controls (17-20):** Concentrate on cybersecurity risk management's human and procedural aspects; diverge from the prior controls.

Despite their benefits, implementing the CIS Controls may pose several challenges. Organizations may encounter difficulties scaling the CIS Controls in line with the size and intricacy of their operations. Implementing CIS Controls could necessitate significant resources, including a skilled workforce and specific tools. Also, ensuring the effectiveness of these controls demands continuous monitoring and timely updates, which some organizations might find challenging.

Nevertheless, the advantages of adopting CIS Controls are substantial. Conceived, honed, and validated by a global community of leading experts, they offer a comprehensive collection of prioritized, highly effective defensive actions, setting forth a **must-do, do-first** approach to cybersecurity. They assist organizations in prioritizing the most effective countermeasures to mitigate risks from the most common and significant cyber threats.

To implement the CIS Controls effectively, organizations may adhere to the following steps:

1. **Define the environment:** Identify the systems, data, networks, and applications deemed critical to operations.

2. **Implement basic CIS Controls:** Begin by implementing the basic CIS Controls, which establish essential security foundations.

3. **Progress to foundational CIS Controls:** After solidifying the basics, concentrate on the foundational CIS Controls to further augment our cybersecurity posture.

4. **Implement organizational CIS Controls:** These controls, focusing on people and processes, aid in improving overall cybersecurity risk management practices.

5. **Monitor and update:** Commit to continuously monitoring the implemented controls and enacting necessary updates in response to risk environment and technology shifts.

Within a DevSecOps context, the CIS Controls can supply a robust and systematic approach to ensuring cybersecurity throughout the development lifecycle, empowering the team to detect and address security issues promptly and effectively.

Payment card industry data security standard

The **Payment Card Industry Data Security Standard (PCI DSS)** is a security protocol to guarantee that all businesses accepting, processing, storing, or transferring credit card information uphold a secure environment. From a DevSecOps perspective, PCI DSS is a blueprint for protecting sensitive cardholder data throughout the software development lifecycle.

PCI DSS pertains to all entities participating in payment card processing, encompassing merchants, processors, acquirers, issuers, and service providers. Furthermore, PCI DSS applies to entities that store, process, or transmit data of cardholders or sensitive authentication data. In DevSecOps, all applications managing cardholder data must adhere to PCI DSS, irrespective of whether the development is in-house or outsourced.

The implementation of PCI DSS comes with challenges. The requirements are comprehensive and detailed, rendering compliance a complex task. Unlike a one-time assessment, it mandates ongoing compliance, posing a challenge for organizations without a mature DevSecOps process. Embedding security within every stage of software development and operations, a cornerstone of DevSecOps may be challenging while ensuring PCI DSS compliance.

The advantages of PCI DSS are compelling. It furnishes robust standards for safeguarding cardholder data throughout its lifecycle. Organizations can reduce the risk of data breaches and financial and reputational damage by aligning with PCI DSS.

To implement PCI DSS effectively, organizations may follow these steps:

1. **Scope assessment:** Identify the systems that store, process, or transmit cardholder data and thus fall within the purview of PCI DSS.

2. **Gap analysis:** Execute a gap analysis to discern the current state of compliance and the measures necessary for achieving full compliance.

3. **Remediation:** Address the gaps identified in the analysis by implementing necessary controls.

4. **Validation:** Confirm the compliance status by conducting an internal audit or through a **Qualified Security Assessor (QSA)**.

5. **Reporting:** Submit compliance reports to the acquiring bank or card brands.

Within the DevSecOps framework, the security controls delineated by PCI DSS should be integrated into all stages of the development pipeline. Automated testing tools can be leveraged to verify PCI DSS compliance as code is written and deployed, ensuring continuous compliance and facilitating early detection and rectification of potential issues.

Control objectives for information and related technologies

Control Objectives for Information and Related Technologies (COBIT) is a comprehensive framework developed by ISACA intended for managing and governing IT. COBIT's objective is to assist organizations in achieving their governance and management goals for enterprise IT, effectively bridging the gap between control prerequisites, technical complications, and business risks. Within DevSecOps, COBIT equips organizations with principles, practices, analytical tools, and models to effectively manage the risks inherent in IT and software development.

COBIT covers a vast scope, encapsulating all IT governance and management elements. It is utilized by organizations of varying sizes across diverse sectors, helping them realize strategic goals through effective and innovative IT utilization while mitigating risks and meeting compliance requirements. In the context of DevSecOps, COBIT's scope includes managing IT-related risks throughout the development and operations lifecycle and ensuring that IT processes are congruent with business objectives.

The implementation of COBIT is challenging. The deployment demands substantial time, effort, IT governance, and management proficiency. Harmonizing COBIT with other standards and frameworks in the organization can pose challenges.

Despite the challenges, the benefits of COBIT are substantial. It facilitates alignment between IT and business strategies, a cornerstone of DevSecOps. COBIT offers a structured approach to managing IT-related risks, a significant aspect of the DevSecOps paradigm, where swift development and deployment could potentially introduce new risks. Moreover, it furnishes a framework for IT governance and assists organizations in meeting compliance requirements.

The implementation of COBIT can be structured into the following steps:

1. **Scope and objectives definition:** Commence by defining the scope of the COBIT implementation and the specific objectives to be achieved.

2. **Gap analysis:** Execute a gap analysis to comprehend the existing state of IT governance and management and identify areas requiring improvement.

3. **Implementation plan:** Draft a plan for implementing COBIT that includes specific actions, responsibilities, and timelines.

4. **Implementation:** Carry out the plan, integrating COBIT practices and controls into DevSecOps processes.

5. **Review and improvement:** Regularly evaluate the efficacy of the COBIT implementation and make necessary improvements.

COBIT can be instrumental in establishing governance and management processes integrated into the software development lifecycle. It ensures that risks are well-managed and IT processes align with business objectives. Additionally, it provides tools for performance measurement and monitoring, which can be harnessed to enhance the DevSecOps process continually.

Health Insurance Portability and Accountability Act

The **Health Insurance Portability and Accountability Act (HIPAA)** is a regulatory standard in the United States designed to safeguard patients' medical records and other health-related information. This information is typically shared with health plans, medical professionals, hospitals, and other healthcare providers. HIPAA, crafted by the Department of Health and Human Services, encompasses security stipulations that mandate businesses to secure their electronic health data.

In DevSecOps, HIPAA has become an integral guideline for teams working on systems that manage **Protected Health Information (PHI)**. Entities covered by these rules include healthcare providers, health insurance companies, and businesses that offer services to these entities or have access to PHI.

When applied to a DevSecOps context, HIPAA presents several challenges. The rapid pace of DevSecOps, characterized by continuous integration and deployment, may inadvertently introduce vulnerabilities that could risk PHI exposure. Therefore, maintaining data privacy and security in such an environment can be challenging. Achieving HIPAA compliance entails setting up secure workflows and procedures and maintaining and providing evidence of this compliance. Documenting and proving compliance can be complicated in a dynamic, automated DevSecOps environment. The DevSecOps team, including developers and operations teams, must thoroughly understand HIPAA requirements and their relevance to their tasks. Therefore, ensuring comprehensive training for the entire DevSecOps team can be significant.

Nonetheless, HIPAA comes with several advantages when successfully implemented within DevSecOps. It encourages high data privacy and security, a big boon within DevSecOps. The teams that can display HIPAA compliance are likely to inspire greater confidence among customers and stakeholders in the healthcare industry.

Implementing HIPAA within a DevSecOps context involves several steps:

1. **Identify PHI:** Start by pinpointing where and how our systems process or store PHI.

2. **Define controls:** Based on the stipulations of HIPAA, establish security controls and procedures required for protecting PHI.

3. **Train the team:** Ensure our DevSecOps team is well-versed in HIPAA compliance, highlighting how it influences their roles.

4. **Automate where possible:** Embed security checks and measures into our DevOps pipelines. For example, employ automated tools to review code for security flaws, monitor system configurations, and record and manage any changes.

5. **Regular audits:** Conduct regular audits of our processes and systems to guarantee ongoing compliance. These audits should include the CI/CD pipeline to ensure security controls are correctly implemented and functioning as desired.

6. **Documentation:** Record all processes and procedures to provide evidence of HIPAA compliance. It should include documenting the outcomes of regular audits and any steps to address identified issues.

It is essential to understand that HIPAA compliance is an ongoing requirement, not a one-time event. With its focus on continuous improvement and automation, the DevSecOps approach can significantly aid in maintaining compliance with HIPAA's data protection rules.

System and Organization Controls 2

System and Organization Controls 2 (SOC 2) represents a set of standards that assess the effectiveness of a service organization in managing and regulating its data. These standards apply to technology-based service organizations storing customer data in the cloud, making SOC 2 highly pertinent to businesses offering **Software as a Service (SaaS)**.

A SOC 2 report refers to an independent audit that evaluates the control measures of a service organization concerning security, availability, processing integrity, confidentiality, and privacy. To achieve SOC 2 compliance, organizations must devise and adhere to strict policies and procedures related to information security.

Developed by the **American Institute of Certified Public Accountants (AICPA)**, SOC 2 is an audit that ensures service providers handle data security to protect their organization's interests and their client's privacy. In the context of DevSecOps, SOC 2 is especially relevant for organizations delivering SaaS products or cloud computing services. SOC 2 evaluates five trust principles: security, availability, processing integrity, confidentiality, and privacy.

There are challenges while going for SOC 2 compliance. It can be complex and time-consuming, particularly within a DevSecOps framework. It necessitates consistent and continuous compliance demonstration across all systems and processes. Moreover, regular audits by external parties are mandatory. It can pose a challenge in a dynamic DevSecOps environment where systems and workflows often change. Also, establishing, implementing, and maintaining controls required to meet the five trust principles can be complex, especially in the fast-paced DevSecOps environment.

SOC 2 compliance can enhance trust among customers and stakeholders, demonstrating the organization's commitment to data protection. Implementing controls can help identify and mitigate potential risks and vulnerabilities. SOC 2 compliance can set a company apart, mainly for SaaS and cloud service providers.

Implementation steps for SOC 2 compliance include the following:

1. **Understanding the principles:** First, comprehend the five trust principles and their application to our business context.

2. **Risk assessment:** Conduct a risk assessment to identify system and process vulnerabilities.

3. **Define and implement controls:** Establish and implement the necessary controls to address identified risks and meet the trust principles. It should align with DevSecOps practices, integrating controls into CI/CD pipelines, automating checks wherever possible, and ensuring continuous compliance.

4. **Documentation:** Record all policies, procedures, and controls to maintain a clear audit trail. Also, ensure that any changes are tracked and documented.

5. **Regular audits:** Conduct regular audits, both internal and external, to ensure continued compliance and to identify any potential issues that need rectification.

6. **Training:** Educate all members of the DevSecOps team to ensure they understand the significance of SOC 2 compliance and its impact on their roles.

Working with different frameworks

Equipped with information regarding different frameworks, let us understand their subtle differences in applicability and relevance for our specific needs. *Table 6.2* is a comparison table incorporating all the discussed frameworks, including ISO/IEC 27001, NIST Cybersecurity Framework, CIS Controls, PCI DSS, COBIT, HIPAA, and SOC2:

Framework	Applicability	Complexity	Advantages
ISO/IEC 27001	Broad applicability to any organization that wants to manage its information security risks	Moderate-high complexity, depending on the size and nature of the organization	Provides a robust model for managing information security risks, recognized internationally
NIST Cybersecurity Framework	Primarily designed for critical infrastructure sectors but broadly applicable	Low-moderate complexity, the framework is flexible and can be tailored to specific needs	Provides a prioritized, flexible, repeatable, and cost-effective approach to managing cybersecurity risk

Framework	Applicability	Complexity	Advantages
CIS Controls	Broad applicability to any organization needing a defined set of actions for cyber defense	Low-moderate complexity focused on a core set of actions	Provides a well-defined guide to the most critical cybersecurity tasks
PCI DSS	Applicable to organizations that handle branded credit cards from major card schemes	Moderate complexity, depending on the size and type of transactions the organization handles	Enhances payment card data security globally
COBIT	Applicable to any organization seeking to align IT objectives with business goals	Moderate-high complexity, depending on the size and nature of the organization	A comprehensive framework for IT governance and management
HIPAA	Applicable to healthcare providers, health plans, and healthcare clearinghouses	High complexity requires a thorough understanding of the healthcare sector and patient data management	Provides robust data protection for patient health information
SOC 2	Applicable to service providers storing customer data in the cloud	High complexity requires ongoing compliance and regular audits	Helps build trust with stakeholders by demonstrating commitment to data security

Table 6.2: A comparison of different security frameworks

It is essential to recognize that the complexity associated with these security frameworks can significantly vary based on factors such as the organization's size, its pre-existing systems and processes, and the specific nature of its business operations. Implementing thorough security measures using one or multiple frameworks can present a significant challenge. Our choice of one or more frameworks should be influenced by several factors, including the nature of our business, the type of data our organization manages, any regulatory requirements we must meet, and our acceptable risk level.

We shall discuss two scenarios and the factors that drive the adoption of one or more frameworks in such scenarios. Let us discuss the case of a **Small to Medium-sized Enterprise (SME)**.

Understanding our requirements is the first step. We shall clarify the type of data our business manages and our specific business needs. For instance, PCI DSS will be crucial for handling credit card data. For companies operating in the healthcare sector, HIPAA is mandatory. If we aim to manage our information security risks, ISO/IEC 27001 or the NIST Cybersecurity Framework may be suitable starting points.

Then, we take stock of our capabilities to execute a chosen framework. We assess whether we have the required in-house expertise or if we need to employ an external consultant. We should consider whether our budget can accommodate investments in new security technologies or training. The process should be gradual. We shall start on a smaller scale and broaden our scope. Initially, we should focus on the most vital aspects of our chosen framework(s). Our security processes can expand.

Training to staff members is critical for the maintenance of compliance. We must ensure all our organization's members know the security processes and responsibilities. Regular training sessions help to ensure our staff understands the security protocols.

Finally, we should regularly examine our security processes and make necessary adjustments based on evolving threats or changes in our business environment. *Figure 6.1* illustrates the steps for implementing security frameworks for an SME:

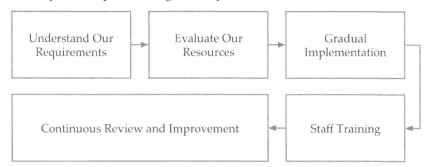

Figure 6.1: *Steps to implement security frameworks for an SME*

In the second scenario, for an enterprise, we shall encounter the presence of officials at different levels who will plan, implement, monitor, and evaluate. In such scenarios, the strategy for adoption will be different. However, in most cases, the **Chief Security Officer (CSO)** is responsible for this. *Table 6.3* elaborates on these responsibilities:

Responsibility	Description
Alignment with business objectives	Confirm that the security framework(s) we select align with our enterprise's business goals.
Cross-functional team establishment	Assemble a team of representatives from various departments to ensure comprehensive coverage of all areas of the enterprise during the security framework implementation, addressing all stakeholders' needs.
Gap analysis	Perform a gap analysis to determine our organization's current state concerning the selected framework(s). It can help us identify necessary changes for compliance achievement.

Responsibility	Description
Roadmap for implementation	Based on the gap analysis results, create a detailed roadmap for the implementation process. It should include key milestones, responsibilities, and timelines.
Implementing controls	Execute the required controls as outlined by the chosen framework. Depending on the framework's stipulations, it could involve changes in processes, implementations of new technologies, or other actions.
Training and awareness	Ensure all employees understand the significance of the latest security measures and how they can contribute.
Regular audits and reviews	Regular audits are necessary to ensure compliance with the chosen framework(s). Utilize these audits to identify areas requiring improvement.

Table 6.3: Responsibilities of the CSO for implementing security frameworks in an enterprise

In both scenarios, it is crucial to remember that security framework implementation is not a one-off task but a continuous process of improvement and adaptation in response to evolving threats and business needs.

Let us now discuss a few case studies:

- **Case study 1: Microsoft's use of the STRIDE model**

  Microsoft has long been at the forefront of threat modeling and is the originator of the STRIDE model. One example is their development of the Office 365 platform. During development, they utilized STRIDE to identify potential threats to the system, specifically focusing on possible avenues for information disclosure and elevation of privilege. They combined this with a **Red Teaming** approach, essentially employing internal teams to act as hackers to validate their threat models. This approach helped Microsoft to identify and remediate potential issues early in the development process, thereby enhancing the security of the Office 365 platform.

- **Case study 2: Financial institution's adoption of NIST Cybersecurity Framework**

  A prominent international bank adopted the NIST Cybersecurity Framework to manage its cybersecurity risk. The bank used the framework's core functions (identify, protect, detect, respond, recover) to evaluate its existing security measures and identify areas of improvement. It used the guidelines to enhance its threat detection capabilities, improve the response plan, and set up a recovery plan. Applying the NIST Framework helped the bank bolster its security posture and increase its resilience against cyber threats.

- **Case study 3: Healthcare providers' compliance with HIPAA**

  A large healthcare provider in the US must comply with HIPAA rules to protect sensitive patient data. To ensure compliance, they introduced data encryption, user authentication, and access controls across their IT systems. They also conducted regular audits and risk assessments to identify potential threats or vulnerabilities. Training programs were conducted to educate staff on the importance of data privacy and the consequences of non-compliance. Through this proactive approach, the healthcare provider has successfully avoided data breaches and complied with HIPAA.

- **Case Study 4: E-commerce Company's Use of PCI DSS**

  A global e-commerce company has effectively implemented PCI DSS standards to protect customer cardholder data. They have established a secure network by installing firewalls and encryption of cardholder data. They maintain a vulnerability management program, which includes regularly updating antivirus software and developing secure systems and applications. Regular testing of security systems and processes is carried out, and an information security policy is maintained. With these measures, the company provides a secure shopping platform for millions of customers worldwide.

These case studies demonstrate how successfully implementing security frameworks can help organizations protect their valuable assets and data, ensuring compliance with relevant regulations and a robust defense against cyber threats.

In a DevSecOps context, these frameworks guide integrating security at each stage of the development and deployment process, empowering teams to work within accepted parameters and adhere to industry best practices. In the subsequent sections, we will explore how these and other frameworks are implemented in a DevSecOps context, concentrating on their role in compliance, auditing, risk management, and threat modeling.

Compliance as code and its importance

In a DevSecOps environment, where agility and rapid deployment are critical, the traditional manual methods of ensuring compliance are no longer sufficient or adequate. Compliance must be as dynamic and adaptable as the code it governs. That is where the concept of Compliance as code comes into play.

Compliance as code (CaC) manages and maintains compliance requirements using code and automation. Much like infrastructure as code or security as code, it involves codifying compliance specifications into executable scripts or configurations that can be applied consistently and automatically across our infrastructure.

The importance of CaC comes from the need to manage complex compliance requirements in a fast-paced, ever-changing DevSecOps landscape. A few fundamental reasons organizations should consider adopting CaC are:

- **Efficiency:** Automating compliance checks can significantly reduce the time and resources required to ensure that systems are compliant.

- **Consistency:** With CaC, the same standards are applied universally across the infrastructure, reducing the chance of human error and inconsistency.

- **Scalability:** CaC is a scalable solution that can accommodate the growth of an organization's infrastructure without the need for a proportional increase in manual oversight.

- **Transparency and accountability:** With CaC, all compliance rules and their enforcement are documented and visible, promoting transparency and accountability.

Let us consider an example scenario where a company must comply with GDPR and ensure that all data stored in the cloud is encrypted at rest and in transit. With a traditional approach, an IT professional would manually check each storage unit to verify that encryption protocols are in place. This process would need to be repeated each time new data is stored or moved, which can be time-consuming and prone to error.

With CaC, the company could write scripts that automatically check whether the appropriate encryption is in place whenever data is stored or moved. These scripts could be integrated into the company's CI/CD pipeline, ensuring compliance checks are performed during every deployment.

Another example might involve a financial institution required to comply with PCI DSS. They could use CaC to ensure their firewall configurations, encryption protocols, and access controls align with PCI DSS standards. These checks could be automated and performed each time an update is made to their systems, ensuring ongoing compliance.

Let us now discuss different relevant tools for CaC. Usually, these tools form part of the larger DevSecOps toolset and are designed to automate the application of compliance policies across infrastructure and software development environments:

- **Chef InSpec:** This is an open-source framework for testing and auditing our applications and infrastructure. Chef InSpec allows us to write controls that represent compliance requirements. These controls can then be executed as code to check if our systems comply. For example, we can write a control that checks if our servers are configured with the correct SSH settings.

- **Open Policy Agent (OPA):** OPA is an open-source, general-purpose policy engine that allows us to codify policy across our stack. With OPA, we can write policy as code and integrate it into our platform as microservices. OPA can enforce microservices, Kubernetes, CI/CD pipelines, API gateways, and more policies.

- **Puppet:** Puppet Enterprise provides a language (Puppet DSL) that allows us to define the state of our IT infrastructure and then automatically enforce the correct state. It includes ensuring compliance with specific standards. For example, we could use Puppet to enforce CIS Benchmarks across our infrastructure.

- **Terraform:** While primarily an infrastructure as code tool, Terraform can also be used for CaC. We can write Terraform configurations that define the compliant infrastructure and then apply those configurations to enforce compliance. HashiCorp, the company behind Terraform, also offers Sentinel, a policy-as-code framework that integrates with Terraform to enforce compliance rules further.

- **AWS Config:** If we are working in the AWS environment, AWS Config allows us to assess, audit, and evaluate the configurations of our AWS resources. We can codify and apply our compliance requirements as AWS Config rules across our environment.

These tools, among others, help us write compliance requirements as code and apply them automatically, ensuring that our infrastructure and applications are always compliant with the necessary standards. The tools we choose will depend on our specific requirements and the environment we are working in. The key is automating as much as possible, ensuring compliance is maintained consistently and efficiently.

CaC offers a solution to managing complex compliance requirements in a dynamic DevSecOps environment. By automating compliance checks and integrating them into the CI/CD pipeline, organizations can ensure that they remain compliant while still enjoying the benefits of agility and speed that DevSecOps provides.

Understanding security audit workflows

A security audit workflow is a series of steps that are taken to assess the security posture of a system, application, or environment. Depending on the requirements, these steps can be manually performed or automated and aim to identify potential vulnerabilities, weaknesses, and threats.

The first step in the security audit workflow is to determine the scope of the audit. This scope could be a specific application, a group of servers, an entire environment, or even the complete software development lifecycle. For example, a financial institution may define the scope of an audit as all systems and applications that handle customer data.

Next, the compliance requirements need to be identified. This could involve industry standards like PCI DSS for payment card data, HIPAA for healthcare information, or GDPR for European data protection. It could also involve internally defined security policies. For instance, a SaaS company might need to comply with SOC2 to assure customers about their security measures.

Figure 6.2 illustrates the security audit workflow, in particular, the scanning and reporting process:

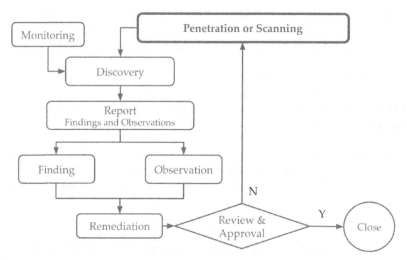

Figure 6.2: *The scanning and reporting process for the security of digital infrastructure and software applications*

The audit involves scanning and testing based on the defined scope and compliance requirements. Tools like Nessus or Qualys can be used for vulnerability scanning, while manual penetration testing might be carried out to validate findings and explore potential exploitation paths.

In the DevSecOps world, scanning and reporting mechanisms serve as the eyes and ears of the system. They continuously monitor and scrutinize every aspect of the application and its environment, detect anomalies and vulnerabilities, and alert the team to any potential issues.

The scanning is of different types. As discussed earlier, **Static Application Security Testing (SAST)** is used to analyze application source code for security vulnerabilities that might lead to attacks. It is performed at a very early stage of the development process and helps to catch vulnerabilities before they become embedded in the code. Tools like SonarQube, Veracode, and Checkmarx provide SAST capabilities.

Unlike SAST, DAST works by examining applications in their running state during the operation or testing phase. This methodology helps identify vulnerabilities that only become visible during a live execution environment. OWASP ZAP and Burp Suite are examples of DAST tools.

Software Composition Analysis (SCA) tools analyze open-source components and libraries for vulnerabilities. This analysis is crucial because modern applications often use many open-source libraries, which can become attack vectors if they contain vulnerabilities. Examples of SCA tools include WhiteSource and Snyk.

Container security scanners analyze Docker and other container images for vulnerabilities, secrets, and configuration issues that might pose a security risk. Tools like Anchore, Clair, and Docker Bench for Security are used for container security scanning.

Finally, infrastructure as code scanning involves scanning **Infrastructure as code (IaC)** templates for misconfigurations and potential security risks. Tools like Checkov and tfsec provide this capability.

Once the scanning is complete, the results need to be analyzed. This analysis identifies vulnerabilities, potential threats, and areas of non-compliance. It also helps prioritize remediation efforts based on the risk associated with each finding. For example, a detected SQL injection vulnerability on a public-facing website would likely be assigned a high priority for remediation due to the potential for data loss.

After the analysis, the process of remediation begins. Remediation activities include patching vulnerabilities, modifying configurations, implementing additional controls, or changing development practices to prevent recurrence.

Now, let us discuss the reporting. It is a crucial aspect of the DevSecOps approach. Reporting tools help present scan results in an actionable manner, clearly understanding the risk landscape and aiding in prioritization efforts. It involves generating reports showing vulnerability trends, compliance status, and security posture at any moment. It can help an organization prioritize security tasks based on risk. Tools like Splunk, Elasticsearch, and Kibana are widely used for creating visualizations and dashboards.

Integration is the key for all these mechanisms to work seamlessly. The scanning tools should be integrated into the CI/CD pipeline to ensure continuous feedback. Similarly, reporting tools should be able to collect data from various scanning tools to comprehensively view the system's security.

To illustrate, consider a scenario where a development team uses Jenkins as their CI/CD tool. They can configure SonarQube for SAST, OWASP ZAP for DAST, and Anchore for container scanning. These tools can scan the application source code, running application, and container images as part of the Jenkins pipeline. Vulnerabilities detected by these tools can be sent to a tool like Splunk, which can create visualizations and dashboards to help the team understand and act upon the results.

A formal security audit report documents all findings, actions taken, and outstanding issues are documented in a formal security audit report. This report provides an audit record and can be used for future reference or to demonstrate compliance to stakeholders or regulatory bodies. Tools like **Governance, Risk and Compliance (GRC)** platforms can assist in producing comprehensive audit reports.

The workflow described above is cyclical and should be performed regularly as part of an organization's security strategy. In a DevSecOps context, these steps can be largely automated, and the results feed back into the development process, allowing teams to address issues as they arise and reduce the risk of security vulnerabilities making it into production. In a mature DevSecOps environment, these audit workflows become a part of everyday operations, making security a shared responsibility across all teams.

Threat modeling

Threat modeling is a structured approach used to identify, quantify, and address the security risks associated with an application. It is a proactive measure taken during the design phase of the application development lifecycle. The process includes identifying potential threats, categorizing them, and implementing strategies to mitigate those threats. Several types of threat modeling techniques are often used in the industry:

STRIDE

Spoofing, Tampering, Repudiation, Information Disclosure, Denial of Service, and Elevation of Privilege (STRIDE) is a threat modeling methodology developed by Microsoft. It is used to identify threats by categorizing them into one of the six categories mentioned above. For instance, an e-commerce application may face the risk of **Spoofing**, where an attacker might pretend to be a legitimate user to gain unauthorized access.

Process for attack simulation and threat analysis

Process for Attack Simulation and Threat Analysis (PASTA) is a seven-step, risk-centric methodology. It provides a dynamic threat identification, enumeration, and scoring process. The focus of PASTA is on business impacts and includes a strong emphasis on attack simulation and analysis. For example, in an online banking application, PASTA might help identify a business risk where an attacker manipulates transaction data, leading to financial loss.

DREAD

Damage Potential, Reproducibility, Exploitability, Affected Users, and Discoverability (DREAD) is part of the risk assessment phase used in Microsoft's **Security Development Lifecycle (SDL)**. For example, for a cloud storage service, DREAD can be used to assess the risk of data being accessed by unauthorized users (Damage potential), the likelihood that an attack could happen repeatedly (Reproducibility), the ease with which the attack could be performed (Exploitability), the proportion of users who would be affected (Affected users), and the ease with which the vulnerability could be discovered (Discoverability).

OCTAVE

Operationally Critical Threat, Asset, and Vulnerability Evaluation (OCTAVE) is a suite of tools, techniques, and methods for risk-based information security strategic assessment and planning. It identifies and evaluates security risks across technological, operational, and human factors. For example, OCTAVE could be used to assess the security risks related to using outdated technology within an organization.

Attack trees

Attack trees provide a systematic way of describing the security of systems based on varying attacks. We represent attacks against a system in a tree structure, with the goal as the root node and different ways of achieving that goal as leaf nodes. For example, an attack tree might be used to illustrate different ways an unauthorized user could gain access to a system, for example, by guessing a password, exploiting a vulnerability, or socially engineering a legitimate user.

Understanding the types of threats an application or system might face and the potential impacts of those threats are essential steps in building secure software. By implementing threat modeling, teams can proactively mitigate security issues before they result in serious breaches.

These techniques and our comprehensive deliberation on different security frameworks will enable us to understand the subtilities of compliance and risk management with DevSecOps. Before discussing our use case of IoT application, let us briefly review the evolving guidelines coming from the globally accepted body, the **Cloud Security Alliance (CSA)**.

CSA's six pillars of DevSecOps

CSA gave guidance in December 2022 through a white paper (**https://cloudsecurityalliance. org/artifacts/six-pillars-of-devsecops/**) regarding how to start with DevSecOps in an organization. With the wide acceptance of DevSecOps, Cloud Computing (we have discussed extensively in earlier chapters), and digital transformation (to be discussed in detail in *Chapter 7, Digital Transformation and DevSecOps*), there has been an exponential increase in the attack surface for the digital systems and a need for real-time defense mechanisms. The guidance has identified six pillars of DevSecOps, as illustrated in *Figure 6.3*:

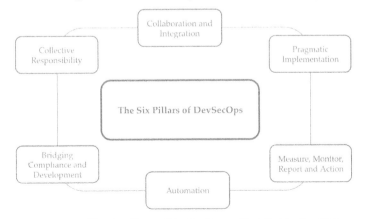

Figure 6.3: The six pillars of DevSecOps as identified by the CSA

Let us take a closer look at these six pillars identified by the CSA for successfully implementing DevSecOps:

- **Collective responsibility:** In a DevSecOps environment, the responsibility for security does not just fall on a dedicated security team. Instead, it is a shared responsibility across all teams. Developers, operations personnel, and security professionals should work together to ensure the security of the digital system. By taking a collective approach, security can be integrated seamlessly throughout the development lifecycle rather than being a separate process handled after the fact. This collective responsibility extends beyond the core DevSecOps team to other stakeholders, including business leaders, legal, HR, and so on. They must all understand and appreciate the importance of security in the overall project.

- **Collaboration and integration:** A key aspect of DevSecOps is the close collaboration and integration between development, operations, and security teams. It may include daily stand-ups, shared tools and platforms, and cross-functional training. By working closely together, these teams can understand the perspectives of one another, learn from one another, and identify potential security issues much earlier in the software process. Collaboration and integration also foster a culture where everyone owns the system's security.

- **Pragmatic implementation:** With this, DevSecOps does not advocate for a one-size-fits-all approach but encourages a pragmatic implementation that suits the specific needs and constraints of each organization. Adopting certain aspects of DevSecOps more quickly than others may be recommended, using different tools or methods or focusing on certain security areas first. The key is to make continual improvements over time and to learn and adapt from experience.

- **Bridging compliance and development:** Compliance (discussed earlier in this chapter) is often seen as a hurdle in fast-paced development environments. However, in a DevSecOps model, compliance requirements are integrated directly into the development process. We can achieve this through automated compliance checks, embedding compliance requirements into user stories, or using compliance as code approaches. By bridging compliance and development, organizations can ensure that they meet regulatory requirements while maintaining the speed and agility of their development process.

- **Automation:** Automation is a critical part of DevSecOps. By automating as many processes as possible, organizations can reduce the risk of human error, speed up the development process, and free up team members to focus on more complex tasks. This can involve automating everything from security checks and compliance audits to deploying software patches and updates.

- **Measure, monitor, report and action:** Finally, an essential pillar of DevSecOps is the continual measurement, monitoring, reporting, and taking action on security-related metrics. By continuously tracking these metrics, organizations can clearly understand their security posture, identify potential issues early, and make data-driven decisions about their security strategy. Furthermore, this pillar involves continuous learning and adaptation based on these metrics and reports, allowing for proactive responses and improvements over time.

These six pillars provide a holistic framework for integrating security into the DevOps process. By fostering collective responsibility, promoting collaboration and integration, implementing pragmatic solutions, bridging compliance and development, leveraging automation, and continually measuring and improving, organizations can build secure, compliant, and resilient systems in a DevSecOps model.

With all this understanding, let us delve into our use case in the next section.

Compliance and risk management for our IoT application

Implementing security audit, compliance, and risk management in our scenario would involve a multi-pronged approach covering the project's different aspects, from the IoT sensor network and cloud data pipeline to the real-time dashboard and ERP integration. A security audit should be carried out across all project components:

- **IoT sensor network:** Inspect the sensors and RFID tags for possible vulnerabilities. Ensure that data transmitted by these devices is encrypted and that the devices themselves are securely configured.

- **Cloud infrastructure:** Conduct a security assessment of the cloud infrastructure to ensure that data is protected in transit and at rest.

- **Dashboard and ERP integration:** Perform a web application security assessment of the dashboard and ERP integration. This should include tests for common vulnerabilities like injection attacks, cross-site scripting, and so on.

- **Data processing:** Ensure that the data processing steps respect privacy regulations and do not expose sensitive information.

The audit process should be repeated periodically and after any major changes to the system. Automated security scanning tools can be incorporated into the CI/CD pipeline to ensure continuous security auditing.

Figure 6.4 illustrates our approach while taking into account both compliance and risk management and aligning them with the organizational perspective:

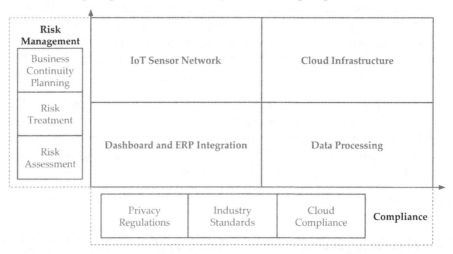

Figure 6.4: *Illustrating the process of achieving compliance and adequate risk management level*

Compliance involves ensuring the system meets relevant legal and industry standards. This includes:

- **Privacy regulations:** Ensure the system complies with privacy regulations such as GDPR. This is particularly important as the system involves personal data from workers.

- **Industry standards:** The manufacturing industry may have specific standards or guidelines for worker safety, data handling, or IoT devices. Compliance with these standards should be ensured.

- **Cloud compliance:** The selected cloud provider should have the necessary certifications to guarantee the security and compliance of the hosted services and data.

Risk management involves identifying and mitigating risks associated with the system. Here is how it could be done:

- **Risk assessment:** Identify potential risks such as data breaches, system downtime, faulty sensors, and so on. Analyze these risks based on their potential impact and likelihood of occurrence.

- **Risk treatment:** Develop strategies to treat identified risks. This could involve mitigating risks (for example, by improving security measures), transferring risks (for example, through insurance), accepting risks, or avoiding risks.

- **Business continuity planning:** Develop a business continuity plan to ensure the system can quickly recover from major incidents. This should include data backup and recovery plans, system redundancy, and disaster recovery plans.

Implementing security audits, compliance, and risk management is not a one-time task but an ongoing process. As the system evolves, the audit, compliance, and risk management processes should evolve, ensuring that the system remains secure and compliant at all times.

The DevSecOps approach facilitates this continuous security mindset, integrating security into every stage of the development and operations process. By applying the principles and practices of DevSecOps, the project team can build a secure, compliant, and resilient system that meets the needs of FitPractice Inc.

Conclusion

In this chapter, we delved into many vital aspects surrounding DevSecOps, covering a breadth of security frameworks and best practices crucial to maintaining robust security within an enterprise. We explored security frameworks such as ISO/IEC 27001, NIST Cybersecurity Framework, CIS Controls, PCI DSS, COBIT, HIPAA, and SOC2. These frameworks offer unique advantages and can be utilized according to an organization's specific requirements, regulations they must comply with, and their risk profile.

Next, we addressed the concept of CaC and its role in embedding compliance within the DevSecOps pipeline. Various tools like Chef InSpec, Puppet, and Open Policy Agent facilitate achieving CaC, enhancing security, and reducing manual effort.

Subsequently, we delved into the integral mechanisms of scanning and reporting and their pivotal role in identifying and addressing vulnerabilities. Then, we dissected the intricacies of security audit workflows, exploring how they maintain systematic checks and balances in the DevSecOps lifecycle.

We discussed managing risks in DevSecOps and how mitigating these risks is paramount in ensuring system security. An in-depth introduction to threat modeling, its types, and applications offered insights into proactive security measures.

The chapter concluded with case studies that demonstrated the successful implementation of these security frameworks, providing a practical understanding of how these concepts work in real-world scenarios.

In the next chapter, we will delve into the nuances of implementing and managing digital transformation projects through a lean approach, emphasizing the cultural aspects of DevSecOps, understanding technical liabilities due to the use of open-source software, and outlining measurable goals for secure development and operational practices. The roles, responsibilities, and skills required in this dynamic landscape will also be examined to provide a comprehensive understanding of the DevSecOps ecosystem.

By mastering the principles in this chapter and applying them in the following sections, readers will be well-equipped to effectively implement and manage a secure DevSecOps pipeline, providing a solid foundation for successful digital transformation projects.

Questions

1. Can you name at least three security frameworks commonly implemented in DevSecOps?

2. What are the key advantages of the ISO/IEC 27001 security framework?

3. What differentiates the NIST Cybersecurity Framework from the CIS Controls?

4. What is CaC, and why is it important in DevSecOps?

5. Can you mention a tool that is often used to achieve CaC?

6. How does CaC contribute to reducing manual effort in security management?

7. What is the role of scanning in the DevSecOps pipeline?

8. How do reporting mechanisms contribute to the security of DevSecOps?

9. Can you name a tool used for scanning vulnerabilities in DevSecOps?

10. What is a security audit workflow, and how is it relevant in DevSecOps?

11. How does a security audit workflow maintain systematic checks and balances?

12. Can you describe an example of an action that might trigger a security audit workflow?

13. How does risk management contribute to the overall security of a DevSecOps pipeline?

14. What are some common risks that are associated with DevSecOps?

15. Can you explain a risk management strategy that is commonly used in DevSecOps?

16. What is threat modeling, and how is it applied in DevSecOps?

17. Can you identify and explain three types of threat models?

18. How does threat modeling contribute to proactive security measures?

19. Can you describe an example of a successful implementation of a security framework?

20. What challenges were faced in the case study, and how were they addressed?

21. What were the key results or outcomes from the successful implementation in the case study?

## CHAPTER 7

Digital Transformation and DevSecOps

Introduction

In the last chapter, we explored the various security frameworks and their management within the DevSecOps landscape. We will now focus on the exciting digital transformation realm in this chapter. The thrust of this chapter is a streamlined approach to envisioning and overseeing digital transformation initiatives, with the spotlight on creating a robust framework for managing DevSecOps.

This discussion underscores the importance of cultural shifts within DevSecOps, highlighting the crucial skills required, individuals' roles, and their responsibilities. We will explore the potential implications of leveraging open-source software, including technical liabilities and current strategies to mitigate or minimize such risks. The goal is to build a firm foundation around secure development and operational practices delineated by clear, measurable objectives and expectations.

Structure

In this chapter, we will discuss the following topics:

- The nature of digital transformation
- DevSecOps: Roles, responsibilities, and skillsets

- Cultivating a new culture: The human element

- Open-source software balancing opportunities and challenges

- The journey towards cloud-native capabilities

Objectives

Our objective in this chapter is to introduce and detail a lean approach to implementing and managing digital transformation projects in the context of DevSecOps. The aim is to present a holistic view of the DevSecOps landscape, examining the cultural shifts, skill requirements, roles, and responsibilities integral to it. Furthermore, we will address the technical liabilities arising from using open-source software and provide best practices to mitigate such risks. This chapter will pave the way toward creating a secure environment for development and operations, underlined by precise and measurable goals and expectations.

The nature of digital transformation

The term **Digital Transformation** describes the comprehensive integration of digital technology into all aspects of an organization. It fundamentally alters how businesses operate and deliver value to their customers. The process often involves a cultural change requiring organizations to continually challenge the status quo, experiment, and adapt to failure.

We must adopt a significant change to our business process. Essentially, it is two-pronged: profitability and production. Organizations drive their decision to change their strategy by looking at either one or both. *Figure 7.1* illustrates both factors apart from other important factors:

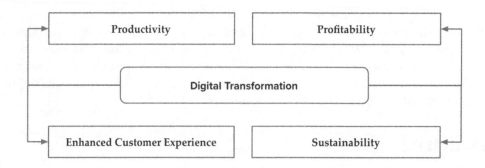

Figure 7.1: Factors driving organizations to opt for digital transformation

Let us look at these two benefits with some statistics. First, it is about improved productivity. According to a 2020 McKinsey report, automation could raise productivity growth globally by 0.8 to 1.4 percent annually. Accenture states that 79% of organizations increasingly use data to drive critical, automated decision-making. Data analytics, AI, and machine learning can help businesses better understand their performance, customers, and the market, leading to more effective decisions and strategies.

Organizations can significantly decrease costs and improve revenue by digitalizing and automating routine tasks. According to an IDC report, companies that are digital leaders in their industries are achieving gross margins 55% higher than those of digital laggards. Digital transformation allows businesses to create new revenue streams through innovative products and services and better meet customer needs. According to a Gartner survey, 56% of CEOs said digital improvements led to increased revenue. Digitally transformed businesses can respond more rapidly to changes in the market environment, giving them a competitive edge.

As per a 2017 Salesforce report, 70% of buying experiences are based on how customers feel they are being treated. Digital tools can enable personalized, convenient, and high-quality customer experiences, increasing customer loyalty and satisfaction.

Digitally transformed companies can also contribute more to sustainability. For example, a Capgemini report found that AI could help industries reduce greenhouse gas emissions by up to 4% by 2030 if deployed at scale.

The goal of digital transformation is not merely to update a company's technology tools. Instead, it is about rethinking old operating models, becoming more agile, and continuously innovating to respond to changes in customer behavior, societal shifts, and industry disruption. Thus, implementing is a big challenge for organizations expecting to reap the benefits.

The main challenge is that the digital transformation is more than a one-size-fits-all solution. Every organization will have different needs and will require different approaches. Let us look at a few famous examples of organizations that have opted for digital transformation:

- **Walmart (retail industry):** Recognizing the growing competition from e-commerce platforms, Walmart embarked on a digital transformation journey to provide a seamless online and in-store shopping experience. They revamped their website and mobile app, implemented a new online grocery pick-up and delivery service, and integrated AI-powered technology in their physical stores to help with inventory management and customer assistance.

- **Mayo Clinic (healthcare industry):** The Mayo Clinic used digital transformation to improve patient outcomes. By integrating AI into its clinical practice, the institution improved diagnostic accuracy, particularly in complex cases. It also created a more personalized patient experience through telemedicine and digital health records, enabling remote health monitoring and consultations.

- **DBS bank (banking industry):** Singapore's DBS bank underwent a comprehensive digital transformation to transition from a traditional financial institution to a digital bank. They achieved this through a cloud-first strategy, implementing a microservices architecture, and using AI and machine learning for risk management, fraud detection, and personalized marketing.

As we can see, the specifics of digital transformation differ. However, it will be great to know that the underlying principle remains the same: leveraging digital technologies to create or modify existing business processes, culture, and customer experiences to meet changing business and market requirements. This process makes organizations more agile, innovative, customer-focused, and resilient. In the following sections, we will examine how these digital transformation principles apply to DevSecOps and how organizations can effectively manage this transformation.

DevSecOps: Roles, responsibilities, and skillsets

If we look at the expectations from DevSecOps, we realize that they converge with what Digital Transformation envisages. It is imperative to identify that the organizations opting for Digital Transformation adopt the DevSecOps process. As organizations transition to a DevSecOps model, understanding the roles, responsibilities, and required skill sets within the team is crucial. As we know, DevSecOps brings development, operations, and security together to work more effectively. While some roles may remain relatively unchanged, adopting DevSecOps often necessitates new roles and additional skill sets to maximize the approach's effectiveness.

Figure 7.2 shows how different roles associated with DevSecOps work in conjunction with the application and its different environments and software management tools:

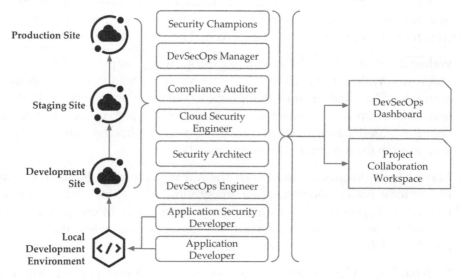

Figure 7.2: *The ecosystem of the application environment, software management systems, and different user roles*

Let us now discuss the roles:

- **Application developer:** The traditional application developer must now be equipped with tools and techniques associated with DevSecOps. A professional working in this role should have adequate awareness of software and privacy demands that are posed by cloud-based applications.

- **Application security developer:** These professionals have a developer background but specialize in application security. They work with development teams to write secure code and identify and fix security flaws in the development phase. They should possess strong coding skills, knowledge of secure coding practices, and familiarity with software security tools.

- **DevSecOps engineer:** A DevSecOps engineer is a professional who works with developers, operations staff, and other IT team members to oversee code releases. They are responsible for integrating security in the DevSecOps pipeline and automating security controls, defenses, and countermeasures. Essential skills include expertise in coding, scripting, systems architecture, open-source technologies, data management, and cloud services.

- **Security architect:** The security architect designs secure network architectures, defines and implements security controls, develops strategies and systems to protect infrastructure, and ensures compliance with data privacy regulations. Knowledge of cybersecurity frameworks, coding, threat modeling, and cloud and network security is required.

- **Cloud security engineer:** Cloud security engineers ensure the security of an organization's cloud-based systems and data. They design, implement, and manage cloud security measures and are involved in compliance and incident response. Understanding cloud architectures, knowledge of cloud-specific vulnerabilities, and experience with cloud security solutions are must-have skills for this role.

- **Compliance auditor:** This role involves monitoring and recording software processes for compliance with regulatory standards. They ensure the organization meets its legal obligations and internal security policies. They require an understanding of legal and regulatory requirements, IT audit procedures, and knowledge of security controls and frameworks.

- **DevSecOps manager:** This role oversees the integration of development and operations teams. They often act as a bridge between the teams and help instill a culture of collaboration and shared responsibility for security. They require strong people skills, a broad understanding of development, operations, and security practices, and experience in project management.

- **Security champions:** Security champions are not necessarily a separate role but members of development teams with a strong interest in security. They help foster good security habits within their teams and act as a liaison between their team and security teams.

By understanding the roles and how they interact with different aspects of the DevSecOps process, organizations can align themselves better with the CSA's six pillars (as discussed in *Chapter 6, Frameworks and Best Practices*) and ensure a more secure and efficient software delivery process. Let us discuss these:

- **CI/CD pipeline interaction:** In the DevSecOps context, the CI/CD pipeline is vital to integrating and deploying changes swiftly and reliably. The application developers and application security developers play crucial roles here. They regularly check their code into version control systems, instigating an automated build and test process. If the code clears these tests, it is ready for deployment. The DevSecOps engineer, symbolizing the automation pillar, is responsible for integrating security and ensuring the deployment is automated, as per CSA's collective responsibility pillar.

- **Environment security:** Security architects and cloud security engineers are the guardians of all environments, development, testing, staging, and production. These roles work in tandem to design and enforce security policies in line with the bridging compliance and development pillar. Additionally, the compliance auditor monitors these processes to ensure the organization meets its regulatory obligations, showcasing the collaboration pillar.

- **Project workspace management tools:** The project workspace management tools are common ground for all team members. Everyone is involved in managing tasks, tracking issues, or collaborating. The DevSecOps manager plays a pivotal role here, fostering a culture of collaboration and shared responsibility for security in alignment with CSA's collaboration pillar.

- **DevSecOps dashboard:** The DevSecOps dashboard is essential for providing insights into the entire development process. It becomes a window into code check-ins, build status, security vulnerabilities, and deployment status. The DevSecOps engineer ensures the dashboard effectively tracks progress and manages the project in tune with the pragmatic implementation pillar.

- **Threat investigation:** In the event of a potential threat, the application security developer, security architect, and cloud security engineer take the lead. They utilize security tools to monitor the application and its environment, in line with the threat investigation pillar. Any identified vulnerabilities are passed on to the application developers for remediation.

- **Automation:** Automation is the linchpin of a successful DevSecOps strategy. All roles, especially the application developers, DevSecOps engineers, and security architects, should aim to automate their tasks using their respective tools. This collective effort to automate aligns with CSA's automation pillar.

Table 7.1 presents key responsibilities in a tabular format that can make them easier to understand at a glance:

Role	Key responsibilities
Application developer	Writing, testing, and integrating code; automating tasks; collaborating in CI/CD process
Application security developer	Writing secure code; identifying and fixing security flaws; using software security tools
DevSecOps engineer	Overseeing code releases; integrating security into the DevSecOps pipeline; automating security controls
Security architect	Designing secure network architectures; defining and implementing security controls; protecting infrastructure
Cloud security engineer	Ensuring the security of cloud-based systems and data; designing and implementing cloud security measures
Compliance auditor	Monitoring software processes for compliance, ensuring the organization meets its legal obligations
DevSecOps manager	Integrating development and operations teams; fostering a culture of collaboration; managing projects
Security champions	Promoting good security habits within development teams; acting as a liaison between development and security teams

***Table 7.1**: Different DevSecOps roles and their key responsibilities*

We must note that these are only key responsibilities, and actual duties may vary depending on the specific organization and the project's complexity. However, in the DevSecOps model, all roles need a fundamental understanding of security principles and the ability to apply them in their work. Communication, collaboration, and continuous willingness to learn are crucial in this ever-evolving field. Organizations can create an effective DevSecOps team that promotes a proactive security culture through clear roles and responsibilities and the right mix of skills.

Cultivating a new culture: The human element

DevSecOps represents a profound transformation beyond technological or procedural shifts. It initiates a fundamental change in organizational culture, fostering a new mindset where the roles of application developers, application security developers, DevSecOps engineers, security architects, cloud security engineers, compliance auditors, DevSecOps managers, and security champions collaborate as a cohesive unit. The shared objective is to deliver secure, high-quality software rapidly.

Collective responsibility

Aligned with CSA's collective responsibility pillar, DevSecOps culture recognizes that security is everyone's responsibility. From application developers adopting secure coding practices to cloud security engineers implementing robust cloud security measures, every role should be woven with the thread of security considerations. For example, in a DevSecOps-enriched company, a DevSecOps engineer would not merely oversee code releases; they would also consider their security implications. Likewise, a security architect would design secure network architectures while cooperating closely with other roles to understand their needs and constraints.

Open communication and collaboration

Breaking down silos lies at the heart of DevSecOps, reflecting CSA's collaboration pillar. It advocates for open communication lines and emphasizes collaboration. Regular meetings, shared objectives, and joint problem-solving should become the norm. For instance, if an application developer is uncertain about a security policy, they should feel comfortable approaching the application security developer for clarification, expecting a helpful, constructive response.

Pragmatic implementation and continuous learning

Consistent with CSA's pragmatic implementation pillar, the ever-evolving technological landscape demands continuous learning and improvement. Regular training sessions, workshops, and learning resources should keep everyone updated on the latest security best practices and threats. For example, a company embracing DevSecOps might host recurring, company-wide security training sessions or encourage team members like the application security developer to partake in relevant online courses or industry conferences.

Automation and empowerment

In resonance with the automation pillar, DevSecOps requires faith in the ability of all roles to handle their expanded responsibilities. Empowerment should replace micro-management, cultivating an environment of ownership and motivation. For instance, management might trust a DevSecOps engineer to integrate security into the DevSecOps pipeline without constant oversight while equipping them with the necessary tools and resources to do so effectively.

Threat investigation and embracing failure

The final pillar, threat investigation, aligns with the DevSecOps ethos of treating failure as a learning opportunity. Teams should feel confident in taking calculated risks, knowing that mishaps will be treated as learning experiences, not penalized. For example, suppose a deployment by a cloud security engineer causes an issue. In that case, teams should work together to understand what happened, how to fix it, and how to prevent it from happening again. This approach stimulates innovation and continuous improvement.

Table 7.2 describes the relationship between each pillar and the corresponding cultural shift:

CSA's six pillars	Cultural shifts	Relationship
Collective responsibility	Shared security responsibility	The collective responsibility pillar fosters a mindset where all roles participate in security, leading to shared security responsibility.
Collaboration	Open communication	The collaboration pillar necessitates breaking down silos and promoting teamwork, leading to a culture of open communication.
Pragmatic implementation	Continuous learning	Pragmatic implementation encourages adaptation to the evolving technological landscape, leading to a culture of continuous learning.
Automation	Empowerment	Automation calls for faith in the capabilities of team members, leading to a culture of empowerment and ownership.
Threat investigation	Embrace risk	Threat investigation aligns with an ethos that encourages taking calculated risks and treating failure as learning opportunities.
Embracing failure	Treating failure as a learning	Embracing failure promotes a mindset where setbacks are considered opportunities for learning and improvement.

Table 7.2: Relationship between each pillar and the corresponding cultural shift

By nurturing collective responsibility, open communication, continuous learning, empowerment, and embracing failure as a learning opportunity, organizations can cultivate a thriving DevSecOps culture. While this shift may be challenging, it is fundamental for effectively implementing DevSecOps.

Open-source software balancing opportunities and challenges

Open-source software (**OSS**) has made significant inroads into various aspects of technology, providing users with versatile, customizable, and cost-effective solutions. The utilization of OSS has been a game-changer in the DevSecOps landscape, primarily due to its ability to speed up development, foster collaboration, and enhance transparency. Yet, while OSS offers abundant opportunities, it also introduces challenges that need to be navigated wisely.

Opportunities presented by open-source software

DevSecOps presents vast opportunities for organizations, and OSS plays a significant role in this domain. From driving speed and efficiency to fostering community and collaboration, OSS plays a critical part in shaping the DevSecOps landscape. It offers unmatched transparency and trust, promotes innovation and flexibility, and significantly reduces costs. Let us delve into the opportunities presented by OSS in the context of DevSecOps, the availability of high-quality tools developed by the open-source community:

Innovation and flexibility

Open-source software offers an incredible degree of flexibility, which in turn drives innovation. However, the source code is freely available, and developers can adapt, customize, and extend the software to suit their specific needs. This freedom to innovate is a key reason why open-source has been at the forefront of most technological advancements in recent years. For example, DevSecOps practices have been significantly boosted by open-source tools like Jenkins for **continuous integration/continuous delivery** (**CI/CD**), Ansible for configuration management, and Docker for containerization have significantly boosted DevSecOps practices. These tools provide a flexible framework for developers and operations teams to collaborate and streamline the software development process.

Reduced costs

As OSS is freely available, it helps organizations significantly reduce costs associated with software licensing and subscriptions. Moreover, the communal effort around OSS leads to shared maintenance costs, further reducing the total cost of ownership. In a DevSecOps context, organizations can leverage open-source security tools like OWASP ZAP for dynamic security testing or **SonarQube** for continuous inspection of code quality to ensure application security without incurring high costs.

Availability of high-quality tools

Open-source communities have developed a vast array of high-quality tools that cover nearly every aspect of the software lifecycle, from development and testing to deployment and monitoring. In the context of DevSecOps, there are open-source tools available for every step of the development pipeline. For instance, Git or subversion is used for version control, Selenium for automated testing, Puppet for configuration management, and **ELK Stack** (**Elasticsearch**, **Logstash**, **Kibana**) for log analysis and visualization. These tools enrich the DevSecOps ecosystem and foster the development of best practices.

Driving innovation in DevSecOps

Open-source communities have been at the forefront of driving innovation in the DevSecOps field. Their contributions range from developing security-focused tools to pioneering practices that integrate security into the DevOps workflow. The tools mentioned earlier, like Jenkins, Ansible, Docker, OWASP ZAP, and SonarQube, are all products of open-source innovation. Furthermore, initiatives like the **Open Web Application Security Project** (**OWASP**) not only provide tools and resources but encourage the adoption of security-minded practices in the DevSecOps culture. open-source communities will undoubtedly continue to play a crucial role in shaping the future of DevSecOps.

Challenges of open-source software

When leveraging OSS within a DevSecOps context, it is crucial to acknowledge and navigate potential challenges. These can range from security risks and dependency management to variability in quality and maintenance. Additionally, there is the need to factor in technological liability and how to manage the potential risks and responsibilities associated with using technology. Let us elaborate on these challenges, accompanied by examples.

Security risks

while fostering trust and collaboration, OSS's transparency can also inadvertently aid malicious actors. By studying the open-source code, attackers might uncover and exploit vulnerabilities, posing security risks. The Heartbleed bug in OpenSSL, an open-source project, is a case in point. This bug resulted in substantial security concerns worldwide, demonstrating the potential threats tied to OSS's open-access nature. With tech liability in mind, organizations must regularly review and secure their open-source components against such threats to avoid legal and financial repercussions.

Dependency management

OSS often depends on other open-source components, creating a complex dependency chain. A security flaw or bug in one of these dependent components could compromise the entire software. Managing these dependencies, ensuring their regular updates, and verifying their security can be complicated. The 2018 event-stream incident provides a stark reminder of these risks, as a widely-used Node.js package was compromised. Organizations must address these issues proactively, considering their operational impact and the broader tech liability implications.

Quality and maintenance variability

The quality and reliability of OSS can vary significantly, primarily influenced by their maintenance practices. Some projects enjoy the backing of extensive, dedicated communities, while a few individuals might maintain others. This inconsistency can lead to variability in problem-solving speeds, impacting the software's overall reliability. Consider an organization that depends on a small open-source project; they might find it no longer maintained, leaving them with the tech liability and the responsibility of maintaining the software or finding an alternative solution.

Technological liability

Utilizing OSS entails potential tech liability, as organizations must bear the responsibility for the security and stability of the open-source tools they use. It includes keeping abreast of software updates, patching security vulnerabilities, and ensuring compliance with relevant regulations. For example, suppose an organization uses an OSS tool for data processing, and it has a security flaw leading to a data breach. In that case, the organization may face legal implications due to this. Therefore, it is critical to factor in tech liability when integrating OSS into the software development lifecycle.

Towards successful open-source initiatives in DevSecOps

As we discussed, embracing OSS in DevSecOps presents vast opportunities for innovation, efficiency, and cost-saving. However, it is accompanied by challenges such as security risks, dependency management, variability in quality and maintenance, and technological liability. To optimize the benefits of OSS while mitigating these risks, organizations should consider a detailed, proactive approach:

- **Implement robust security measures:** Given the security risks associated with OSS, it is critical to have robust security measures in place. Regular code reviews, vulnerability assessments, and penetration testing can help identify and address potential security threats early. For instance, using open-source tools like OWASP ZAP for dynamic security testing can help identify vulnerabilities that malicious actors can exploit.

- **Manage dependencies actively:** Dependency management is critical in using OSS. It is essential to map out and keep track of all open-source components and their dependencies in our project. Tools like **Dependency-Track** can alert when a component is being used. It allows proactive management of potential risks and ensures the integrity of software.

- **Vet the OSS projects:** Before integrating an OSS into the DevSecOps pipeline, vet the project's quality and robustness. A large, active community and regular updates indicate a well-maintained project. Also, look at the project's history of handling security issues, which can provide insight into the potential future reliability of software.

- **Manage technological liability:** Understanding the tech liability that comes with OSS use is crucial. It includes ensuring compliance with software licensing, maintaining updated software versions, and patching security vulnerabilities promptly. Tools like FOSSA can help with automated license compliance and vulnerability management, aiding in managing tech liability.

- **Foster a culture of learning and collaboration:** We should encourage our team to actively participate in open-source communities. It can provide valuable learning opportunities, keep the team updated with the latest best practices, and foster a sense of ownership and responsibility. It also allows the organization to give back to the community.

- **Develop a comprehensive open-source policy:** Have a clear policy that outlines how OSS should be used within the organization, covering aspects like selection, approval, tracking, and maintenance of OSS. It can serve as a guideline for developers and help ensure that OSS usage aligns with the organization's strategic objectives and compliance requirements.

- **Leverage automation:** Whenever possible, use automation to streamline the integration of OSS into the DevSecOps pipeline. It can help manage the complex web of dependencies and ensure that all components are up-to-date and secure.

By implementing these strategies, organisations can leverage the power of open-source to drive innovation in DevSecOps while managing the associated challenges effectively. With a proactive and balanced approach, OSS can serve as a cornerstone in the organization's journey toward creating a robust, agile, and secure DevSecOps environment.

Equipped with a solid framework for handling DevSecOps and digital transformation, let us look at the way we should go for implementation with cloud-native capabilities.

The journey towards cloud-native capabilities

In the wake of rapid digital transformation and the ever-growing importance of DevSecOps, the shift towards cloud-native capabilities becomes not just a favorable choice but a strategic necessity. Cloud-native capabilities involve developing applications with an inherent design to exploit the benefits of cloud computing environments. This transition is not simply about adopting new technologies but demands a complete transformation of processes, team dynamics, and the overall organizational culture. The road to becoming cloud-native unfolds across several stages, each providing unique opportunities and posing distinctive challenges.

Traditionally, many applications were built as monolithic entities, large, indivisible units where different application components are interwoven. Due to their tightly integrated infrastructure, these applications pose significant challenges regarding scalability and adaptability. Suppose we take an **enterprise resource planning** (ERP) system built as a monolithic application. Scaling or migrating such a system or implementing updates can become a complex task due to the intertwined nature of its various components and the underlying infrastructure.

The containerization process provides uniformity across varied environments, which means an application behaves the same way from a local developer's workstation to the production environment, thus eliminating the infamous it works on my machine problems. For example, Docker has emerged as a popular platform for containerization, providing developers with lightweight, isolated, and reproducible environments, which can significantly accelerate the application development and deployment process.

Microservices architecture offers enhanced flexibility for scaling, permits independent deployment of services, and allows for various technology stacks for different services. Netflix, the streaming giant, has successfully implemented microservices architecture to manage its extensive scale. The platform consists of multiple microservices, each handling tasks like user authentication, video encoding, and delivering personalized recommendations.

With an increase in the number of containers and microservices, managing them manually becomes unfeasible. Orchestration tools automate the process of deployment, scaling, and managing containerized applications, thus simplifying overall management. Kubernetes helps manage containerized applications across different hosts, dealing with various tasks, including load balancing, automatic scaling, and secret management.

Serverless computing offers a computing model where the cloud provider dynamically allocates machine resources, freeing the developers from the hassles of server management. The billing is based on actual resource consumption rather than pre-allocated capacity. Serverless platforms like **AWS Lambda** and **Google Cloud Functions** allow developers to run their code without the need to provision or manage servers, thus speeding up the development process and reducing operational overheads.

Finally, it is about the integration of DevSecOps into our mainstream processes. With cloud-native development practices gaining traction, integrating security into the development lifecycle becomes crucial, thus leading to the emergence of DevSecOps. This approach embeds security protocols right into the CI/CD pipeline, enabling continuous security monitoring and ensuring compliance checks. For example, in a cloud-native DevSecOps setting, tools like Aqua Security (**www.aquasec.com**) can enhance container security, and SonarQube can be employed for continuous checks on code quality and security.

It is important to note that the transition towards cloud-native capabilities is a journey and not a single-step process. Each organization will discover its unique path depending on specific requirements, resources, and constraints. However, the overarching aim remains constant: delivering value faster, more reliably, and securely while fully harnessing the flexibility and power cloud technologies offer.

Conclusion

In this chapter, we have embarked on a journey through the digital transformation landscape, with DevSecOps as our guiding principle. We began by understanding the nature of digital transformation, acknowledging its comprehensive and disruptive influence across industries. It is a process that transcends the boundaries of technology alone, profoundly impacting business models, operational structures, and the very culture of organizations.

In the context of DevSecOps, we investigated the different roles, responsibilities, and skills instrumental in this paradigm shift. This journey through DevSecOps roles was more than an exploration of job titles or descriptions. It examined the essential human element and the skills and mindsets required for success in the evolving digital landscape.

Cultural transformation, a vital yet often overlooked aspect, was brought to the fore. We recognized that technology, processes, and tools are only as effective as the people wielding them, emphasizing the significance of fostering a culture that encourages learning, collaboration, and transparency, where security is everyone's responsibility.

As we tread the open-source path, we acknowledge the balance between the opportunities it presents and the challenges it might bring forth. OSS offers extensive advantages, including cost efficiency, flexibility, and rapid innovation. However, they can also introduce certain risks, and we delved into strategies to mitigate these liabilities while reaping the benefits.

Finally, we turned our gaze toward the future, exploring the journey towards achieving cloud-native capabilities. In an era where the cloud is quickly becoming the norm rather than the exception, understanding this transition's intricacies is vital to ensuring a resilient, scalable, and efficient digital infrastructure.

The ultimate objective of this chapter and, indeed, this entire exploration has been to equip us with the knowledge and insight required to navigate our organization's path toward secure digital transformation underpinned by DevSecOps. By cultivating the right skills, nurturing an appropriate culture, leveraging the right tools, and implementing robust security frameworks, we can drive our organization toward a future where security, development, and operations converge seamlessly.

As we conclude this chapter, we understand that the journey is continuous and ever-evolving. The next step involves constantly learning, adapting, and innovating. The scope is expansive, and the opportunities are infinite in DevSecOps.

Questions

1. What does digital transformation mean, and how does it impact how businesses operate and deliver value to their customers?

2. What role does culture change play in digital transformation, particularly in challenging the status quo and adapting to failure?

3. How do profitability and production drive an organization's decision to undergo digital transformation?

4. Please elaborate on the impact of automation on productivity growth. How can data analytics, AI, and machine learning contribute to this productivity growth?

5. How does digital transformation enable businesses to create new revenue streams and better meet customer needs? Please provide some examples.

6. How does digital transformation affect customer experiences, and how is it reflected in buying experiences?

7. How can digitally transformed companies contribute to sustainability by reducing greenhouse gas emissions?

8. How does digital transformation go beyond updating a company's technology tools? What does it entail in terms of rethinking old operating models and innovation?

9. Please discuss an organization's challenges when implementing Digital Transformation.

10. How does the approach to digital transformation vary across different organizations? Please give examples from various industry verticals like retail, healthcare, and banking.

11. What are the fundamental principles underlying digital transformation, and how do they apply to different businesses and market requirements?

12. Please explain how the principles of digital transformation apply to DevSecOps.

13. What strategies can organizations use to manage digital transformation within DevSecOps effectively?

14. Please describe different roles and their key responsibilities in DevSecOps. What changes are expected in traditional roles with the adoption of DevSecOps? How does the convergence of development, operations, and security teams affect the roles and responsibilities within an organization adopting DevSecOps?

15. How does understanding the roles within DevSecOps help an organization align with the CSA's six pillars?

16. How do the key responsibilities of different roles vary across different organizations and projects?

17. How important are communication, collaboration, and continuous learning in a DevSecOps environment, and how do these skills contribute to a proactive security culture?

18. Discuss the critical cultural shifts that take place in a DevSecOps environment.

19. How does the DevSecOps culture align with the CSA's pillars, and how does this manifest in different roles?

20. How does OSS contribute to innovation and flexibility in the DevSecOps landscape?

21. Please discuss some high-quality tools developed by the open-source community that are instrumental in a DevSecOps context.

22. What is the impact of OSS on cost reduction, especially in terms of software licensing and maintenance?

23. What are the potential security risks associated with the use of OSS, and how can these be mitigated?

24. How does dependency management become a challenge in the context of OSS, and how can it be addressed?

25. How can the variability in quality and maintenance of different OSS projects pose a challenge to their implementation?

26. How does technological liability factor into using OSS, and what steps can be taken to manage this responsibility effectively?

27. What measures can be taken to balance the opportunities and challenges presented by OSS in the DevSecOps context?

28. How does cloud-native application development differ from traditional application development methods?

29. How should organizations transition towards cloud-native capabilities considering their specific requirements and resources?

Index